TREATING
DISSOCIATIVE
IDENTITY
DISORDER

TREATING DISSOCIATIVE IDENTITY DISORDER

The Power of the Collective Heart

Sarah Y. Krakauer

BRUNNER-ROUTLEDGE
Taylor & Francis Group

USA	Publishing Office:	BRUNNER-ROUTLEDGE
		A member of the Taylor & Francis Group
		325 Chestnut Street
		Philadelphia, PA 19106
		Tel: (215) 625-8900
		Fax: (215) 625-2940
	Distribution Center:	BRUNNER-ROUTLEDGE
		A member of the Taylor & Francis Group
		7625 Empire Drive
		Florence, KY 41042
		Tel: 1-800-634-7064
		Fax: 1-800-248-4724
UK		BRUNNER-ROUTLEDGE
		A member of the Taylor & Francis Group
		27 Church Road
		Hove
		E. Sussex, BN3 2FA
		Tel: +44 (0) 1273 207411
		Fax: +44 (0) 1273 205612

TREATING DISSOCIATIVE IDENTITY DISORDER: The Power of the Collective Heart

1 2 3 4 5 6 7 8 9 0

Printed by Edwards Brothers, Ann Arbor, MI.
Cover design by Rob Williams.

A CIP catalog record for this book is available from the British Library.
∞ The paper in this publication meets the requirements of the ANSI Standard Z39.48-1984 (Permanence of Paper).

Library of Congress Cataloging-in-Publication Data

Krakauer, Sarah Y.
    Treating dissociative identity disorder : the power of the collective heart / Sarah Y. Krakauer.
      p. cm.
    Includes bibliographical references and index.
    ISBN 0-87630-975-9 (case : alk. paper)
    1. Multiple personality--Treatment. I. Title.

  RC569.5.M8 K73 2001
  616.85'2360651--dc21   00-065184

ISBN 0-87630-975-9

This book is lovingly dedicated
to my father, Cyrus H. Gordon,
who taught me to embrace new ideas and to take joy in sharing them;

to my mother, Joan Kendall Gordon, of blessed memory,
whose nurturing spirit has been with me
throughout each phase of the project
and is with me now at this time of completion and joy;

and to my husband, Henry Krakauer,
and our children, Ilana, Mark, and Ben,
whose love and unfaltering belief in the value of this work
have given me more than they will ever know.

CONTENTS

PREFACE

The purpose of the book is to introduce a new model for the treatment of dissociative identity disorder (DID), explore its relationship to existing models, present preliminary support for its assumptions and efficacy, and invite further implementation and development of the model and assessment of its utility. This model may reflect a shift in the treatment of dissociation characteristic of the turn of the 21st century. The last decade of the 20th century was a time of challenge to clinicians treating DID. In fact, it was challenging in both senses of the word: characterized by contentious encounter and confrontation on the one hand, and by stimulation to transcend previous limitations, on the other.

In response to these challenges, a consensus has emerged within the professional community regarding the treatment of individuals presenting with posttraumatic symptoms, dissociation, and/or memories of childhood abuse. A growing number of traumatic stress scholars and clinicians agree that a stance of supportive neutrality is appropriate with regard to the authenticity of recovered memories. They also concur that carefully paced, phase-oriented treatment is indicated so that the therapy fosters increased stability and enhanced functioning and avoids undue or premature focus on traumatic memories. Cautious clinical practice, with scrupulous avoidance of suggestive therapy techniques, has been emphasized. There is widespread agreement that therapists should avoid implying that an abuse history can be inferred on the basis of symptomatology. While most therapists treating dissociation are now skeptical about the use of regressive hypnotherapy techniques in the context of memory retrieval, there is still debate regarding the appropriateness of hypnosis in other therapeutic contexts.

The consensual model, with its emphasis on restraint, is a mixed blessing for clients and therapists. Attention to careful, respectful treatment is certainly in everyone's best interest. However, some therapists feel that they can no longer use with impunity some of the techniques, particularly hypnosis, that they had come to view as their most effective tools in the treatment of dissociative disorders.

I believe that we are standing at the threshold of a new era in the treatment of dissociative and posttraumatic disorders. This new era will be characterized by more potent intervention strategies and by equal attention to avoiding countertherapeutic suggestions and ensuring therapeutic suggestions. At present, suggestiveness is a dirty word. We have been led to believe that we must, at all costs, avoid suggestive practices. But "suggestive" is not synonymous with "misleading." If there is adequate support for the assumptions underlying clinical practice, there is nothing wrong, and everything right, with making suggestions. Most therapists strive to instill hope and empower clients through enhancement of their self-esteem and do so, in part, by means of suggestive language. We believe and suggest that our clients are worthwhile human beings, deserving of our attention and capable of effecting significant changes in their affective states and the quality of their lives. It would be naive to suppose that we need to avoid all manner of suggestiveness in order to provide cautious, ethical, and effective psychotherapy. What is essential is that we be careful about the language and imagery we use so that we are responsible about what we suggest.

The Collective Heart treatment model presented in this book incorporates the cautions articulated during the last decade of the 20th century and introduces new intervention strategies designed to emphasize the recovery of personal authority rather than of memories. This model retains the traditional interventions that are felt to be relatively risk free and presents a number of innovative techniques. It is based on three fundamental assumptions. The first is that every individual, no matter how damaged and fragmented at the level of personality, has an intact inner core that can guide the individual to a state of harmonious functioning. The second assumption is that severely traumatized, fragmented clients typically need assistance with mobilizing this inner core, or collective heart, and that this assistance involves exposure to therapeutic techniques in the context of a respectful professional relationship. The third assumption is that highly dissociative clients have easy access to the guidance of the intact inner core. Their dissociative tendencies can be utilized therapeutically, and they can quickly learn to enter a meditative state in order to experience internal guidance in a vivid, sensory manner.

This model emerged from my experiences working with dissociative clients over a period of 11 years. I developed an interest in dissociative disorders during my clinical psychology internship in 1989, while on rotation in the Admissions/Acute Treatment Unit at Eastern State Hospital in Williamsburg, Virginia. My supervisor, Richard Griffin, introduced me to the assessment and treatment of dissociative disorders and assigned me a dissociative case early in my rotation. During my second internship rotation, I was able to continue treating this patient on an outpatient basis, under the supervision of Paul Dell. Dr. Griffin's and Dr. Dell's dedicated supervision of my work with this complex and interesting patient provided the fundamental understanding and skills that have guided my work in this area.

In the early 1990s, after I had returned to Eastern State Hospital as a staff psychologist, I had two clinical experiences that challenged me to think about dissociation in new ways. In retrospect, I can trace the distinctive features of the Collective Heart model back to these two experiences. One involved a client who reported in session that two of her alter personalities had gone off somewhere to seek guidance. I wanted to know more. Where had they gone? What sort of guidance were they seeking, and from whom? The host reported that they had gone somewhere deep within her to ask for help with making an important decision. Having learned about higher order alters known as internal self-helpers (ISHs), I assumed that this client's alters were consulting an ISH, and asked if this alter would be willing to speak with me. The source of the guidance then informed me that I was mistaken in my assumption that this was a member of the personality system. I was informed that this source of inner guidance was not an alter.

The second experience involved a dissociative patient who appeared to be experiencing suicidal ideation associated with an anniversary reaction. I consulted with her outpatient therapist, Earl Flora. He suggested that, while the patient was in trance, I ask the patient's "subconscious" to present visually on an internal screen three suggestions for resolving the current crisis. The first suggestion offered by the client's subconscious was that I assemble art materials to be used by the child alter who was experiencing the anniversary reaction, so that he could convey his distress. The resulting intervention enabled us to resolve the suicidal crisis and discharge the patient to continue her therapy on an outpatient basis.

From these two experiences, I learned that an inner resource could be called upon to assist with treatment planning and effect healing. In addition, I learned that it may be most helpful to conceptualize this inner resource as transcending the personality system with its rigid compartmentalization. Over the years, I found that clients can contact this intact core, or inner wisdom, without the aid of a hypnotic induction. I also found that the inner wisdom can generate visions of hope for the future and can mediate the flow of other unconscious material into consciousness and the flow of information between members of the personality system.

I described this potent inner resource as "the inner wisdom of the unconscious mind," or simply "the inner wisdom." One DID client, feeling that "wisdom" was too cerebral, suggested "collective heart" to highlight the experiential component of her innermost being. She reported in session one day that she had reassured her mother, who was distressed by the discovery of the client's abuse history, with the following: "All of the alters from our collective heart know that if you could have done anything to help, you would have."

The collective heart can be understood as an internal compass which each of us possesses. It directs us toward optimal psychological and behavioral functioning, that is, toward both what we ought to do and what we most profoundly want to do. How is it possible that a congruence exists between the two? Because when we grasp the long-term consequences to ourselves and others, we choose the course that is most personally rewarding, which is also the morally right path. Here the highly dissociative individual is at an advantage: By using her innate capacity to enter an altered state of consciousness with ease, she can vividly experience and compare various courses of action and can determine for herself which promotes the greatest sense of well-being in the long run.

The examples of dissociative pathology presented in this volume are based on observations of over two dozen dissociative clients I have assessed or treated. However, case vignettes illustrating the model are drawn from the therapies of the 12 clients with whom I have used this model in a private, outpatient setting. In all cases, care has been taken to omit or alter identifying characteristics. Additional measures have been taken to protect those clients who have been given names (pseudonyms) in chapters 7 through 12. In these cases, extensive clinical material is used to illustrate the various interventions, with quotations taken from process notes or videotape transcriptions. In order to provide such details without harming my clients, I have taken the usual measures to alter identifying characteristics, omitting the abuse history altogether when it is irrelevant to the intervention strategy. Furthermore, I presented each client with the portion of the manuscript depicting his or her case material for review, encouraged the client to voice any concerns, and obtained informed consent to use the material in this volume. The consent form that I used addressed the adequacy of efforts to preserve anonymity and the faithful rendering of clinical developments despite these efforts. In addition, the client's signature affirmed that no incentives were used to encourage consent, that the client knew that she could decline consent without fear of consequences such as disappointing the therapist or negatively impacting the therapy, and that the entire personality system freely offered full consent.

In light of the fact that 9 of these 12 clients (and the majority of DID clients generally) are female, the female pronoun is used in this volume whenever the prototypical client is described. The male pronoun is used only in case vignettes depicting male clients. In referring to the therapist,

I vary the personal pronoun to avoid the awkwardness of the "s/he" construction.

Chapters 1 through 3 contextualize and introduce the Collective Heart model. Chapter 1 discusses the nature of dissociation and summarizes the early history of hypnosis and dissociation. Chapter 2 addresses traumatology and the treatment of dissociative states, emphasizing developments during the last third of the 20th century. The delayed memory controversy is discussed and the current standards of care are introduced. Chapter 3 provides an overview of the Collective Heart treatment model with attention to theoretical principles, stages, goals, and intervention strategies. Some distinctive characteristics of the model are noted.

Chapters 4 through 6 describe specific features of the assessment and treatment processes and elaborate upon the nature of the therapeutic relationship, which supports the therapy experience. Chapter 4 presents a detailed guide to diagnostic assessment as well as evaluation of potential for harm to self and others. Patience, caution, and respect for the client's comfort level are underscored. Chapter 5 introduces relaxation and meditative techniques (with verbatim instructions) that clients master and then use independently. This chapter also describes three visualized inner structures that facilitate experiences of increased safety and control, improved internal communication, and receptivity to inner guidance. Chapter 6 addresses the nature of the therapeutic relationship, emphasizing mutual respect and trust. Empowerment of the client through reduction of the power differential, the use of informed consent or refusal, and accurate empathy are accentuated. The importance of honoring what is often viewed as "resistance" is highlighted. Suggestions are offered regarding the formation of relationships with the alters. Also included are contracts regarding preservation of life.

Chapters 7 through 12 illustrate the various stages of therapy with extensive case vignettes. The case material demonstrates how clients draw upon the inner wisdom, or collective heart, to obtain guidance and heal their fragmented personality systems. Numerous examples illustrate that as clients are able to envision rewarding possibilities for their future, they choose to live and not to die, and that as they are able to envision more potent forms of empowerment, they choose to relinquish destructive ways of exercising control. Emphasis is placed on helping clients discover that, as adults, they have the power to create the conditions for their own growth and healing. They learn that they can make it safe for their alters to evolve and mature, eventually joining the host as a seamless, harmonious whole.

Finally, Chapter 13 evaluates the current status of the model. It stresses that the approach is still in its infancy and has not yet been subjected to broad clinical application or empirical evaluation. The demographics of the clinical series are presented, and a preliminary, qualitative evaluation is made on the basis of anecdotal observations. Issues explored include compliance with the consensual standards of care and preliminary evidence supporting the theoretical assumptions and clinical efficacy of the model. The model is also compared with other treatment models. Commonalities and distinctive features are elaborated.

What I hope to convey in these pages is that something deep within traumatized individuals remains intact, balanced, and hopeful despite the psychologically devastating effects of trauma. In treating these clients, our most potent tools are those that empower the client to gain conscious access to this unconscious resource. Even for people who are suffering in extremis, this work confirms the essential healthy core of the human heart.

ACKNOWLEDGMENTS

Without the contributions of teachers, colleagues, family members, and friends this book could not have been conceived, nurtured, and delivered. My first words of gratitude go to those who introduced me to dissociative identity disorder and the innate healing potential of the unconscious mind, Dr. Richard Griffin and Dr. Paul Dell. Dr. Griffin supervised my training in the assessment and treatment of dissociative disorders during my clinical psychology internship and taught me that the unconscious mind is the part of us that possesses the answers sought by the conscious mind. Dr. Dell supervised my training in the outpatient treatment of dissociation. Drs. Griffin and Dell generously shared their expertise with me and conveyed a belief that I have what it takes to work effectively with dissociative individuals. I am also indebted to Dr. Earl Flora for his recommendations regarding the capacity of the unconscious mind to suggest productive treatment strategies.

Armed with all I had gleaned from this rich training experience, I began treating dissociative clients on an outpatient basis. Over time, I realized that I had developed a model which was in some ways distinct from other models in the literature. Buoyed by successful clinical outcomes, I decided to write a book. I knew nothing about the world of publishing so I am fortunate to have a friend, neighbor, and colleague who encouraged me to pursue a contract. Dr. Michael Nichols provided thoughtful and encouraging responses to an early draft of a sample chapter, mentored me during the writing of the prospectus, and made recommendations regarding the submission of the proposal. I especially appreciate his generous emotional support because his expertise is not in the treatment of dissociative disorders, and I expected to encounter skepticism rather than enthusiasm. Michael also deserves thanks for infusing my writing experience with his good humor.

I am grateful that Lansing Hays, then Acquisitions Editor at Brunner-Routledge, felt the project had potential, and offered me a contract. Although he soon left Brunner-Routledge, I feel blessed that he was there, confident in my work at a crucial moment. He was succeeded as

Acquisitions Editor by Bernadette Capelle, under whose much appreciated guidance this project has been brought to completion. I would also
like to thank her Editorial Assistant, Erin Seifert, for her many behind-
the-scenes efforts, Jenn Gunning, for her skillful work as Production Editor, and Rebecca Lazo, Marketing Representative, who saw to it that the
book would reach its intended readership.

It was my good fortune that my capable Developmental Editor, Jim
Kehoe, enlisted the assistance of Dr. Christine Courtois as external re-
viewer of the manuscript. She was the first scholar with expertise in the
treatment of posttraumatic disorders to read any part of the manuscript.
Her thoughtful responses directed me towards the clarification of crucial
concepts and distinctions, better organization of the first two chapters,
and more adequate acknowledgment of the contributions of pioneers in
the field. I am grateful for her valuable suggestions.

After revising the manuscript, I was fortunate to meet three scholars
whose support and assistance are deeply appreciated. I wish to thank
Dr. Laura S. Brown for her encouragement and her willingness to read
the manuscript. I am indebted to Dr. Onno van der Hart for his generosity
in reading the preface and three crucial chapters. His astute responses
led to important modifications that will enhance the effectiveness of
the volume. Equally important, I am grateful for Onno's warm support
and availability at a sensitive moment in the production process. Finally,
I wish to thank Dr. Carolyn Zerbe Enns for her enthusiasm about the
book and her generosity in agreeing to write the foreword. In addition to
highlighting strengths of the book, her fine foreword invites the reader to
engage in a critical evaluation of diagnostic, theoretical, and procedural
aspects of the model.

I am grateful to my daughter, Ilana, for taking time from her busy
schedule as a doctoral student in clinical psychology to read several chapters and offer suggestions that improved the manuscript both substan-
tively and stylistically. I thank my dear friends Drs. Sylvia Scholnick and
Deborah Morse, who read drafts of chapters, and whose responses enhanced the book's organization and readability. In addition, Sylvia spent
countless hours walking around town with me, listening as my ideas took
form, helping me to articulate and illustrate them more effectively. I am
grateful to her for celebrating with me as I reached major milestones in
the publication process.

I deeply appreciate my husband's eagerness to read and respond to each
chapter as I completed it. Henry affirmed the effectiveness of the evolving
manuscript while challenging me to sharpen my theoretical formulations
and explore stylistic alternatives. I can't thank him enough for his steady
confidence in the value of my treatment model and in my ability to
present it in a compelling manner. What was really remarkable was not

the enthusiasm he conveyed in the brighter moments, but his capacity to sustain it for several years as the manuscript evolved. Not once did he express doubt that the project was worth the sacrifices it entailed. In fact, he is hardly aware that it entailed sacrifices.

We are blessed with three dear children—Ilana, Mark, and Ben—now all in their twenties. I thank them for their love and support, and for valuing my work just as the creative work of each family member is valued, whether it is scholarly, artistic, or clinical.

Finally, for the clients whose stories are told in these pages, I feel a sense of gratitude that is nearly beyond words. They are my greatest teachers. They thank me for telling them about the inner wisdom but, in truth, almost everything I know about the inner wisdom I learned from them. For all they have revealed to me, and for their willingness to collaborate with me in their healing work, I feel a gratitude that can be conveyed only in the language of the heart.

FOREWORD

I began reading this manuscript with both anticipation and curiosity. I am a feminist therapist, a person who has studied and written about the delayed/recovered memory debate, and a professor of psychology. However, I have limited familiarity with dissociative identity disorder, and thus looked forward to gaining more in-depth understanding of the challenges and complexities of working with those who experience a shattered identity. I was not disappointed!

Dr. Sarah Krakauer presents her collective heart model in a personal, engaging, and highly readable fashion. Intrigued by the phrase "collective heart," I discovered that this descriptive title was co-created with a client and refers to an inner core or internal compass that can provide clients with sound guidance. Dr. Krakauer proposes that dissociative clients, who are easily able to enter an altered state of consciousness, may be especially well equipped to tap this inner guidance through meditative states. Thus, the very dissociative and trance-like qualities that often lead to coping difficulties or erratic behavior can also become assets for creative healing and empowerment. Dr. Krakauer's case illustrations and description of her approach together portray a highly creative, artistic, and committed therapist who holds a great deal of optimism about and faith in the healing capacities of her clients.

Some of the key strengths of this book include its even-handed discussion of the delayed/recovered memory debate and how the lessons we have learned from this debate need to inform the ethical treatment of traumatized individuals. Building on the observations of prominent researchers and clinicians, she emphasizes the importance of abiding by rigorous standards of practice and ethical treatment. Dr. Krakauer views the major goal of therapy as the recovery of personal authority and mastery over one's life rather than the recovery of memory. In light of this goal, she outlines the importance of careful, comprehensive, non-leading assessment; and emphasizes the centrality of facilitating the current coping skills of her clients. Given the primacy of coping and client stabilization, any efforts to work through or reprocess painful or traumatic memories are placed on hold until the client demonstrates readiness to engage in this work.

The therapeutic alliance plays a crucial role in this model. Consistent with the values of feminist therapy, Dr. Krakauer highlights the importance of decreasing power differentials between the client and therapist. Respect, trust, flexibility, and collaboration are key features of the model. To support client empowerment, she puts forth the view that underlying the client's fragmentation is a powerful capacity for growth. It seems likely that one of the most powerful aspects of this model is its emphasis on the role of the therapist in facilitating the expectation that each person has the capacity to experience healing.

I applaud Dr. Krakauer's courageous choice to present this model at a time when the very notion of dissociative identity disorder, its etiology, and its diagnosis remain controversial. For example, a recent survey of psychiatrists found that there is "little consensus" (p. 321) about the validity of the dissociative disorders (Pope, Oliva, Hudson, Bodkin, & Gruber, 1999). I confess that I am somewhat uncomfortable with the use of the diagnostic label of dissociative identity disorder, fearing that it may lead some clients and therapists to overemphasize symptoms associated with multiple identities and to inadvertently miss a wide range of other issues and distressing symptoms that often occur in conjunction with dissociation. I prefer the label complex posttraumatic stress disorder, which attends to alterations of identity and consciousness, but also focuses on other alterations of experience, such as affect regulation, relationships with others, and systems of meaning (Herman, 1992). Although I may not share all of Dr. Krakauer's assumptions about diagnosis, I share her beliefs about the general focus and goals of therapy. I value Dr. Krakauer's respect for her clients and her emphasis on current coping and client strengthening.

Recognizing the controversial use of hypnosis and age regression in the treatment of dissociation, Dr. Krakauer chooses not to employ therapist initiated hypnosis, but instead, trains interested clients to use self-generated meditative and visualization states. Visualization exercises are designed to help clients enhance their sense of safety, clear their minds of troubling images and thoughts, and replace negative images with metaphoric images that inspire confidence. She utilizes a visualized internal theater, which allows clients to play out scenarios on an imaginary screen, and also introduces several unique techniques. To decrease the likelihood that clients will confuse reality with fantasy, Dr. Krakauer explains that the movie theater is not an objective reality but an opportunity to experiment with possibilities. Clients can pace themselves through the movie by learning to control images with an imaginary remote device that has play, stop, pause, amplification, and rewind buttons.

In recent years, some forms of imagery and visualization exercises have been compared to hypnosis and identified as potentially risky techniques. Recent research findings (e.g., Terrance, Metheson, Allard, & Schnarr, 2000) reveal that guided imagery may be associated with similar mechanisms and effects as hypnosis. Some uses of visualization and memory may increase the likelihood of pseudomemory formation, and these possibilities may be more likely in clients who are highly susceptible to dissociation or hypnosis.

Dr. Krakauer is cognizant of these types of concerns and has used them to inform her work. She does not use therapist generated guided imagery with clients; however, when they are interested, she teaches clients to enter meditative states that allow them to use visualized inner structures to deal with the challenges of living. These inner structures include the theater tool, rooms in a hall of safety, the conference room, and the anger rock. Compared to many forms of visualization and imagery, she proposes that these tools are less intrusive, more cautious, less suggestive, more empowering, and less likely to lead to confusion of reality and fantasy. These novel and promising ideas and techniques, which are demonstrated effectively in Dr. Krakauer's work with 12 clients, merit further exploration with a wider range of clients. Since mechanisms of and distinctions between hypnosis, guided imagery, and meditative states are still unclear, it will be important to explore the similar and different effects associated with hypnosis, imagery, and the client-directed meditative states used by Dr. Krakauer.

In light of unresolved questions, concerns about memory, and the recommendations of Dr. Krakauer, it seems most appropriate to use meditative states, visualization, and imagery for specific purposes such as managing anxiety, strengthening self-soothing skills, containing or altering negative images, and increasing client self-confidence. As one component of informed consent, it is also important for therapists to explain to clients that spontaneous memories which emerge during visualization experiences may be distorted or influenced by imagined events.

When I first read this manuscript, I experienced some uneasiness with terms like "collective heart" and "inner wisdom." The phrases initially reminded me of terms I would encounter in a popular psychology book. As a self-identified scientist-practitioner, "inner wisdom" sounded overly subjective, fuzzy, and untestable. Thus, it was of interest to me that some of Dr. Krakauer's clients have also expressed discomfort with the phrase "inner wisdom." She noted that one client thought the term sounded too spiritual and another found the term too cerebral! I appreciate the fact that Dr. Krakauer has shown respect for her client's discomfort and has worked collaboratively with them to formulate language that is personally meaningful. On further reflection, I have also concluded that the notion of "inner wisdom" seems related to numerous humanistic and existential concepts such as inner-awareness, congruence, inner flow, the "felt sense" associated with the technique of focusing, evocative unfolding, being in process, human potential, inner experiencing, and inner vision (Bohart, 1995; Bugenthal & Sterling, 1995). The concept of "inner wisdom" reflects a strong humanistic value system. Dr. Krakauer's approach calls on the therapist to be a fellow explorer rather than an expert on the client's life. Even with severely traumatized individuals, therapy is less about repairing damage and more about exploring and creating new possibilities that are based on the client's underlying, healthy core.

I find the notion of an inner intact core and "inner wisdom" to be intriguing and compelling. Conventional views suggest that due to traumatic experiences, persons with dissociative identity disorder may not develop a core sense of self during the earliest periods of life (e.g., Pica, 1999). According to this traditional view, the basic self is presumed to be marked by internal fragmentation, and thus, it would be unlikely that individuals with dissociative identity disorder could count on a core "inner wisdom" for guidance. While Dr. Krakauer accepts the conventional view that trauma disrupts the development of a core sense of self in these individuals, her model challenges the assumption that their ability to access unconscious inner wisdom has been similarly disrupted. From a feminist perspective, I still wonder whether it is possible, in a world marked by violence, sexism, racism, and many other "isms," for traumatized individuals to retain a healthy and whole self-knowledge, especially when much of the damage to the self occurred during the earliest years of life. Another question is whether there are occasions when encouraging individuals to tap this intuitive wisdom might allow them to think less critically and carefully about their behavior and goals.

As a part of a bold and exciting alternative to these typical views and questions, Dr. Krakauer proposes that while the personality systems of dissociative clients have been damaged, they retain a healthy core that can help them understand that they are worthy and lovable individuals, capable of repairing damage to the self and of experiencing positive memories and emotions. Through case studies and anecdotal data, Dr. Krakauer demonstrates how clients have successfully tapped an inner healthy core and used it to sort through the challenges of living. The case examples presented in the second half of the book provide in-depth insights about how clients build on this inner core. Finally, in response to the anticipated criticism that this approach may be overly endorsing of a client's "inner wisdom," Dr. Krakauer notes that she consistently encourages clients to evaluate, test, and, when appropriate, challenge their "inner wisdom."

This volume will serve an important role in disseminating and facilitating the testing of new models of treatment. Major strengths and contributions include Dr. Krakauer's careful attention to ethical behavior, her respect for clients, her helpful case studies, and her detailed descriptions of the sample on which she has based her model and book. I believe this volume will enrich clinical understanding as well as stimulate important theoretical and research developments. I am certain that this model will be useful to those who treat dissociative disorders. Moreover, I expect that the innovative techniques described in this book will also be useful to persons who work with a wide range of psychological difficulties. I look forward to reading more about the evolution of this model.

Carolyn Zerbe Enns
Professor of Psychology, Cornell College

☐ References

Bohart, A. C. (1995). The person-centered psychotherapies. In A. S. Gurman & S. B. Messer (Eds.), *Essential psychotherapies: Theory and practice* (pp. 85–127). New York: Guilford.

Bugenthal, J. F. T., & Sterling, M. M. (1995). Existential-humanistic psychotherapy: New perspectives. In A. S. Gurman & S. B. Messer (Eds.), *Essential psychotherapies: Theory and practice* (pp. 226–260). New York: Guilford.

Herman, J. L. (1992). *Trauma and recovery*. New York: Basic Books.

Pica, M. (1999). The evolution of alter personality states in dissociative identity disorder. *Psychotherapy, 36*, 404–415.

Pope, H. G., Oliva, P. W., Hudson, J. I., Bodkin, J. A., & Gruber, A. (1999). Attitudes toward *DSM-IV* dissociative disorders diagnoses among board-certified American psychiatrists. *American Journal of Psychiatry, 156*, 321–323.

Terrance, C. A., Matheson, K., Allard, C., & Schnarr, J. A. (2000). The role of expectation and memory-retrieval techniques in the construction of beliefs about past events. *Applied Cognitive Psychology, 14*, 361–377.

The Nature and Early History of Hypnosis and Dissociation

It is of course easier to reject *en bloc* a teaching that has incorporated errors than to undertake the difficult task of selecting the grain from the chaff, and, as Janet had to conclude, "hypnotism is dead ... until the day it will revive."

— H. F. Ellenberger, *The Discovery of the Unconscious*

In 1784, a member of the French aristocracy made a remarkable psychological discovery. Amand-Marie Jacques de Chastenet, Marquis de Puységur, who had been trained by Franz Anton Mesmer in the technique of animal magnetism, found that he was able to induce a "magnetic sleep" state in which the subject displayed enhanced insight and lucidity. Puységur reported that, in this state, his subject was able not only to diagnose his own medical and interpersonal problems and determine their etiology, but also to foresee the appropriate course of treatment and mobilize the resources necessary for successful implementation (Ellenberger, 1970).

This book introduces a treatment model for dissociative identity disorder (DID) that relies heavily on the human capacity discovered by Puységur. In illustrating the Collective Heart treatment model, I use case material from several dissociative cases to demonstrate that Puységur was right, at least for individuals with DID, who can learn to enter an altered state of consciousness with ease. Without the use of heterohypnosis,

I have been able to facilitate in dissociative clients the enhanced insight and lucidity, the capacity to direct and pace their own treatment, that Puységur achieved via his "magnetic sleep" induction.

This chapter addresses the nature of dissociation and reviews historical developments bearing on dissociation and hypnosis. The following chapter summarizes major 20th century developments in traumatology and the treatment of dissociative states, discusses the nature of memory, and highlights the delayed memory debate and its impact on clinical practice. Together, these two chapters provide an historical overview to contextualize the Collective Heart treatment model.

☐ The Nature of Dissociation

The psychological term "dissociation" refers to the disconnection or lack of integration between the normally integrated functions of memory, identity, or consciousness (American Psychiatric Association, 1994). The concept of a dissociative continuum has been used to describe responses ranging from nonpathological dissociation—reflected in such experiences as daydreaming—to pathological dissociation, with DID (formerly known as multiple personality disorder, or MPD) as the endpoint of the continuum. However, as Courtois (1999) argued, the construct of the dissociative continuum may be of limited utility because pathological dissociation is not merely a more extreme manifestation of the tendency underlying normal dissociation. The important distinction is that normal dissociation doesn't involve the inaccessibility of specific memories that characterizes pathological dissociation. Four characteristics distinguish pathological from normative dissociation: Only in pathological dissociation do we encounter loss of executive control, change in self-representation, amnestic barriers, and loss of ownership over behavior (Kluft, 1993b).

The capacity to dissociate is normally distributed in the population. Traumatized individuals may utilize whatever dissociative ability they possess to defend against otherwise unbearable experiences. DID, the most severe manifestation of dissociative pathology, is a complex posttraumatic condition that can develop when a highly dissociative child is traumatized, most commonly before the age of 5 (Loewenstein, 1994), and almost always by 9 or 10. The greater the severity, chronicity, and emotional complexity of the trauma, the more complex the DID condition tends to be. These two factors, the innate capacity to dissociate and the experience of childhood trauma, are the two fundamental etiological factors in DID. An ancillary factor has been suggested: the absence of supportive responses within the social environment that might help the child process traumatic experience and thereby serve a mitigating function. While this is true in the vast majority of cases, I have treated one DID client whose nurturing caretakers would almost certainly have assisted the child had the trauma been detected.

Subsequent chapters will convey the phenomenology of DID to readers unfamiliar with the inner landscape characteristic of this disorder. However, before the history of hypnosis and dissociation is summarized, a brief description of the core features is provided for purposes of introduction. "Dissociation can be conceptualized," wrote Loewenstein (1994), "as a basic part of the psychobiology of the human trauma response. In dissociation, there is thought to be a protective activation of altered states of consciousness as a reaction to overwhelming psychological trauma" (p. 3). Highly dissociative individuals are able to "leave the body," effectively disconnecting the "observing self" from the "experiencing self" (van der Kolk, 1996, p. 192).

DID originates when the child dissociates, using this innate capacity to distance or remove herself psychologically in order to avoid experiencing otherwise unbearable trauma. Another personality is created to endure the experience and hold the memory, thereby sparing the original personality, or *host*, the knowledge of what has occurred. This additional or alternate personality, commonly known as an *alter*, continues to function as a distinct compartment within the individual's collective mind, actively seeking to protect the host from repeated trauma and to avoid disclosure of the forbidden knowledge to the host. Should additional trauma occur, and should the alter be unable to endure it herself, additional personalities may be created in order to take over for the overwhelmed alter. The host and alters are referred to collectively as the *personality system*. As pointed out by van der Kolk, van der Hart, and Marmar (1996), dissociation in response to early traumatization increases the likelihood that a child will continue to rely on dissociation when stressed and decreases the likelihood that alternative coping strategies will be developed. The poorly developed nondissociative coping strategies, in combination with dysfunctional learning and the search for mastery and meaning, may explain the likelihood of revictimization in survivors of childhood abuse (Sandberg, Lynn, & Green, 1994).

Occasionally alters are formed in a nontraumatic context. For example, they may be created to perform a specialized function, such as numbing the host emotionally or helping the host cope with academic or occupational demands. In the event of abuse (in contrast with naturally occurring trauma such as accidents, fires, earthquakes, and the like), alters may also be created to ensure that secrets are guarded from those outside the personality system, such as family members, teachers, neighbors, and so forth. These alters, who may have internalized threats made by perpetrators regarding the consequences of disclosure, often use quite intimidating methods to ensure that the abuse is not reported.

A personality system can be large or small, but regardless of size, certain types of alters are typically present in DID clients. Kluft (1984b), Coons, Bowman, and Milstein (1988), Ross, Norton, and Wozney (1989), and Putnam (1989) all offer useful typologies. In my clinical experience, almost all DID clients have at least one *child alter*, and the more complex cases often have numerous child and adolescent alters. Child alters may be fearful, pleasing, helpful, and so forth. Also nearly universal in DID cases are *angry alters*, who have sometimes been labeled "persecutors." These alters are best understood as fiercely protective, and they become tremendous assets in the therapeutic process once their fundamentally protective nature is affirmed and alternative means of safeguarding the system are discovered. Most DID clients also have at least one *acting-out alter*, who may engage in high-risk behaviors, such as sexual promiscuity, substance abuse, spending money recklessly, speeding while driving, gambling, and the like. In female clients, these alters may be highly flirtatious and provocative. Severely *depressed alters* are not uncommon. Frequently, there is at least one overtly *nurturing alter*. There is often an *efficient, "take-charge" alter* who excels at managing the task demands of daily life, but may not be skillful at handling affect. *Internal self-helpers* (ISHs) are discussed in Chapters 2 and 13. They are mentioned here because they are conceptualized as alters by many experts. Alters can be any age, including ages older than the host, and either gender. Putnam (1989) reported that "at least half of all MPD patients have cross-gender alter personalities" (p. 110). Male alters in female clients are common. Although in 1980, Coons noted that "only one case of a male multiple personality with a secondary female personality has been reported" (Coons, 1980, p. 331), within a decade it was reported that the majority of male MPD patients appeared to have female alters (Putnam, 1989). The sexual orientation of an alter can sometimes differ from that of the host. Alters can also differ in terms of race. I have treated three DID clients who had certain alters who were racially different from the host. Needless to say, when an alter emerges in the body, an observer sees him or her as having the age, race, and gender consistent with the body, despite the subtle or obvious changes in posture and demeanor determined by the alter's personality type, role, and needs. The full range of internally-perceived physical characteristics of any alter, including age, gender, race, hair color, stature, body type, and so forth, is, of course, derived from a psychological representation of the alter.

What begins as a creative survival strategy for an otherwise completely vulnerable child becomes disruptive as the child experiences amnesia for the times when the alters assume executive control of the body, and becomes confused by evidence of activities carried on outside of aware-ness. Discrepancies between the child's experience and responses of oth-ers in the environment such as parental accusations that the child did things the child has no memory of having done, contribute to the child's growing sense of personal deficiency or defectiveness. Some alters resent having to endure traumatic experiences, and they express considerable anger toward the host for not being adequately self-protective. The host's experience of hearing voices inside the head offering advice or criticism or arguing with one another, combined with the increasing awareness that other people don't seem to hear such voices, compounds the child's sense that something is amiss. In addition, the alters experience flash-backs, which have been described as "brief dissociative episodes during which the trauma is reexperienced in sensorimotor form or as intrusive cognitive recollections" (Pope & Brown, 1996, p. 54). One first-person account of DID described flashbacks as "intrusions of recollection so vi-olent and so vivid that the past nearly obliterates the present" (Phillips, 1995, p. 78). The alters' flashbacks may infiltrate the host personality's consciousness, terrifying the confused host, who is unable to determine whether the flashback material reflects actual experience or merely imag-ination. However, the symptoms of DID are most likely to motivate the individual to seek psychotherapy in adulthood, when discontinuities in memory, behavior, and sense of personal identity tend to preclude fulfill-ment of societal expectations and to result in suicidal behavior and other manifestations of severe psychopathology.

☐ The History of Dissociation and Hypnosis

The Early History of Dissociation and Hypnosis

Long before dissociation was understood from a psychological perspec-tive, cases of "demonic possession" were observed and reported. By care-fully reexamining the documentation of these cases in the late 19th century when posttraumatic disorders were first understood psychologi-cally, Désiré Bourneville, a colleague of Pierre Janet, was able to identify the essential clinical features of "doubling of the personality," later re-named MPD and DID, in these cases of demonic possession (van der Hart, Lierens, & Goodwin, 1996). One such case that was reexamined by Bourneville is the intriguing case of Jeanne Fery, a 16th century Domini-can Nun who had been treated for demonic possession via exorcism in 1584 and 1585. This case has been described in detail by van der Hart, Lierens, and Goodwin (1996) as "perhaps the earliest historical case in which DID can be diagnosed retrospectively with confidence" (p. 18) because the trauma history as well as all the core clinical manifestations of the disorder were documented meticulously.

Modern psychological theories of dissociation are best informed by a series of developments beginning in the last quarter of the 18th century. Ellenberger's (1970) fascinating historical analysis, *The Discovery of the Unconscious: The History and Evolution of Dynamic Psychiatry* provided a thorough chronology of these developments. Ellenberger (1970) has traced the origins of dynamic psychiatry from 1775, when the Austrian physician Franz Anton Mesmer challenged the renowned German Exorcist Father Johann Joseph Gassner by introducing a secular treatment for the convulsions, seizures, and other symptoms that were previously understood to reflect possession states. Mesmer argued that these apparent possession states were actually caused by insufficiency, imbalanced distribution, or poor quality of a mysterious physical fluid that fills the universe, linking individuals to one another and to the earth and the heavenly bodies. He claimed that his technique of animal magnetism cured these states by redistributing the fluid in the afflicted individual through the action of his own plentiful and superior fluid, thereby eliciting "crises" and restoring health. Mesmer's theory, by substituting a physical entity (the universal fluid) for a spiritual process (possession), was consistent with the Enlightenment *Zeitgeist* in which reason was valued over superstition and blind adherence to tradition. Despite Mesmer's use of magnets and specially designed devices to facilitate treatment, he attributed his therapeutic success to his animal magnetism, the high concentration of the mysterious fluid within his body. Furthermore, Mesmer believed that all such therapeutic successes, including Gassner's, were ultimately attributable to animal magnetism, no matter how they were conceptualized by the practitioner.

Mesmer moved to Paris, where he treated wealthy patients and trained students in the technique of magnetism. Among his disciples was the Marquis de Puységur, a member of one of the most illustrious families of the French aristocracy. Puységur modified Mesmer's method, abandoning the notion that the crisis was caused by the redistribution of physical fluid, and attributing his therapeutic successes to the magnetizer's will. (Despite the rejection of a physical entity as the active ingredient in the cure, the term "magnetizer" was retained.) Puységur, through the conception of the "magnetic sleep" state, became the father of "artificial somnambulism," which was later called "hypnosis." Thus we see that Mesmer, in treating what we would now generally classify as somatoform disorders, introduced the first secular treatment, and Puységur introduced the first truly psychological treatment. Although Mesmer's name has entered our vocabulary (we find ourselves "mesmerized") while Puységur's has fallen into obscurity, Puységur's contribution "equals or even exceeds the importance of Mesmer's own work" (Ellenberger, 1970, p. 70).

Let us take a closer look at the nature of Puységur's discovery, and then explore what Ellenberger and other historians of psychology emphasize as Puységur's major contributions and the extent to which Puységur's discovery may transcend these acknowledgments. One of Puységur's first patients was a young peasant named Victor Race. In magnetizing Race, who presented with a mild respiratory disease, Puységur expected to observe the typical crisis that Mesmer encountered in his work, a crisis characterized by convulsions or other sudden, disordered movements. Instead, Puységur observed that Race fell into a strange sleep state in which he displayed greater lucidity than in his normal waking state. He spoke, responded to questioning, and was able to diagnose his disease, foresee its course of evolution, and articulate the appropriate treatment. Puységur called the distinctive crisis achieved during magnetic sleep "the perfect crisis." He found that the patient was amnestic for the crisis following the magnetic sleep state. However, Puységur discovered that when magnetic sleep was once again induced in Race toward the end of his life, he recalled in extraordinary detail the crises he had experienced decades earlier (Ellenberger, 1970).

Interestingly, during a magnetic sleep state, Race was able to gain insight into interpersonal difficulties as well as medical problems. For example, during magnetic sleep Race once confided to Puységur that he was distressed about conflict with his sister. Puységur, having observed Race's capacity for lucidity, suggested that Race look for a solution within himself. This intervention proved successful, and Race implemented the inner guidance he received and resolved the sibling tension. This extension of Puységur's work into the interpersonal realm is especially significant because the psychological concerns we now consider commonplace weren't articulated in his day. Ellenberger (1970) stated that Race "would never have dared talk about" (p. 72) the sibling conflict with anyone except during this remarkable state of magnetic sleep.

Puységur utilized his magnetic sleep techniques with a great many patients, always gratuitously, and received much acclaim. However, it was from his work with Victor Race that Puységur learned not only the technique but also the appropriate applications. After an attempt to use Race for a demonstration of magnetic sleep, Race became more symptomatic. Race was able to discover during magnetic sleep that magnetism should only be used therapeutically and not for purposes of experimentation and demonstration (Ellenberger, 1970).

Puységur founded a professional society in Strasbourg, the *Société Harmonique des Amis Réunis*, to train magnetizers, establish treatment centers, and document treatment accurately. Members, who numbered over 200 by 1789, agreed to provide treatment free of charge, meticulously record case material, and submit these records to the *Société*, which published annual reports. One can only imagine the wealth of data this *Société* would have generated had its activities not been disrupted by the French Revolution in 1789. When therapeutic activities resumed following the defeat of Napoleon, the new generation of magnetizers used Puységur's method rather than Mesmer's, while retaining the term "mesmerizing" to describe the induction of the lucid sleep state.

Despite his influence, Puységur's contributions were forgotten after his death in 1825. It wasn't until 1884 that Charles Richet rediscovered Puységur and was able to demonstrate that all the core elements of hypnosis, which Richet's esteemed contemporaries claimed to have discovered, were actually apparent in Puységur's writings. These core elements include the notion of therapeutic rapport between the magnetizer and the subject, the altered state of consciousness with its appearance of wakefulness, the amnesia following the altered state of consciousness, and the lucidity of certain subjects as manifested by their ability to obtain, while in the altered state, information not otherwise available to consciousness. It is interesting to note, however, that the theory of crises, which anticipated the 20th century hypnotic technique of abreaction, predated Puységur's contributions. In Gassner's method the crisis was evidence of demonic possession and the first step in exorcism, and in Mesmer's method the crisis was the artificially produced manifestation of the disease and the means to its cure (Ellenberger, 1970).

So we see why Ellenberger (1970) credited Puységur, "one of the great forgotten contributors to the history of the psychological sciences" (p. 74), with discovering the core elements of what would later become hypnosis. The relatively few references to Puységur that appear in the literature following Ellenberger have credited Puységur for founding hypnosis by refining Mesmer's technique through the elimination of reference to bodily fluids, and his identification of the magnetizer's will as the active agent in facilitating the "perfect crisis" with its alert, sleeplike state, and subsequent amnesia. Crabtree (1993) made the important observation that Puységur's discovery brought about a paradigm shift. Previously, mental disturbance could be explained only by means of what Crabtree labeled the *intrusion paradigm*, in which an external entity exerts influence, or the *organic paradigm*, in which a physical disturbance affects the brain or nervous system. Puységur's discovery, Crabtree noted, introduced the *alternate-consciousness paradigm*. "This state of divided consciousness," Crabtree observed, "became the basis for all modern psychotherapies that accept the notion of unconscious mental activity" (p. 67).

Puységur made another profound contribution: In modifying Mesmer's technique both theoretically and procedurally, Puységur was able to discover within some of his subjects a capacity to become agents of their own healing. Crabtree (1993) aptly noted that in so doing, Puységur anticipated the ISH phenomenon noted in the 20th century (see chapters 2 and 13). Let us look at Puységur's own description of his discoveries to explore to what extent he himself realized the full significance of his accomplishments. In 1785 he addressed the Masonic society in Strasbourg, concluding his presentation with the following:

> I believe in the existence within myself of a power. From this belief derives my will to exert it. The entire doctrine of Animal Magnetism is contained in the two words: *Believe* and *want*. I *believe* that I have the power to set into action the vital principle of my fellow-men; I *want* to make use of it; this is all my science and all my means. *Believe* and *want*, Sirs, and you will do as much as I. (A. M. J. Chastenet de Puységur, 1807, cited in Ellenberger, 1970, p. 72)

At first blush, this statement appears to emphasize the will of the magnetizer as the key to the cure. However, consider the phrase "the power to set into action the vital principle of my fellow-men." Puységur was apparently aware of capabilities within his subjects that he could help potentiate, but that essentially resided within them. His concluding statement, "*Believe* and *want*, Sirs, and you will do as much as I," conveys the belief that he had no unusual gifts. Furthermore, since Puységur observed the phenomenon of lucidity in some of his subjects, but not in others, while his will presumably remained constant, he must have believed that the magnetizer's will was a necessary, but not sufficient, condition for lucidity. Therefore, it seems fair to conclude that Puységur was aware of having discovered something within at least some of his subjects that was even more remarkable than his means of potentiating it. Moreover, while the term "magnetizer's will" may connote manipulation if not frank coercion, Puységur's reference to "the vital principle of my fellow-men" clarifies that he was not speaking of an egotistical, self-serving will, but a will that is consonant with the deepest yearnings of the subject.

Puységur and his peers, notably Bertrand, referred to collectively as the "early magnetizers" and acknowledged by Ellenberger (1970) as the founders of the first dynamic psychiatry, had a tremendous impact on European society. For example, before the end of the 18th century, it had become a widespread practice in Germany for those seeking practical advice, medical assistance, or spiritual guidance to consult a somnambulist. However, the practice also met with a great deal of ridicule. Opposition tended to be somewhat culture specific. In 1784 a French governmental inquiry into mesmerism, focusing not on *whether* treatment was effective but *why* it was effective, concluded that there was no evidence for the existence of a "magnetic fluid." Although magnetism fell into disrepute in France in the early 19th century, it continued to enjoy favor in Germany. Mesmer's theory was harmonious with the German Romantics' vision of the universe as a living organism infused with soul interconnecting its superficially distinct parts. They hoped that somnambulic lucidity would facilitate contact between the human mind and the world soul. In 1812, the Prussian government appointed a commission of inquiry whose findings resulted in the institution of chairs of Mesmerism at the universities of Berlin and Bonn.

When interest in mesmerism eventually declined in Germany in the mid-19th century under the impact of rationalism and positivism, it began in England. James Braid, a Manchester physician, is commonly credited with having renamed magnetism "hypnotism." He proposed a theory based on brain physiology, emphasizing the patient's role and insisting on training the patient in self-hypnosis. Other British physicians, Elliottson and Esdaile, reported success with using hypnosis as a surgical anesthetic, replicating Récamier's success using magnetism for this purpose in 1821 (Ellenberger, 1970).

In fact, as Gravitz (1993) pointed out, Braid was not the first to use the "hypn-" prefix in reference to the altered state of consciousness. Although Braid did, in 1842, use the term "neuro-hypnology," the French had used the name of the Greek god of sleep, *Hypnos*, as the basis for their nomenclature as early as 1809, having observed that artificial somnambulism was perceived as a sleeplike state. Gravitz (1993) highlighted the role of E. F. d'Hénin de Cuvillers in using and disseminating terms incorporating the "hypn-" prefix, such as "hypnotiste" (hypnotist), "hypnotiseur" (hypnotizer), and "hypnologie" (the field itself). Cuvillers was among the followers of Mesmer who, undaunted by the results of the 1784 French governmental inquiry into mesmerism, continued studying, practicing, and refining Mesmer's method, emphasizing the imaginative or mental, and denying the physical (i.e., the existence of a magnetic fluid), as the basis for the altered state of consciousness (Gravitz, 1993).

Later, another Frenchman was similarly tenacious in the face of societal skepticism. Although magnetism had fallen into disrepute in France between 1860 and 1880, the French physician Liébeault wasn't dissuaded from using the method. He offered his patients a choice: He would treat them with magnetism gratis or with conventional medical treatment for the usual fee. Before long he had a huge practice yielding almost no income (Ellenberger, 1970)!

Liébeault's student, Bernheim, published his well-received textbook in 1886 and became the leader of the Nancy School. Bernheim distinguished between good and poor hypnotic subjects, good subjects being characterized by habitual passivity (typified, he felt, by old soldiers and factory workers) and poor subjects being characterized by greater wealth and social status and, presumably, the relative autonomy that financial and social power afford. He believed that hypnosis didn't reflect the pathology of hysteria, but rather the effect of suggestion, to which all people respond to some degree. Eventually he came to believe that the hypnotic state wasn't essential to the therapeutic process originally associated with it and introduced an approach the Nancy School called "psychotherapeutics," in which hypnotic effects were obtained in normal waking consciousness (Ellenberger, 1970).

The era of Bernheim's leadership of the Nancy School was characterized by increased status for hypnotism (previously practiced as artificial somnambulism or magnetic sleep) in France. Two of the most prominent contributors to the field of hypnosis, Pierre Janet and Jean-Martin Charcot, were engaged in creative theoretical and clinical work. Despite the significance of their contributions, it is important to bear in mind, as Janet himself acknowledged, that the groundwork had been laid by the early magnetizers a century earlier. Janet claimed that it was inappropriate to refer to Puységur and his contemporaries as "precursors" when they had actually founded the science of hypnotism, anticipating all of the major features identified in the late 19th century. He noted that the following had been understood by the early magnetizers in the 18th century: that rapport was the crucial feature of magnetism and somnambulism; that the effect of rapport was experienced during the session, and that its counterpart, "influence," was sustained between sessions; that reciprocal influence was established between the practitioner and the subject; that the rapport carried the risk of intense interpersonal attraction; and that subjects were capable of executing posthypnotic suggestions. Janet also identified the errors of the early magnetizers, which jeopardized their acceptance by the medical profession. First, instead of focusing on the most basic manifestations of magnetic sleep, they attempted to demonstrate the validity of their practice by means of extraordinary phenomena. Second, most magnetizers lacked professional training and some instructed their uneducated subjects to diagnose and treat disease in other people, an illegal practice that antagonized the medical establishment. Finally, the procedure was easily exploited by quacks who sought to profit from lucrative stage demonstrations, inviting ridicule of all who practiced magnetism, including those who provided their services gratuitously and altruistically (Ellenberger, 1970).

Although Charcot and Janet weren't the first to identify the fundamental tenets of hypnotism, they added much to our understanding of the mind and its organization. Charcot, a French physician who was hailed as the greatest neurologist of his day, developed an interest in mental phenomena and became the powerful leader of the Salpêtrière

School, rival of the Nancy School. He observed the fragmentation of the stream of consciousness in hysteria (Putnam, 1989) and undertook the challenge of distinguishing between hysterical and epileptic convulsions. Hysteria had long been considered one of the "magnetic diseases," along with lethargy, somnambulism, catalepsy, maniacal ecstacy, and ecstatic visions. Accordingly, Charcot became interested in hypnotism and developed an understanding of hysteria. He demonstrated that hysterical, posttraumatic, and hypnotic paralyses were essentially the same phenomenon and distinguishable from organic paralyses. He found the same was true for amnesias, and distinguished the reversible "dynamic amnesias" (i.e., hysterical, posttraumatic, and hypnotic amnesias) from "organic amnesias," in which nothing is recoverable (Ellenberger, 1970). In applying medical methodology to hypnotic phenomena, Charcot was the first to synthesize the traditions of hypnosis and official psychiatry. His prestige in neurology brought credibility to hysteria, which had long been associated with malingering (Herman, 1997).

Charcot identified three successive stages in his hypnotized patients and presented a well-received paper at the *Académie des Sciences*. The success of his paper generated renewed interest in hypnotism, which led to numerous scholarly publications and ultimately to new prestige for the study and practice of hypnotism. It was Janet who pointed out the irony that the *Académie des Sciences* was the same institution that had condemned hypnotism three times in the previous century under the name of magnetism (Ellenberger, 1970).

Unfortunately, there were certain practices that Charcot had instituted at the Salpêtrière that contaminated his conclusions regarding the successive stages of therapy. His students, eager to please Charcot with their clinical acuity, would rehearse their demonstrations before showing their patients to Charcot. Following the demonstrations, Charcot would discuss the cases with his students in the presence of the patients. Under the circumstances, the likelihood of mutual suggestion between Charcot, his students, and the patients cannot be underestimated. Six years after Charcot had passed away, a few of his hysterical female patients remained at the Salpêtrière Hospital who would, "for a small remuneration, act out for the students the full-fledged attack of the *grande hystrie*" (Ellenberger, 1970, p. 101). Blanche Wittmann, who was among Charcot's most renowned patients at the Salpêtrière, exhibited an alter personality, Blanche II, who reported having witnessed the primary personality acting out Charcot's three stages of hypnosis. So it is apparent that Charcot's work was tainted by what we now call confirmation bias: His expectations influenced his patients' behavior, and their behavior, in turn, confirmed his confidence in his theoretical formulations. This difficulty didn't always escape the attention of his contemporaries. Bernheim reported that of the thousands of patients he had hypnotized, only one exhibited the three stages of hypnosis, and this patient had spent three years at the Salpêtrière (Ellenberger, 1970).

Janet was another of Charcot's contemporaries who was disturbed by the manner of Charcot's interaction with his patients. It was Janet who founded the objective study of dissociation. Part of his giftedness in objectivity apparently resided in his awareness of the role of subtle influences. He demonstrated that Charcot's alleged three stages of hypnosis were simply the result of unconscious training that his patients received at the Salpêtrière. He pointed out how much hypnotic behavior is shaped by expectation, the hypnotist unwittingly preparing the subject to perform a role, and the role varying somewhat from practitioner to practitioner and epoch to epoch. He described the intense attachment the subject felt for the hypnotist as *besoin de direction*, the need to be directed. Properly utilized, this need on the part of the patient could be a potent therapeutic tool (Ellenberger, 1970).

Janet (1889/1973) recognized the clinical sequelae of trauma. He argued in *L'Automatisme Psychologique*, published in 1889, that dissociation may occur when a person experiences powerful emotions such as terror, which constrict attention and disrupt the capacity to integrate experience into consciousness (Cardeña, 1994). The experience of vehement emotions, he proposed, can interfere with the process of matching frightening experiences with established cognitive schemata (van der Kolk, Weisaeth, & van der Hart, 1996). Janet believed that traumatized individuals become phobic about memory because they have failed to develop narratives about their traumata, instead experiencing posttraumatic amnesias and hyperamnesias (van der Kolk, Brown, & van der Hart, 1989). Terrifying or otherwise overwhelming experiences, he claimed, result in memories and affects that are not integrated into the person's identity but maintain a separate existence as "fixed ideas," "simultaneous psychological existences," or "successive existences" (alter personalities). Thus we see that Janet had grasped the core characteristics of what we now call posttraumatic stress disorder (PTSD) and DID. His treatment approach involved bringing compartmentalized memories and feelings into consciousness where they could be processed therapeutically. He anticipated contemporary treatment strategies with his three-phase therapy model (van der Hart, Brown, & van der Kolk, 1989).

In addition to his contributions in the fields of hypnosis and dissociation, Janet had a profound impact on the psychological sciences more generally. Ellenberger (1970) described Janet as standing "at the threshold of all modern dynamic psychiatry" (p. 406). It was Janet who coined the term "the subconscious." Originally trained as a philosopher before studying medicine, he distinguished the subconscious from "the unconscious," an existing philosophical concept. Bleuler's understanding of schizophrenia was informed by Janet's concept of psychasthenia with its reduction in psychological tension. Jung drew on Janet's "subconscious fixed idea" in developing the notion of the complex. Adler's notion of the feeling of inferiority, or "organ inferiority," was derived from Janet's *"sentiment d'incomplétude"* (sense of incompleteness or deficiency). Freud referred to Janet's "function of the real" in defining his psychoanalytic term, "the reality principle." Finally, the Freudian notion of transference bears a striking resemblance to Janet's concept of somnambulic influence and the need for direction (Ellenberger, 1970).

These many enduring contributions to the theories of others notwithstanding, Janet's formulations regarding the role of trauma in hysteria enjoyed wide acceptance for only a brief time. As we will see, despite Freud's early recognition of the impact of childhood trauma, his subsequent theory substituted sexual fantasies for actual incest in the etiology of hysteria. Psychoanalysis crowded out competing theoretical models, and Janet's most important discovery was forgotten until the dissociative defense was rediscovered in the 1980s as a key element in PTSD (van der Kolk, Weisaeth, & van der Hart, 1996).

Magnetism was introduced into the United States via the French-American city of New Orleans. While Janet was losing status in France, he was admired in the United States, where he was invited to attend the opening ceremonies for a new building at Harvard Medical School and deliver a series of lectures in 1906 (Ellenberger, 1970). In the United States during the first three decades of the 20th century, major contributions to the study of consciousness, hypnosis, and dissociation were made by William James, his student Boris Sidis, and Morton Prince (Putnam, 1989). Prince, who wrote on the unconscious, hypnosis, and dissociative phenomena, is best known for publishing the multiple personality case of Christine Beauchamp (pronounced "Beecham," according to Prince's footnote) in *The Dissociation of a Personality* (Prince, 1905/1930).

The Role of Hypnosis in the Discovery of the Unconscious

Bearing in mind these historical developments, we turn our attention to the role of hypnosis in emerging conceptions of the unconscious. Long before Freud's time, the early magnetizers clearly understood the existence of the unconscious mind. We have seen how Puységur elicited in Race and other patients the capacity to draw on intelligence not ordinarily available to the conscious mind. Two of Puységur's contemporaries, Bertrand and Noizet, both argued that some mental contents are only manifested through their effects and not through personal awareness. Ellenberger (1970) observed that

> Hypnotism provided a first model of the human mind as a double ego, a conscious but restricted ego that the individual believes to be the only one, and a subconscious, much wider ego, unknown to the conscious one, but endowed with unknown perceptive and creative powers. (p. 168)

Although hypnosis experienced waves of favor and disfavor at various times in various countries, artificial somnambulism was the primary means of gaining access to the unconscious from 1784 to about 1880. In fact, hypnotism was referred to as the *via regia*, or royal road, to the unconscious. Two models of the human mind emerged from the study and practice of magnetism and hypnotism: the concept of the duality of the mind, also known as dipsychism or double ego, and later the concept of the mind as composed of a cluster of subpersonalities or parts, also known as polypsychism. These two models had a tremendous impact on dynamic psychiatry. Janet's concept of the subconscious and Freud's first formulation of the unconscious as the totality of repressed memories and tendencies were derived quite clearly from the notion of dipsychism. Freud's later tripartite model is, of course, an example of polypsychism. Despite these important contributions, hypnotism fell into disfavor at the end of the 19th century, when anything that related to hysteria, hypnosis, or suggestion was eyed with increasing suspicion (Ellenberger, 1970).

Trends in the Status of Dissociation

Just as the status of hypnotism has waxed and waned, the study of dissociation has had periods of professional and cultural support and periods of dismissal and even condemnation. Dual personality was noted during the 18th and 19th centuries and was understood within the general context of hysteria, a common "magnetic condition." "I believe it satisfactorily established, in a general way," wrote Binet in 1887, "that two states of consciousness, not known to each other, can co-exist in the mind of an hysterical patient" (cited in Ellenberger, 1970, p. 143). Janet conceptualized hysteria as a permanent state of dual personality.

The early published cases of what we now call DID were all reports of dual personality. Soon after instances of demonic possession disappeared from the literature, cases of dual personality began to appear in the mesmerist writings. In 1791, Eberhardt Gmelin published a case he described as *umgetauschte Persönlichkeit*, or "exchanged personality," in which the two personalities had distinct national characters (French and German) and accompanying language skills and accents. During the 19th century, other cases of divided or dual personality were noted. The famous case of Mary Reynolds was thought to have been published by Dr. John Kearsley Mitchell around 1815. However, it is perhaps better known through the elaboration of the case by Mitchell's son, Dr. Silas Weir Mitchell, who, in 1889, published *Mary Reynolds, A Case of Double Consciousness*, a more comprehensive case history based on his father's records. In 1840, Despine Sr. published what Ellenberger (1970) called the first "truly objective study of multiple personality" (p. 129) with the case of Estelle, an 11-year-old girl who was celebrated as *"la petite ressuscitée"* ("the little resurrected one") after Despine fused her primary personality, who was paralyzed, in pain, and could tolerate few foods, with her secondary personality, who was lively and had a voracious appetite and varied diet. Although Estelle's primary and secondary personalities are highlighted in Despine's textual account, Kluft (1993c) observed that Despine included additional personalities in an intriguing appendix. (Incidentally, Despine decided to use magnetism to treat his young patient after her mother informed him that Estelle was comforted by a choir of angels, indicating that this was an "ecstatic disorder," which should be amenable to a magnetic cure.) Janet was among the first hypnotists to attempt systematic experiments with patients presenting sets of subpersonalities. By 1880, multiple personality was of great interest in psychiatric and philosophical circles. No longer was the focus limited to dual personality. Morton Prince's 1905 publication of the renowned case of Christine Beauchamp described "personality clusters" (Ellenberger, 1970).

During this period of interest in dissociation, a number of theories and classification systems were developed. There were two theoretical camps in the 19th century: The *associationists* argued that dissociation resulted from a mental split or disconnection between the two main gears of associations, and the *organicists* promoted the notion that the brain itself had been organically modified. With subsequent developments in medical technology, it became possible to test the brain function of dissociative individuals, and in 1953 Morselli published his findings of distinct electroencephalograms in the two personalities of his patient, Marisa (Ellenberger, 1970).

Among the many issues explored during the 19th century was the relative moral and psychological status of the personalities in dual or multiple personality. A number of hypnotists observed, as Despine had in treating Estelle, that the secondary personality appeared to be healthier than the primary one. Eugene Azam, a professor of surgery at the Bordeaux Medical School, coined the term *"dédoublement de la personnalité"* ("doubling of the personality") to describe the dual personality phenomenon. In 1887, he published the case of Félida X, whose secondary personality was highly intelligent and was aware of the full life history, while the primary personality was of average intelligence and suffered from severe hysterical symptoms, headaches, and neuralgias. Frederick Myers, William James, and Pierre Janet all supported Azam's generalization that the primary personality is unhealthy and the secondary personality represents the healthy premorbid state, and that through fusion the resources of the secondary personality effect the health of the patient (Ellenberger, 1970). However, the view that the secondary personality is suspect was not without its supporters. Sidis, for example, believed that the secondary personality, whom he called the "subwaking self," was amoral, quite subject to emotional arousal, and, therefore, capable of performing any act (Putnam, 1989).

These competing views of the relative status of the personalities found their way into fiction. During the second half of the 19th century, many writers were inspired by the topic of dual personality, which appeared in literature as "the double." Stevenson's *The Strange Story of Dr. Jekyll and Mr. Hyde*, published in 1886, is the most notable example of a literary work influenced by dual personality, but earlier well-known works include Gozlan's best-selling French novel, *Le Médecin du Pecq*, published in 1839, and Dostoevski's *Dvoinik (The Double)*, published in 1846. In each of these works the secondary personality is threatening. The dramatic tension derives from the conflict between the personalities, the primary personality terrified by the prospect of losing control at any time to a stranger within himself who is capable of doing anything. *William Wilson*, published by Edgar Allen Poe in 1839, illustrates the other approach: The primary personality lives a life of debauchery and eventually murders his morally superior secondary personality, thereby killing himself as well (Ellenberger, 1970).

The Impact of Freudian Theory on the Study of Dissociation

During the 1930s, the study of dissociation lost status within the scientific community and was no longer viewed as a legitimate clinical interest (Putnam, 1989). This shift was due, in very large part, to the powerful impact of Freudian theory.

Early in his career, Freud, working independently of Janet, arrived at similar conclusions regarding the origins of hysteria. In collaboration with Breuer, he announced his discovery of the traumatic origins of hysteria. With Breuer, Freud published an article in 1893 in which they stated clearly that hysterical symptoms are related to psychic trauma, whether obviously related or symbolically disguised. They explained that the trauma may have occurred while the patient was in a state of autohypnosis or it may have been excluded from consciousness altogether. Under hypnosis the trauma is reexperienced vividly, and the traumatic material, once brought into consciousness, is worked through verbally and affectively (Breuer & Freud, 1893/1959). Freud (1924/1953b), in a eulogy of Charcot, criticized Charcot for overestimating heredity in the etiology of hysteria and underestimating the role of trauma. "So greatly did Charcot over-estimate heredity as a cause," he claimed, "that no loophole was left by which nervous disease could be acquired" (p. 23).

Unlike Janet and Breuer, Freud believed that all "traumatic reminiscences" were sexual in nature (Herman, 1997). In 1896, Freud wrote in *The Aetiology of Hysteria* (reproduced in Freud, 1924/1953a):

> I put forward the proposition, therefore, that at the bottom of every case of hysteria will be found one or more experiences of premature sexual experience, belonging to the first years of childhood, experiences which may be reproduced by analytic work though whole decades have intervened. I believe this to be a momentous revelation. (p. 198)

Not long after Freud proclaimed his theory of hysteria as a great discovery, he reported that he had been misled by his patients' fantasies. Apparently threatened by increasingly frequent patient reports of incest allegedly occurring within his own social and intellectual circle, and distressed by professional rejection, Freud repudiated the traumatic theory of hysteria. For the rest of his life he devoted his professional energy to exploring fantasies rather than reconstructing his patients' personal histories through the uncovering of suppressed, repressed, or dissociated memories. By 1904, he had rejected hypnosis and replaced it with the psychoanalytic technique of free association as a means of exploring patients' fantasies. His theory of infantile sexuality, referring to the sexual drives and wishes of infants, replaced the seduction hypothesis, thereby denying the reality of childhood sexual abuse. Herman (1997) pointed out that, while Freud has been blamed for his recantation of the traumatic theory of hysteria, a broader social perspective affords the recognition that there was no societal or political support in Freud's day for a serious inquiry into the origins of hysteria.

In considering the impact of psychoanalysis on the study of dissociation, the most striking feature is the preeminence of the intrapsychic and the associated tendency to dismiss the impact of highly significant environmental threats. Freudian theory, despite its powerfully stimulating influence not only within psychology and psychiatry but also on culture and the arts, nonetheless had an inhibitory effect on our understanding of the human response to trauma and, consequently, on our efforts to address the needs of traumatized individuals. In illuminating the dynamics of the intrapsychic realm, Freud failed to attend adequately to the reality of interpersonal violence and its intrapsychic repercussions.

It is quite fascinating to observe the nearly exclusively intrapsychic focus that characterizes Freudian theory playing itself out in Freud's personal life. As Hitler rose to power, Freud's friends urged him to emigrate to the United States or England. For years he remained adamantly opposed to such a move, even after the Nazis had murdered many of his fellow Jews and had systematically destroyed his books and suppressed the psychoanalytic societies in Germany. Freud was "strangely blind to the pervasiveness of the Nazi danger" (Ellenberger, 1970, p. 855). It wasn't until the Nazis actually occupied Vienna that Freud agreed to leave the city for England in the last year of his life.

The Impact of Freudian Theory on the Notion of a Creative Unconscious

Just as Freud's model had an inhibitory impact on the status of dissociation and traumatization, it also thwarted professional and societal appreciation of the creative powers of the unconscious mind. Freud's purely regressive id, with its antisocial impulses, is a far cry from the unconscious healing potential discovered by Puységur. One cannot underestimate the suggestiveness inherent in these formulations of the unconscious. The pervasive psychoanalytic tradition emphasizing the regressive—rather than the creative—nature of the unconscious mind not only shapes training programs and treatment modalities, but, in the final analysis, it has a profound influence on how patients view their innermost nature.

It's interesting to note that Jung, even before articulating his concept of the collective unconscious, conceived of the personal unconscious as quite distinct from Freud's exclusively regressive one. Jung's analytic or complex psychology emphasizes an unconscious that is a rich source of guidance to the patient undergoing the process of individuation, which results in harmonious living and the realization of the patient's truest self (Jung, 1959). Unfortunately for the status of the unconscious, Jung's model, though influential, hasn't had nearly the impact of Freud's in psychiatry, psychology, and most aspects of intellectual and cultural life.

CHAPTER

Traumatology and the Treatment of Dissociative States: Major 20th Century Developments

The 20th century witnessed the birth of traumatic stress studies, or traumatology, and the codification of PTSD and the dissociative disorders. This chapter addresses these developments. It summarizes the contributions of the early pioneers in the treatment of MPD/DID and highlights the delayed memory debate and its impact on clinical practice. The chapter concludes with the emerging consensus regarding the need for cautious, respectful, and empowering treatment of individuals who may have been traumatized in childhood.

☐ Traumatology

The Emergence of Traumatology

We have seen that Janet articulated the psychological sequelae of trauma and that Freud turned his attention, and the world's, to intrapsychic dynamics. A period of declining interest in trauma and dissociation followed. Herman (1997) referred to the study of psychological trauma itself as having "a curious history—one of episodic amnesia" (p. 7). Psychiatry and psychology, like society in general, have experienced amnestic periods in which previously discovered phenomena are forgotten or vehemently denied. Courtois (1999) described the cyclical nature of this phenomenon as a *"fin de siècle"* effect (p. 1), in which the last decades of the 19th and 20th centuries have witnessed an attack on the credibility of accounts of traumatization.

Of course, it's extremely uncomfortable to acknowledge the full reality of traumatization. In order to accept the emotional truth of the traumatized individual, we need to connect empathically with the experience of utter terror and helplessness (Herman, 1997). We have to face the fact that we live in a world where natural disaster and human exploitation are possible, and where those who should protect us (such as our parents and political leaders) are sometimes responsible for the most devastating events in domestic and military life.

Although Janet's pioneering work, and the early work of Freud and Breuer, focused on the effects of trauma within the domestic sphere, with the sexual exploitation of girls as the most common etiological factor in hysteria, the impact of childhood sexual abuse was not the impetus that spawned the field of traumatology in the 20th century. In the first decade of the 20th century, the Swiss psychiatrist Edouard Stierlin studied survivors of an earthquake and a mining disaster, becoming the first researcher in disaster psychology. While his contemporaries maligned the character of traumatized individuals by attributing their symptoms to weakness of will, constitutional predisposition, and even desire for compensation, Stierlin observed that traumatic neurosis was unique among psychogenic conditions in that its etiology doesn't necessarily involve psychopathological predisposition (van der Kolk, Weisaeth, & van der Hart, 1996). However, even this pioneering work failed to mobilize the psychiatric profession, with its strong intrapsychic focus, to recognize the psychologically devastating effects of trauma. There were other efforts to address the traumatized population during the first half of the 20th century, including efforts early in the century to protect children from maltreatment, but momentum was not maintained (Courtois, 1999).

The real catalyst for the field of traumatology was wartime experience. Kardiner, after treating traumatized World War I veterans, challenged the assumptions of his Freudian training and essentially defined, in 1941, what would be codified as PTSD nearly four decades later. He identified the core symptoms of extreme physiological arousal, hypervigilance, reexperiencing of trauma, and altered sense of self in relation to the world (van der Kolk, Weisaeth, & van der Hart, 1996). Hypnosis was reintroduced, for the first time in four decades, to treat combat trauma in World War II (van der Kolk, Weisaeth, & van der Hart, 1996). However, it was in the aftermath of the Vietnam War that new data finally challenged the prevailing view of psychopathology as a predominantly intrapsychic phenomenon, the posttraumatic stress response was identified, and the field of traumatology originated (Courtois, 1996).

In addition to combat trauma, other social developments beginning in the 1960s contributed to the growing interest in traumatology. The human rights and women's movements highlighted domestic violence. The identification of battered child syndrome in 1962 alerted physicians to the physical evidence of abuse they had been overlooking and served as a catalyst to research. In the same year, concentration camp syndrome was identified and preliminary research efforts into the effects of internment, starvation, and exhaustion were initiated (Eitinger, 1962). In the 1960s and 1970s, consciousness-raising groups served to heighten public awareness of the prevalence and severity of various forms of traumatization, notably combat trauma and the sexual victimization of girls and women. By the mid-1970s numerous studies documented the prevalence and developmental impact of child abuse and led to the formulation of intervention strategies. Child Protective Services were upgraded accordingly. Rape Trauma Syndrome was first described in 1974 by Burgess and Holstrom, who were struck by the similarity between the intrusive posttraumatic symptoms of survivors of rape and survivors of combat. That same year, the mandatory reporting of suspected child abuse was implemented via the federal Child Abuse Prevention and Treatment Act (Courtois, 1999). In 1981, Judith Herman wrote:

> Until the resurgence of the women's liberation movement, even the most courageous explorers of sexual mores simply refused to deal with the fact that many men, including fathers, feel entitled to use children for their sexual enjoyment. Nevertheless, this fact is established by now beyond any reasonable doubt. (p. 21)

No longer was the *Zeitgeist* dismissive of traumatized individuals, the legitimacy of their complaints, and the efforts of researchers and clinicians to understand and alleviate their suffering. Accordingly, methodologically sophisticated child sexual abuse studies began emerging in the late 1970s, documenting that child sexual abuse occurs in all social strata (Courtois, 1999). By 1980, the fundamental similarities between the various posttraumatic syndromes—rape trauma, battered woman, Vietnam veterans, concentration camp, and abused child—were recognized, and a new inclusive diagnosis, posttraumatic stress disorder (PTSD), was introduced in the Diagnostic and Statistical Manual of Mental Disorders (*DSM-III*; American Psychiatric Association, 1980). This revision of the diagnostic manual also introduced a new category, the dissociative disorders, with multiple personality (MP) as the most severe form of dissociative psychopathology. MP was renamed multiple personality disorder (MPD) in the *DSM-III-R* (American Psychiatric Association, 1987), when it was described as "not nearly so rare as it has commonly been thought to be" (p. 271), and was subsequently renamed dissociative identity disorder (DID) in the *DSM-IV* (American Psychiatric Association, 1994). Although PTSD is classified as an anxiety disorder rather than a dissociative disorder, MPD/DID can be conceptualized as a special variant of PTSD (Spiegel, 1984), or more specifically, as a complex form of childhood-onset PTSD (Kluft, 1991). As observed by Janet, dissociation is an integral aspect of PTSD (van der Kolk, 1996).

The inclusion in the *DSM* of the dissociative and posttraumatic diagnoses was both a reflection of the accomplishments of traumatologists and a catalyst for future research and treatment model development. The crucial role of terror in the human response to traumatic events had been established. Horevitz and Loewenstein (1994) put it well: "At the core of all traumatic memory is overwhelming terror wherein the past and present cannot be differentiated, and the future does not exist. Pain and survival are the imminent realities of this experience" (p. 307). In response to the dissociated episode of having been overwhelmed by terror, the individual experiences both physiological hyperarousal, with various forms of intrusive recollection, and denial and numbing. Van der Kolk, Weisaeth, and van der Hart (1996) pointed out that while Horowitz defined the biphasic nature of the trauma response in 1978—the alternating phases of intrusive reexperiencing and numbing—it has now been established that the phases do not necessarily alternate, but coexist.

Auerbach (2000) observed that the physiological approach to PTSD, encouraged by the diagnostic criteria, is typically understood as the fundamental approach to the disorder because the physiological correlates are readily amenable to empirical investigation. However, he emphasized the value of the alternative, psychological approach, which explains posttraumatic symptomatology as a consequence of the shattering of schemata concerning the self and the world. Trauma disrupts the meaningful organization of life experience, thereby exerting a debilitating effect on self-perception and ability to face the future. Shay (1995) described the loss of authority over mental function, including trust in one's perceptions and memory, commonly experienced by survivors of combat trauma. Herman (1997) emphasized "disconnection" as a consequence of traumatization and highlighted the importance of reclaiming one's world in the context of a healing relationship and opportunities to reconnect through participation in community.

Documentation of the psychologically damaging impact of childhood trauma is emphasized in the traumatology literature. Problems commonly experienced by victims of childhood maltreatment include depression, anxiety, low self-esteem, difficulty trusting others, substance abuse, sexual maladjustment, and self-destructive behaviors including suicidality (Putnam, 1997). The experience of maltreatment in childhood encourages helplessness, passivity, and dependency, which, in turn, lead to tolerance of interpersonal violence and subsequent revictimization (Briere, 1992).

The traumatology literature also highlights the impact of maltreatment and abuse on a child's self-image. Courtois (1996) identified shame, despair, and feelings of being permanently damaged as symptoms of human-induced trauma. Briere (1992) delineated two mechanisms by which abuse tends to promote cognitive distortions regarding the self and the world: psychological reactions to the terror and helplessness experienced at the time of the abuse, and subsequent efforts to make sense of having been abused. Herman (1997) described how a poor self-image is created and reinforced because it serves a function for the abused child:

> The child must construct some system of meaning that justifies [the abuse]. Inevitably the child concludes that her innate badness is the cause. The child seizes upon this explanation early and clings to it tenaciously, for it enables her to preserve a sense of meaning, hope, and power. If she is bad, then her parents are good. If she is bad, then she can try to be good. If, somehow, she has brought this fate upon herself, then somehow she has the power to change it. If she has driven her parents to mistreat her, then, if only she tries hard enough, she may someday earn their forgiveness and finally win the protection and care she so desperately needs. (p. 103)

Putnam (1992, p. 96) offered a valuable "developmental, behavioral-state" model for conceptualizing MPD and later (1997) described the developmental sequelae of traumatization which results in pathological dissociation:

> Multilevel developmental disturbances are produced by the segregation or compartmentalization of information, skills, and behavior into discrete dissociative states, such that this knowledge is only erratically (as opposed to reliably) available to the individual. Difficulties with the integration of dissociatively compartmentalized information impair metacognitive executive functions and iteratively disrupt the developmental consolidation of sense of self over the life course. (p. 15)

Affect dysregulation, or impaired capacity to modulate affect and respond in an appropriate manner to a variety of environmental demands and challenges, has long-term consequences for the child's self-image (Putnam, 1997). In fact, van der Kolk (1996) described impaired self-regulation as "possibly the most far-reaching effect of psychological trauma in both children and adults" (p. 187), with greater likelihood of ongoing difficulties regulating anger, anxiety, and sexual impulses in cases where there has been earlier onset and greater duration of traumatization. Gold (2000) emphasized the etiological role of pervasive, grossly negligent parental behaviors in the development of these serious psychological disturbances. He argued that, in conceptualizing and treating posttraumatic disorders, focus on discrete acts of sexual and physical abuse should not eclipse the impact of broad deficiencies in the family environment, which are responsible in large part for the child's developmental failures in affect regulation, self-expression, conflict resolution, and so forth.

During the last two decades of the 20th century, tremendous strides were made in traumatology research, elucidating the epidemiology, diversity, and neuropsychology of the posttraumatic response. The existence of chronic dissociative pathology, as opposed to the previously acknowledged acute time-limited dissociative reactions, finally gained wider recognition (Putnam, 1989). Exciting advances in the neurosciences permitted investigation of the psychobiological processes involved in the trauma response. In studying the neurotransmitter functions in PTSD subjects, abnormalities have been documented in catecholamines, serotonin, endogenous opioids, and corticosteroids. Summarizing the research literature on neurohormonal alterations occurring in response to acute and chronic stress, Chu, Matthews, Frey, and Ganzel (1996) noted that we rely on animal models for documentation of many of the stress-responsive neurohormonal changes. However, they continued, "persistent increases in catecholamine activity, alterations in hormonal functions in the HPA axis, and opioid responses have all been documented in patients with PTSD" (p. 4). New brain imaging technologies permit display of the neuroanatomy of PTSD. Finally, researchers have been able to demonstrate empirically, as Janet and Kardiner had long ago observed clinically, that autonomic arousal can evoke in PTSD subjects, but not in controls, visual and affective experiences linked with past trauma (van der Kolk, van der Hart, & Marmar, 1996). The observation that traumatized individuals often display "speechless terror," or alexithymia (loss of words to express emotions), is consistent with results of a PET scan study (van der Kolk, 1996). When PTSD subjects were exposed to stimuli reminiscent of traumatization, there was evidence of increased activity in the areas of the right hemisphere associated with emotional and autonomic arousal, and simultaneous decreased oxygen utilization in the area of the left hemisphere associated with expressive language.

Support for the notion that there are two distinct memory processes, governing normal and traumatic memory, are presented later in this chapter, in the context of the delayed memory controversy. Summarizing the data available at the end of the 20th century, Courtois (1999) wrote: "At present, a substantial body of research derived from clinical, non-clinical, and community samples correlates a history of childhood sexual abuse with a wide range of potential aftereffects and diagnosable mental conditions in approximately 20–40 percent of victims" (p. 123).

Despite these major developments within the field of traumatology, training of mental health professionals continues to neglect the sequelae of trauma (Carlson & Armstrong, 1994; Courtois, 1995, 1999; Enns et al., 1998; Enns, McNeilly, Corkery, & Gilbert, 1995; Pope & Brown, 1996), with the result that posttraumatic and dissociative disorders are still grossly underdiagnosed. Saxe et al. (1993) reviewed hospital charts of psychiatric inpatients, comparing the documentation of histories, symptoms, and diagnoses reflecting trauma and dissociation with findings obtained by the research team, who administered diagnostic tests and blindly interviewed high-scorers on the Dissociative Experiences Scale (Bernstein & Putnam, 1986) and a control group of low-scorers. They found that patients' charts documented only 29% of the dissociative symptoms and 21% of the dissociative and PTSD diagnoses that were detected by the research team.

Courtois (1999) divided the 20th century into three epochs in terms of prevailing views of the impact of trauma on psychological functioning. Citing Armstrong (1978), she called the first two thirds of the century "The Age of Denial," with psychoanalytic theory obscuring the prevalence and consequences of trauma. "The Age of Validation" (Armstrong, 1978, cited in Courtois, 1999) began in the late 1960s, as posttraumatic reactions became apparent in the aftermath of the Vietnam War and as the prevalence of physical and sexual violence against women and children became widely recognized. As we will see, the process of validation sometimes involved an overemphasis on trauma to the exclusion of other appropriate therapeutic foci, setting the stage for "The Age of Backlash" (Armstrong, 1994, cited in Courtois, 1999) beginning in the last decade of the 20th century. This epoch was characterized by charges that recovered memories are artifacts of misinformed and unethical therapy practices. The legitimacy of the traumatic stress and dissociative perspective has once again been threatened.

In order to contextualize the backlash against individuals reporting delayed recall for traumatic life events and against the professional community providing their treatment, we turn our attention now to the impact of traumatology on psychotherapy practices during the last three decades of the 20th century.

The Impact of Traumatology on Psychotherapy

Developments in traumatology contributed to renewed interest in dissociation and its role in response to trauma. There was a great deal of scholarly and clinical activity in the field of dissociation during the 1970s and 1980s. Putnam (1989) pointed out that this renewed interest in dissociative disorders was generated not only by developments in traumatology, but also by Hilgard's "neodissociative" theory of consciousness, which rekindled interest in hypnosis as well as dissociation, and by the publication of Ellenberger's *The Discovery of the Unconscious: The History and Evolution of Dynamic Psychiatry* (1970), which highlighted early cases of multiple personality and the role of hypnosis in pre-Freudian dynamic psychiatry.

Major contributors to treatment model development for MPD during the 1970s and 1980s include Bowers et al. (1971), Allison (1974), Coons (1980), Kluft (1982), Horevitz (1983), Braun (1984a), Wilbur (1984), Fine (1988), Putnam (1989), and Ross (1989). Schreiber (1974) popularized Wilbur's pioneering psychoanalytic treatment of MPD in *Sybil*, although, as Kluft (1993c) observed, it depicted Wilbur's early therapeutic efforts and cannot do justice to the contributions she made later in her illustrious career. Kluft (1993c) also noted that Putnam's 1989 text, *Diagnosis and Treatment of Multiple Personality Disorder*, has been tremendously influential as the most widely respected single volume addressing the treatment of MPD.

A number of MPD treatment models emerged in the 1970s and 1980s, with no one model receiving more empirical support than the others (Kluft, 1993a). Although some models addressed the need to "neutralize" and disempower destructive alters (e.g., Allison & Schwartz, 1998), other models approached conflicts within the personality system in a more even-handed manner. Applications of systems theory to the internal system of the individual helped to focus clinical attention on the importance of recognizing the protective function of each member of a system, and each member's unique role. Many of the MPD treatment models developed in the 1970s and 1980s emphasized the formation of empathic connections with all members of the personality system and the recognition that all personalities are fundamentally protective and are indispensable to the patient's potential for harmonious functioning. This approach contrasts with the 19th century view of dual personality discussed previously, which held that one is the healthy or morally superior personality, and the other is the sick, dangerous, or evil personality.

In addition to internal communication and cooperation, these treatment models also emphasized the uncovering, exploration, and metabolism of traumatic memories and relied heavily on the use of abreaction. This use of deliberate reexperiencing of trauma for therapeutic purposes had been used with survivors of combat trauma, after having been initially introduced by Freud and Breuer. However, it was applied to the treatment of survivors of childhood trauma without empirical support for its efficacy with this population, with mixed results (Courtois, 1999). Although there was diversity of opinion among MPD therapists in terms of whether all traumatic incidents required abreaction, or whether the abreaction of a few representative incidents sufficed (Kluft, 1993a), regressive hypnotic work, in general, and the use of abreaction of trauma, in particular, were characteristic of most MPD therapies in the 1970s and 1980s. Some treatment models incorporated stage and screen techniques, utilized during the hypnotic trance state, to facilitate abreaction (Horevitz & Loewenstein, 1994). For most therapies, the goal was fusion of the personality system into a functional whole, achieved via the integration of split-off memories and affects.

Braun's pioneering work (1984a) broadened the conceptual framework of MPD from an essentially psychological one to one that brought together diverse approaches "under the rubric of neuropsychophysiologic (NPP) state-dependent learning (SDL)" (Braun, 1988, p. 5). He described the process by which numerous environmental interactions occurring while the child is in similar NPP states form a chain of linked information. "This chaining of knowledge, memory, and interactive patterns," he explained, "forms an alter personality with its own response patterns, life history, and range of affect" (1988, p. 5).

Some of the MPD therapy models emerging during this period incorporated the ISH, which was first described by Allison (1974) as "the manifestation of a higher part of the personality which is derivative of the Soul, a part called the Inner Self, the Real Self, or simply the Self" (p. 30). Although Allison and Schwartz (1998) stated explicitly that the ISH is an entity, the "Essence" of the person, rather than an alter, most clinicians and researchers have conceptualized the ISH as an alter personality who can greatly assist the therapeutic process due to his or her knowledge, wisdom, emotional composure, and perspective. Allison describes conversing with the ISH as if the patient were a third party, with the ISH serving as a cotherapist. Some patients presented with more than one ISH. There was no consensus as to whether an ISH is present in all MPD patients (Putnam, 1989).

Kluft (1993c) provided a useful history of the major contributions to the treatment of MPD/DID as well as a nosology of therapeutic orientations, distinguishing successful from unsuccessful approaches. He identified the two most successful orientations, both of which espouse integration of the personality structure as the ideal goal of treatment: (a) *Strategic integrationalism*, derived primarily from the work of Wilbur as augmented by the contributions of Kluft: a psychoanalytically informed approach that effectively challenges the dissociative defenses, and (b) *Tactical integrationalism*, based on the work of Allison, Braun, Caul, and Fine: an approach in which integration is achieved via emphasis on diverse, deliberate tactics involving hypnotic approaches and cognitive-behavioral restructuring. Kluft also acknowledged that a coherent *personality-focused* approach has been effective with many patients. This orientation emphasizes cooperation among the members of the personality system, who are often viewed as an internal family system, with the goal of increased inner harmony and mutual support rather than integration per se.

Although this chapter emphasizes the modifications in clinical practice precipitated by the delayed memory controversy, responsible therapists treating dissociative clients have been refining their methods in response to their own clinical successes and failures and in accordance with developments reported in the professional literature. Coons, Bowman, and Milstein (1988); Schultz, Braun, and Kluft (1989); Ross, Norton, and Wozney (1989); and Putnam, Guroff, Silberman, Barban, and Post (1986) all reported large-scale open (noncontrolled) studies, providing useful preliminary generalizations regarding characteristics of MPD patients and their treatment needs. Among the most significant contributions to the literature is the set of 12 "pragmatic empirical ground rules" formulated by Kluft on the basis of consultation with approximately 1,200 therapists treating MPD patients. His rules were derived from a compilation of errors made by therapists. Applying the rules to subsequent consultations, he confirmed that the patient was unlikely to do well when a serious violation of any of the 12 rules occurred (Kluft, 1993c). The rules concern establishment of firm boundaries, maintenance of a strong therapeutic alliance, focus on patient's achievement of mastery, addressing buried trauma and associated affect, promoting collaboration among the alters, correcting cognitive errors, and restoring shattered assumptions, among other goals.

Unfortunately, some MPD therapists during the 1970s and 1980s became overzealous in their goal of uncovering and processing trauma. It is likely that DID was overdiagnosed at that time. Many therapists too readily endorsed the veracity of recovered memories and were inadequately attentive to the suggestiveness of their interventions. For example, suggestions were sometimes made that the patient's symptomatology suggested a history of abuse and would not improve until the abuse was recalled, articulated, and worked through.

While MPD treatment models were emerging, a lay literature began to appear, and untrained individuals, often themselves survivors of childhood abuse in various stages of their own recovery, presented themselves as abuse specialists and began providing lay services without professional supervision. These lay therapies tended to overemphasize the importance of identification and metabolism of trauma and to underemphasize adaptive functioning and symptom reduction (Courtois, 1999). Courtois (1999), in her exhaustive and even-handed analysis of the recovered memory debate, described how many therapists felt a strong attraction to working with survivors of childhood trauma, and how their behavior contributed to the controversy:

> As part of the attraction, it quickly became the norm for some therapists (professionals as well as lay) to overemphasize abuse to the exclusion of other life and therapy issues, and to rely prematurely and almost exclusively on exploratory approaches to traumatic memory that were inherently destabilizing. When patients exhibited symptoms associated with a history of sexual abuse but had no memory, repressed memory for the abuse came to be viewed as the rule and non-remembering as constituting dissociative amnesia and denial. As the atmosphere of zealotry accelerated, more and more serious and bizarre forms of abuse were regarded as the norm, accepted uncritically, and, in some cases, reinforced. A number of therapists acted out on their countertransference, suspended critical judgment, developed dual-role relationships with patients, and functioned as advocates (and sometimes zealots) rather than remaining in their roles as therapists. (p. 307)

Concurrently, media coverage began to feature the more sensational aspects of MPD. In the 1970s, television documentaries began highlighting cases of the least common and most exotic forms of abuse as if they were the prototype. For example, satanic ritual abuse, alien abduction, and past life abuse were disproportionately portrayed (Courtois, 1999), inviting incredulity in the viewing audience. This biased media coverage, in combination with treatment errors made by both lay and professional therapists, set the stage for the emergence of the recovered memory controversy in the early 1990s.

☐ The Recovered Memory Controversy

In 1990, a legal precedent was set when a 51-year-old American male was convicted of a murder committed 20 years earlier "on the basis of a freshly unearthed repressed memory" (Loftus, 1993, p. 519). Within two years, the False Memory Syndrome Foundation (FMSF) was established with the goal of authenticating what it claimed was a psychological syndrome reaching epidemic proportions. The FMSF contends that "false memory syndrome" is a diagnosable psychological syndrome, akin to a personality disorder, characterized by pervasive investment in, and preoccupation with, a traumatic memory that is objectively false, but held by the individual to be true. The FMSF has launched a vehement attack on the DID diagnosis. Although a group of 17 eminent researchers coauthored a statement in which they challenged the term "false memory syndrome" as "a non-psychological term originated by a private foundation whose stated purpose is to support accused parents" (Carstensen et al.,

1993, cited in Pope & Brown, 1996, p. 72), the FMSF has successfully attracted a Scientific and Professional Advisory Board of distinguished professionals who enhanced the organization's credibility.

The participants in the debate, the proponents of the false memory and traumatic stress positions, were generally from completely different professional backgrounds. Until recently, two separate bodies of literature addressed the issue of delayed memories of childhood abuse, with little cross fertilization or consolidation (Alpert, 1995). One literature was based on scientific memory research and was generated primarily by cognitive psychologists who had no clinical experience or training (the proponents of the false memory position), and the other was based on the scholarly literature of traumatology and child sexual abuse and was generated by clinicians or scientist-practitioners treating victims of trauma and, in some cases, also conducting research (the proponents of the traumatic stress position). The controversy became highly contentious and politicized because the mental health professions lacked, at the time of the establishment of the FMSF, a "trauma-focused clinical paradigm that attend[ed] to the reconstructive nature of memory as well as a memory research paradigm that tend[ed] to traumatic events and their possible impact on memory" (Alpert, 1995, p. 4).

In a common scenario leading to litigation, an individual accuses a family member of having incestuously abused her during childhood and states that she retrieved her traumatic memories in the context of psychotherapy after an extensive period of intervening amnesia. The alleged perpetrator then sues the therapist. The prosecuting attorney seeks, and receives, assistance from the FMSF and arranges for the testimony of memory experts who challenge the theoretical basis of repressed memories as inconsistent with the literature of memory science, arguing that the clinician, by using inappropriate therapy techniques, is responsible for having created pseudomemories. In addition to this type of litigation scenario, there are others in which the alleged victim sues the alleged perpetrator, and still others in which the patient sues the therapist for the implantation of false memories. The professional climate has become highly litigious. Because of financial losses sustained by malpractice insurance companies when therapists are sued, one malpractice insurance company has advised its insureds not to provide psychotherapy to clients presenting with delayed recall of trauma (L. S. Brown, 1997).

Arguments of the False Memory Position

Proponents of the false memory position cite the research of Elizabeth Loftus and her colleagues, which provided ample evidence that false reports can be easily induced in experimental settings. For example, in her famous "lost in the mall" paradigm, Loftus found that subjects can be misled to believe that, during childhood, they once had the distressing experience of having been separated from family members in a shopping mall. She reported that, once the memory is suggested, the subject elaborates sensory components of the event and places great confidence in the authenticity of the memory (Loftus, 1993). Similarly, in other research paradigms, subjects have been influenced to believe they performed actions they actually only imagined performing. Such false reports are easy to induce even when subjects are actively discouraged from modifying their reports based on information supplied after the initial presentation of the event (Belli & Loftus, 1994). These results are consistent with a body of data emerging from eyewitness report research, which indicates that subjects' recall for a scenario presented via videotape can be distorted by the language used in inquiring about the subjects' recollections. Collectively, these data indicate that memory, at least the type of memory explored in these research paradigms, is reconstructive rather than reproductive. Our memory processes are malleable and fallible, so our recall must be, at best, reconstructive. We cannot reproduce a past event in its original, pristine form.

Proponents of the false memory perspective argue that therapists treating patients with recovered memories ignore data regarding the fallibility of human memory and engage in a number of suggestive practices that are likely to contaminate the memory process. They claim that such practices include visualization techniques, hypnosis, and, especially, hypnotic age-regression, which generate perceptual detail for the client, increasing the likelihood that the client will reify the memory based on the vividness of the experience. Proponents of the false memory perspective generally view as suspect all techniques encouraging imagination, such as storytelling (Belli & Loftus, 1994). They claim that certain verbal suggestions are highly risky in terms of pseudomemory production. For example, *The Courage to Heal: A Guide for Women Survivors of Child Sexual Abuse* (Bass & Davis, 1988), a popular self-help book, contains the following statement: "If you are unable to remember any specific instances like the ones mentioned above but still have a feeling that something abusive happened to you, it probably did" (p. 21). Other techniques that are felt to be risky, according to the false memory perspective, include sodium amytal interviews, journal writing, dream interpretation, body work, and the recommendation of self-help books and participation in support groups intended for survivors of abuse (Courtois, 1999).

Spanos (1996, p. 274), arguing that MPD is a cultural phenomenon or "sociocognitive enactment" rather than a true psychological entity, cited Mulhern's (1991) description of hypnotic procedures that have been used with MPD patients to elicit "memories" of satanic ritual abuse:

During hypnotic interviews clinicians explicitly described satanic ritual scenes or displayed pictures of satanic symbols to the patient; then addressed "all parts of the patient's mind" or "everyone inside," requesting that any part who recognized the satanic material so indicate by a nod of the head or by prearranged yes, no, or stop ideomotor signals. (p. 610)

Spanos (1996) claimed that "hypnotic behaviors are goal-directed enactments and . . . highly hypnotizable subjects are cognizing individuals who are attuned to even subtle interpersonal cues and who are invested in meeting the social demands of hypnotic situations to present themselves as 'good subjects'" (p. 38). According to the false memory advocates, whether or not therapists intentionally make suggestive statements, their practices are contaminated by confirmatory bias; that is, they look for what they expect to find and neglect other avenues of exploration.

There is some difference of opinion within the false memory camp with regard to the possibility of authentic recovered memories. Some members of the FMSF Professional Advisory Board claim that repression of significant trauma is impossible. Statements have been published by some false memory proponents indicating that all memories recovered after a period of amnesia are objectively false. However, Belli and Loftus (1994) stated: "We do not deny the possibility of authentic repressed memories" (p. 429), and express concern that society may become suspicious of reports of actual victims given the climate of uncritical acceptance, and even encouragement, of memory production in the course of psychotherapy.

Arguments of the Traumatic Stress Position

Proponents of the traumatic stress position argue that the FMSF has not disclosed the methodology used in identifying and validating the syndrome and in determining the extensiveness of the alleged epidemic (Pope & Brown, 1996). Most of the responses from the traumatic stress community, however, have addressed the claims of the researchers supporting the false memory perspective, rather than the FMSF itself. While proponents of the traumatic stress position do not challenge the data suggesting that memory is malleable and, therefore, fallible, they do challenge the interpretation and generalizability of these research results. Pope and Brown (1996) interpreted Loftus' findings regarding the effects of postevent misinformation as indicating that subjects can be consistently deceived in terms of the peripheral details, but not the central features, of a memory. However, the most pervasive criticism of the conclusions drawn by Loftus and her colleagues pertains to the generalizability of their findings. Traumatic stress proponents claim that not only are real eyewitnesses less susceptible than experimental subjects such as Loftus' (Pope & Brown, 1996), but, given obvious ethical constraints, no research paradigm replicates traumatic events or induces posttraumatic symptoms. Given this limitation, traumatic stress advocates claim, it is inappropriate to generalize from laboratory studies of memories for nontraumatic events to memories for traumatic events.

This claim, that there is limited ecological validity to the findings of Loftus and her colleagues, cannot be evaluated without exploring whether memory always operates according to a single set of rules or whether there are, in fact, two distinct memory processes, one governing traumatic and another governing nontraumatic experiences. Interestingly, Janet distinguished traumatic from nontraumatic memories, arguing that traumatic memories lack the flexibility of nontraumatic memories, cannot be easily integrated with cognitive schemata, are therefore dissociated from consciousness, and manifest as unwelcome, intrusive sensory experiences (Courtois, 1999). The scientific community, stimulated by the efforts of van der Hart and his collaborators (e.g., van der Hart et al.,1989; van der Kolk et al.,1989), has finally begun to investigate the claims made by Janet long ago regarding the nature of posttraumatic and dissociative states.

Currently, scientific memory research is being conducted by both false memory and traumatic stress proponents. While there is still debate among researchers as to whether the same, or different, rules govern memory for traumatic and nontraumatic events, traumatic stress proponents cite emerging neurobiological data suggesting that the experience of trauma has long-term consequences for neurological functioning that are likely to impact both the storage and the retrieval of memories (Pope & Brown, 1996). Due to the influence of individual variables, not all survivors of trauma experience PTSD. However, biological changes have been documented in those trauma survivors who do develop PTSD, and many of these changes have been found to occur in systems intimately involved with memory processes (Courtois, 1999).

Courtois (1999) summarized the research data cited by the traumatic stress proponents as follows:

> A body of research is emerging that documents the psychobiological and psychophysiological alterations involved in both the arousal and numbing phases of PTSD that might underlie the psychological and psychosomatic responses to trauma.... These changes include abnormalities of stress hormone regulation, hyperarousal of the autonomic nervous system, chronically increased levels of cortisol, and changes in the central nervous system (CNS) catecholamine, serotonin, and endogenous opioid systems.... Preliminary research supports the fact that traumatization can lead to measurable, sometimes permanent alterations in brain physiology

and neurochemistry.... Those alterations can, in turn, account for the production of chronic hyperarousal and intrusive symptomatology. (p. 82)

Aside from concern with the interpretation of empirical results and generalizability of research findings to a traumatized population, proponents of the traumatic stress position also challenge the claims of the FMSF by citing data regarding the veracity of memories of childhood trauma. Since memories can only be verified via corroboration, some of the most useful data comes from prospective studies of corroborated abuse. In these studies, individuals whose histories of abuse are documented medically and/or legally are assessed later in life in terms of the existence, accuracy, and continuity of their memories.

Collectively, results of these prospective studies document that a significant percentage of survivors of childhood abuse experience full or partial amnesia (Courtois, 1999; Pope & Brown, 1996). These studies also demonstrate that many childhood survivors actively deny that they experienced abuse; that recovered memories are reasonably accurate in their central features, although often not in their peripheral detail; and that recovered memories are no less accurate than continuous memories (D. Brown, Scheflin, & Hammond, 1998; Courtois, 1999; Harvey & Herman, 1997; Kluft 1997). The consistent finding of substantial underreporting of abuse in cases of previously documented abuse provides strong support for the *possible* veracity of recovered memories after a period of amnesia. Harvey and Herman (1997) alluded to the irony that recovered memories of trauma have evoked so much skepticism, when "amnesia is recognized as one of the cardinal symptoms of posttraumatic stress disorder" (p. 262).

Broad-based clinical observations are consistent with results of prospective studies. Kluft (1997) reported that significant observations regarding recovered memories can be gleaned from his files reflecting a period of 18 years in which he had the rare opportunity to treat a large sample of DID patients in an area with an unusually stable population base. He reported that his records reflect hundreds of corroborated recovered memories.

Corroboration has been obtained in some cases where therapists have used techniques felt to be suggestive, such as journal writing with the nondominant hand to give voice to the "inner child" (Butler, 1996). Furthermore, corroboration has been found in some cases of alleged abuse with improbable features (Courtois, 1999), indicating that the validity of these allegations should not be discounted simply on the basis that they appear bizarre or farfetched. Pope and Brown (1996) advised:

> Each report of recovered memory of abuse must be carefully and fairly evaluated on an individual basis.... The most plausible, coherent, and compelling report of abuse, even when it does not involve a period of forgetting, may

describe something that never occurred in the life of the narrator. The most implausible, internally contradictory, and unpersuasive story, based on memory recovered after a long delay, may reflect abuse that was actually perpetrated on a person. (pp. 20–21)

Even for a given individual, each case of recovered memory must be evaluated on its own merits. This point is underscored by Kluft's (1997) observation that corroboration is sometimes obtained for recovered memories of patients reporting other memories that are disconfirmed.

Neither are recovered memories to be dismissed as false on the basis that they are reported by a person known to be mentally ill. Horevitz (1994) concluded that, the fallibility of the memory process notwithstanding, "the evidence to date suggests that psychopathology itself does not contribute to the distortion of early childhood memories and that the memories of patients in therapy are reasonably accurate" (p. 443).

Proponents of the traumatic stress position have also noted two important asymmetries in the manner in which the FMSF has addressed accuracy of memories. The first is selective attention to false positives and dismissal of false negatives (Courtois, 1999). If memory is not always accurate, the traumatic stress advocates suggest, why ignore the cases when known abuse victims deny abuse history, and assume that all recovered memories constitute false positive reports? The second asymmetry that has been noted in the FMSF stance is consistent suspicion of the alleged victim's report, without scrutiny of the veracity of the alleged perpetrator's denial of guilt. Rubin (1996) proposed that, in addition to psychological denial and desire to avoid social embarrassment, three factors might contribute to possible memory deficits in sex abusers. These factors are behavioral reenactment of the perpetrator's own dissociated childhood trauma, alcohol-induced blackouts (with alcoholism common in incestuous fathers), and antisocial personality features which increase the likelihood of lying.

D. Brown et al. (1998), in their exhaustive analysis of the legal aspects of delayed memory treatment, pointed out that the proponents of the false memory perspective have sometimes displayed "false logic" and irrationality. They noted, for example, that

There is a growing corpus of scientific and clinical data in support of the view that traumatic experiences are encoded and stored both as behavioral memory and verbal memory, and that in certain instances the implicit, behavioral memory [also known as nondeclarative and early memory] for the trauma may take primacy over the verbal memory [also known as explicit, narrative, episodic, declarative, and late memory] in the form of behavioral reenactment and intrusive reexperiencing. While false memory advocates almost never mention the behavioral memory system, they do mention and criticize the more limited case of body memories, which they use as an example of a dangerous memory recovery technique.... Some false memory advocates consistently ignore these data. To ignore the entire corpus of scientific data on implicit, behavioral memory because it might lend credence to clinicians' description of unconscious behavioral reenactments of trauma, which in turn might even justify memory recovery techniques, is poor science. To debunk a poorly understood subset of the phenomenon (body memory) as a way of dismissing the more substantive evidence on the general phenomenon (implicit, behavioral memory) is also poor logic. Dismissing the validity of recovered memories of abuse on the grounds that the memory is accompanied by somatic distress (or a body memory) is neither logical nor scientific. (p. 384)

Other trauma experts have highlighted the lack of appropriate professional restraint on the part of false memory researchers. For example, Harvey and Herman (1997) noted that some proponents of the false memory position

bolster their speculations with demeaning characterizations of psychotherapy patients and practitioners. Whatever research may ultimately reveal about the accuracy of traumatic recall and the authenticity of adult memories of childhood trauma, these polemics go far beyond the reach of available data and cast a chill on serious scientific dialogue. (p. 261)

Other responses to the claims of the false memory position involve distinctions between easily confused concepts. For example, repression is sometimes confused with dissociation. "Those who believe in repression," stated Loftus and Ketcham (1994), as if they were referring to proponents of the traumatic stress position, "have faith in the mind's ability to defend itself from emotionally overwhelming events by removing certain experiences and emotions from conscious awareness" (p. 7). Proponents of the false memory position argue that _repression_ of traumatic material is not possible, but the proponents of the traumatic stress position argue that traumatic experiences may be _dissociated_. The distinction is important because dissociation is an empirically supported, rather than theoretically based, defensive response to trauma, which has documented physiological correlates and accounts for posttraumatic amnesia (Yates & Nasby, 1993).

Similarly, the terms related to delayed memories may be misleading. In the treatment of DID, what is referred to as delayed recovery or retrieval of memories may be more accurately described as the internal sharing of memories. Why is this distinction important? Because when the issue is recovered versus continuous memory, an internally shared memory is both recovered and continuous. A traumatic memory held by an alter personality, for example, and shared with the host in the course of therapy, is a recovered memory from the perspective of the host, but it is a continuous memory from the perspective of the alter, whose life experience to date has been organized around the safeguarding of the memory and responding to the experience of having been traumatized. Although the abuse itself may be uncorroborated, corroboration of the continuity of the alter's memory may be possible.

Consensus of the Task Forces Investigating False Memory Allegations

A number of professional task forces have been established in an effort to resolve the dispute between the false memory and traumatic stress proponents. Courtois (1999) summarized the findings of the various task forces and concluded that a common finding among those examining the existing data in an impartial manner is that delayed memory recovery is possible and that the creation of false memories is also possible. The recommendations of all such task forces include dual cautions: The debate should not be used to conceal the existence of child abuse as a profound social issue, but neither should the seriousness and injuriousness of false accusations be disregarded. The consensus of the task forces also includes encouragement of a more dispassionate approach to the delayed memory issue, with reliance on empirical evidence and increased restraint, tolerance, and sensitivity. The need for additional research activity, professional training, and cautious clinical practice is emphasized by the various task forces.

Cautions Emerging From the Delayed Memory Controversy: Standards of Care and Risk Management

Although the debate has been, for the most part, quite adversarial, it has led to a strong consensus among clinicians who treat posttraumatic conditions. There is now widespread agreement within this professional community that the appropriate response to patients presenting with posttraumatic symptoms is one characterized by a "stance of supportive neutrality" (Horevitz & Loewenstein, 1994) with regard to the authenticity of recovered memories. The clinician is cautioned to avoid the extreme responses of uncritical endorsement and rigid dismissal of the patient's reported recollections, and to encourage patients to explore trauma-related material without drawing premature conclusions regarding the historical accuracy of memories (Courtois, 1999; Enns et al., 1998; International Society for the Study of Dissociation, 1994; Pope & Brown, 1996).

The International Society for the Study of Dissociation's (ISSD) *Guidelines for Treating Dissociative Identity Disorder (Multiple Personality Disorder) in Adults (1994)*, emerging from the committee chaired by Barach, delineated the standard of care judged to be appropriate at the time of its publication. The guidelines reflected consensus as well as diversity of opinion among committee members, modified in light of responses to an early draft by the ISSD membership. They emphasized the fundamental unity of the DID patient: "The DID patient is a single person who experiences him/herself as having separate parts of the mind that function with some autonomy ... not a collection of separate people sharing the same body" (p. 3). The guidelines outlined appropriate treatment goals, including promoting stability, independence, and "moving the patient toward a sense of integrated functioning" (p. 3) and emphasized the risks associated with the use of leading questions, failure to attend to boundary management, excessive focus on past trauma, and premature efforts at integration. They reported "psychodynamically aware psychotherapy, often eclectically incorporating other techniques ... [including] cognitive therapy techniques" (p. 4) as the predominant treatment approach, and discussed hypnosis as a modality typically employed by clinicians experienced in the treatment of DID, with the most common uses being crisis management, soothing, calming, containment, and fostering of ego strength. They supported the use of expressive therapeutic approaches including art, movement, occupational, sand tray, and recreational therapies, provided by appropriately trained professionals.

During the last 5 years of the 20th century, a professional consensus emerged that, in effect, supports the therapeutic recommendations of Janet regarding the structure and pacing of therapy for traumatized patients. A cautious, phase-oriented approach to the treatment of posttraumatic disorders has received wide support (e.g., Chu, 1998; Courtois, 1996, 1999; Herman, 1997; Horevitz & Loewenstein, 1994; Kluft, 1993c; Pope & Brown, 1996). Experts agree that carefully paced treatment is indicated so that the therapy fosters increased stability and enhanced functioning and avoids undue or premature focus on traumatic memories. Therapy for DID typically involves three stages: (1) containment and stabilization, with an emphasis on improved handling of daily challenges; (2) carefully paced exploration and resolution of trauma and dissociative defenses, culminating in integration; and (3) postintegration treatment, addressing ongoing efforts to work through anger and grief, and redirection of energy into personal, interpersonal, and occupational development.

Consistent emphasis has been given to the importance of therapist mastery of the literature on human memory and its fallibility and of patient education regarding normal memory processes. Patients should be informed that memories may represent historical reality, but they may also incorporate elements reflecting nonhistorical elaboration or confabulation, or they may be wholly fantasy based (Courtois, 1999). Patients should also be informed that emotionality, completeness, vividness of detail, and confidence in the memory may be unrelated to its accuracy (Courtois, 1999).

Assessment should include appropriate, but not excessive, attention to a possible history of trauma. Clinicians are advised to inquire, in a straightforward manner, about a broad range of traumatic experiences including neglect, accidents, medical trauma, natural disasters, and physical, psychological, and sexual abuse in the course of history-taking during assessment (Enns et al., 1998). There is no empirical basis for the notion that false memories of traumatic events are formed on the basis of this type of simple, straightforward questioning (Lindsay, 1997).

A number of other recommendations for treating traumatized patients have received wide support. The importance of using the therapeutic relationship to model a "cooperative, collaborative, and supportive partnership" has been emphasized (Enns et al., 1998, p. 248). This collaboration may involve therapist support for a patient's search for corroboration of memories, when initiated by a sufficiently stable patient who is able to explore the likely outcomes and possible consequences of the search (Courtois, 1999). Attention to transference and countertransference is highlighted, especially because patients alleging abuse may evoke in practitioners a desire to rescue, which can lead to therapist overinvolvement and boundary violation, or to therapist burn-out and, eventually, to abandonment of the patient. Clinicians are therefore urged to seek supervision or consultation for help in identifying and managing transference dynamics and experiences of vicarious traumatization (Courtois, 1999).

For purposes of risk management in cases where recovered memories of abuse are at issue, meticulous documentation has been consistently recommended. Clinicians are cautioned to document such memories as "reported" or "alleged," rather than noting them as if the therapist endorsed their veracity. Therapists are also advised to document their responses to these reported memories, including efforts at patient education about the vagaries of memory. Pope and Brown (1996) and Courtois (1999) recommended that this verbal education be augmented by written patient handouts and by patients' written acknowledgment that they have read and discussed information about the memory process. Because the DID diagnosis has been controversial, Courtois (1999) urged therapists to use caution in making this diagnosis, meticulously documenting dissociative symptoms and behaviors.

In addition to these guidelines regarding what therapists should be careful to do in the course of treating patients with posttraumatic and/or dissociative symptoms, there is also a strong consensus regarding what clinicians should avoid doing. First and foremost, therapists should exercise extreme caution in avoiding suggestive interventions, such as regressive therapy techniques, and suggestive language and leading questions presented in the course of assessment or treatment. For example, the following should not be suggested or implied: that the therapist is an expert on the client's experience; that the client's symptom picture suggests an abuse history; that the client's therapeutic progress is contingent on efforts to recall childhood events; and that if the client is emotionally disturbed by hearing or seeing an account of victimization, this suggests that she has been similarly victimized.

Furthermore, therapists are cautioned to avoid using new and relatively unproven treatment techniques (Courtois, 1999), "confrontational methods that attack personal identity or defenses" (Enns et al., 1998, p. 249), and all manner of dual relationships. While ethically minded therapists are careful to avoid engaging in therapeutic relationships involving emotionally and physically intimate attachments, therapists may not have considered the inappropriateness of other types of dual relationships that are at issue when a patient presents recovered memories and may become involved in litigation. Courtois (1999) cautioned therapists not to serve as a forensic examiner or expert witness for a therapy patient because of the conflict of interest inherent in such an arrangement. She also underscored the importance of not recommending that patients confront alleged perpetrators in response to recovered memories and emphasized that family separations, cut-offs, and litigation not be encouraged. She makes it a condition of the written therapy contract that such actions not be taken impulsively and that adequate time be devoted in session to laying the groundwork, should the patient decide to move forward with challenging the alleged perpetrator.

Of all therapeutic techniques felt to be risky, hypnosis is the most controversial. In fact, skepticism regarding the legitimacy of the MPD diagnosis grew out of its association with hypnosis (Horevitz, 1983). While some clinicians believe hypnosis is a necessary tool throughout treatment, others believe it should be used judiciously, and still others believe it must be avoided altogether. Given the empirical evidence that hypnosis can produce false memories, elaborate memories erroneously, and enhance patients' confidence that these memories reflect actual events, the general consensus within the professional community is that hypnosis should at least be avoided in the context of memory retrieval. It has been argued that hypnosis is appropriate when offered as a tool helpful to the patient rather than helpful to the therapy, to be used for purposes of self-control, mastery, anger management, relaxation, and symptom reduction (Horevitz, 1983), and self-soothing, containment, and ego-strengthening (ISSD, 1994). Somewhat more controversial are arguments that hypnosis, while avoided for memory retrieval, can be safely used in other phases of memory work. For example, Brown, Scheflin, and Hammond (1998) and Kluft (1997) believe that the judicious use of hypnotherapy is appropriate for purposes of memory enhancement, memory integration, and the resolution of trauma. Some experts recommend that, if hypnosis is used at all, written informed consent be obtained (Courtois, 1999; Pope & Brown, 1996). Recent recommendations urge more restraint with regard to the use of hypnosis than is reflected in the ISSD (1994) guidelines. In terms of legal ramifications of the use of hypnosis, the ISSD (1994) guidelines state: "Material recalled in trance is not likely to be admissible evidence in any legal action undertaken by the patient" (p. 10). Courtois (1999) extended the warning, adding that the use of hypnosis may result in disqualification of the individual's ability to testify at all and is therefore contraindicated with any patient who is likely to become involved in any legal proceeding. The therapist could be sued by the patient if the patient's testimony is disqualified due to therapeutic procedures that were followed.

Despite the strong consensus that emerged during the last 5 or 6 years of the 20th century, Courtois (1999) cautioned that current recommendations must be viewed as preliminary. A great deal more outcome research is needed to establish the appropriateness and efficacy of the standards of care for traumatized individuals and for patients presenting recovered memories of abuse.

☐ Eliminate the Chaff or Reject Hypnosis *En Bloc*?

We turn our attention back to Ellenberger's (1970) observation that it's easier to reject a flawed practice in its entirety than to pursue the painstaking goal of distinguishing the grain from the chaff. Although there are still conflicting views regarding whether hypnosis may be appropriate for some therapeutic tasks with individuals reporting recovered memories, there is widespread agreement that hypnosis carries risks of contaminating memory retrieval and erroneously inflating the subject's confidence in the veracity of recovered memories. Furthermore, current legal statutes affect psychotherapy practice regardless of the beliefs of the practitioner. The question is whether we can modify the hypnotic procedure to eliminate those features that are now considered excessively risky in working with this particular clinical population and still confer the benefits of hypnosis. If we eliminate the chaff—the risky techniques—are we left with something of value?

I will argue that, in working with DID clients, a highly trance-prone population, we can eliminate the implication that the therapist is an authority on the client's experience, trance induction, age-regressive techniques, and contact between the therapist and the client during the client's altered state of consciousness and still potentiate the capacity for lucidity and self-healing described by Puységur. This should be no surprise. After all, the therapeutic effects of what we now call hypnosis have been attributed to animal magnetism by Mesmer, to the practitioner's will by Puységur, to the effect of suggestion by Bernheim, and so forth. Given these various formulations over time, how can we be confident in attributing the benefits of hypnosis to any given set of procedures?

The treatment model presented in this volume involves training the client to enter a self-induced meditative state in order to obtain inner guidance toward healing. Although this state may be analogous to a hypnotic state in terms of brain-wave activity and narrowing of attention, it is distinct from a heterohypnotic state in terms of suggestion and other manifestations of therapist influence. (See chapter 3 for further discussion of the extent to which this treatment model contains elements of hypnosis.) It is a three-phase model consistent with the current standards of care. The client has ample opportunity to use this meditative technique during the first phase of therapy, long before the internal sharing of memories may become a focus of treatment. The quality of the inner guidance obtained by the client can be evaluated by both the client and the therapist while the guidance is focused on increased stability, improved decision making, internal communication and cooperation, and the like. During the second stage of therapy, the host receives inner guidance to listen to alters who have painful disclosures to make, but typically does not receive traumatic memories directly from the source of the inner guidance, which I refer to as "the inner wisdom of the unconscious mind."

The following chapter presents an overview of the Collective Heart treatment model for DID. This model is informed, on the one hand, by the cautions emerging in response to the recovered memory controversy and, on the other hand, by the observation that DID clients have a remarkable ability. These highly dissociative clients consistently display the capacity, once their internal resources are potentiated, to obtain all the inner guidance they require in order to heal their shattered lives and reclaim their birthrights of harmony, wholeness, and inner authority.

CHAPTER

Overview of the Collective Heart Model: Assumptions, Stages, Goals, and Techniques

Information is power, but only if it is moved where it is needed, when it is needed, and in its most useful form.

—William G. McGowan, Founder and Chairman of
MCI Communications Corporation

The Collective Heart model is based on three fundamental assumptions. The first is that every individual, no matter how damaged and fragmented at the level of personality, has an intact inner core that, once potentiated, can guide the individual to a state of harmonious functioning. A significant feature of this guidance is the unique timetable that determines the pacing of the healing process. The second fundamental assumption is that severely traumatized, fragmented clients typically need assistance with mobilizing this inner core, or collective heart, and this assistance involves exposure to therapeutic techniques in the context of a respectful professional relationship. The third assumption is that highly dissociative clients have easy access to the guidance of the intact inner core. Their trance-proneness, often a liability as it leads to confusion and impaired functioning, can be transformed into a rare asset when they learn to enter an altered state of consciousness at will to experience internal guidance in a vivid, sensory manner. These three assumptions suggest an approach to the treatment of DID that is cautious, paced, and empowering. Treatn follows the three-phase structure consistent with the emerging standards of care summarized in chapter 2.

Instead of asserting either that the DID client is genuinely and fully fragmented or that the fragmentation is illusory, this model differentiates the aspect of the client that has been damaged by trauma from the aspect that has remained intact. Certainly the psychologically devastating impact of childhood trauma has been well established. In some cases there is permanent damage to the physical body as well. The resulting impairment can be considerable. According to the Collective Heart model, however, when life experiences such as childhood abuse damage the individual, the damage affects the neurochemical, cognitive, and personality functioning. Despite this devastation, a deeper aspect of the self remains intact. This deep, intact core can be understood as the collective heart, or as the inner wisdom of the unconscious mind. This inner core serves as a guide to healing the fragmentation that exists at the level of personality.

By conceptualizing the personality (or system of personalities) as only one aspect of the self, it is possible to acknowledge fragmentation or multiplicity without denying the underlying unity of self and its powerful therapeutic implications. The treatment approach based on this conceptual model does not focus on fragmentation and trauma, but on practical techniques to mobilize the inner wisdom, which mediates the transfer of information from the unconscious to the conscious minds of the host and alters as they are ready to utilize it. This approach is consistent with Kluft's (1993c) suggestion that ego strengthening be emphasized in treating dissociative disorders, so that "the patient is taught many techniques to achieve self-efficacy ... in the treatment and in his or her life" (p. 89).

The notion of the inner wisdom may sound vague and elusive. My guess is that it may not be meaningful as a construct until case material (presented in chapters 7 through 12) illustrates and enlivens it. I have struggled to find terms to describe this intact inner core that would convey its meaning clearly. None of the usual psychological terms quite fit. Certainly it's part of what we call the *unconscious*. Beyond that, the term that comes closest is *intuition*. "Intuition" is a good fit in that it encompasses both the emotional (feeling and sensing) and the cognitive (comprehending, grasping, knowing, understanding) aspects of what this inner core contributes. But "intuition" generally denotes insight achieved through unspecified means. It implies a spontaneous "aha" or a vague sense of "just knowing," without knowing how one knows. Most people find that intuition isn't tapped at will. What I am calling "the inner wisdom of the unconscious mind" or the "intact inner core" is the internal resource underlying intuition, which generally manifests as intuition in nondissociative individuals. I have found that dissociative clients are able to tap into this resource intentionally and reliably by using specific therapeutic techniques in a meditative state. During the course of treatment, this inner wisdom manifests increasingly as intuition, although the client maintains the ability to enter a meditative state and seek concrete, sensory guidance as needed. As the treatment model and case illustrations are presented, we will see how this rather mysterious inner resource is the basis for well-defined techniques and how consistent clinical outcomes were observed for the 12 clients who have received this form of treatment to date. Limitations of anecdotal observations notwithstanding (see chapter 13), case illustrations drawn from this initial clinical series convey the manner in which the inner wisdom guides the client throughout the three stages of therapy.

If the inner wisdom guides the therapeutic process, what is the role of the therapist? The therapist must have thorough training in psychotherapeutic principles, as well as specialized training in dissociative disorders, in order to provide competent treatment. The therapist must also be familiar with the literature on human memory processes. The guidance of the inner wisdom is never a substitute for clinical judgment. Both the therapist and the client must evaluate the quality of guidance received. The client is encouraged to consider whether it is helpful, whether it seems accurate given her past experience, and so forth. If she doesn't understand the guidance or doesn't accept it, I suggest that she challenge the inner wisdom with her reservations.

Ultimately, the therapist is ethically, and, in some cases, legally, responsible for actions taken by the client on the basis of suggestions emerging from the therapy hour. For example, the decision regarding hospitalization of a suicidal client cannot be based solely on guidance from the inner wisdom. Although the inner wisdom may offer guidance regarding efforts to address suicidality on an outpatient basis, the therapist's final decision regarding hospitalization is based on sound clinical judgment (see chapter 6). By the same token, the therapist never encourages a client to take any action advocated by the inner wisdom if it appears to be countertherapeutic. Although this type of dilemma is rarely encountered, the therapist must be prepared to explore further any guidance that challenges professional judgment, such as quitting a job precipitously, impulsively confronting an alleged abuser, entering into a hasty marriage, and so forth. Should the client report receiving inner guidance that appears risky or unsound, the client should be encouraged to ask the inner wisdom to help her understand the counsel in light of her own, or the therapist's, misgivings. On rare occasions, alters have tried to pass themselves off as the inner wisdom. Upon inquiry, the deception is easily dismantled.

Clinical skill and judgment are also required in suggesting approaches to the client's meditative work. Clients need help in formulating requests for guidance from their inner wisdom. Although the therapist's suggestions are always phrased as something that the client might want to consider, and is free to decline, the therapist's skill in offering specific suggestions is an important element in a successful therapy. The therapist helps the client shape the questions to be posed to the inner wisdom and the inner wisdom provides verbal and visual answers, which the client and therapist then explore.

☐ Three Stages of Therapy

Stage 1

During the first stage of therapy, the client is introduced to the notion of the inner wisdom of the unconscious mind (or collective heart), is offered techniques and structures for utilizing it, and focuses on resolving problems in daily living. The goals of this first stage of therapy are as follows:

- increasing safety and stability,
- establishing an effective therapeutic alliance,
- accepting the diagnosis,
- increasing internal communication,
- improving decision-making skills and self-care to enhance daily functioning,
- decreasing self-injurious behavior,
- improving interpersonal communication,
- increasing initiative, confidence, and self-esteem,
- mobilizing hope,
- experiencing self-healing capabilities.

As explained in chapter 4, the notion of the inner wisdom is introduced during the assessment process. In a relaxed, meditative state, the client is able to receive a happy memory, formerly unavailable to consciousness (Dolan, 1991), as a gift from the inner wisdom. This is a novel and powerful experience for the client, who most likely dreads the unconscious as a repository of painful memories, things too awful to be allowed into conscious awareness.

As soon as the initial assessment procedure has been completed and the diagnostic criteria have been satisfied, the treatment approach is explained to the client. I describe the disorder and the inner wisdom in the following manner. If the client has reported a history of early trauma and is aware of having more than one distinct personality, I begin by explaining the vagaries of human memory and the nature of dissociation. I inform the client that, whether or not the reported memories accurately reflect life events, she apparently had cause to use her innate ability to dissociate. In order to survive overwhelming experiences, I explain, some people dissociate, "shut down," or temporarily "go away," and another personality can be created to deal with the traumatic experience and hold the traumatic memory. As a result, the person becomes divided or fragmented in terms of personality and may feel that personal identity has been shattered. (If the client is not aware of early trauma or personality fragmentation, but meets the diagnostic criteria for DID, I simply say that all of us have had some difficult childhood experiences and, to an extent, our personalities form in response to our experiences.) I go on to say that we tend to think of ourselves psychologically in terms of our personality and our abilities (intellectual, athletic, artistic, and so forth), as if that is the sum total of our identity. I then share my observation that there's an aspect of self which is far more profound than personality or abilities. This can be thought of as the innermost being, and it remains intact no matter what life events the client may have experienced and no matter what negative personality traits or behaviors she may have developed in response. At this deep level, the client is a harmonious whole. The major task of therapy is to allow this healthy and resilient inner core to guide the client toward a harmonious and satisfying life. I explain that I will sometimes address her as "you personally and you collectively," to remind her that each personality is part of a larger whole.

To convey the notion that wisdom resides in a part of the client's mind not always available to consciousness, I sometimes liken depression to being under a dark cloud. I speak of how we may wake up to dark, rainy skies and say to ourselves, "I wish it were a sunny day. I'd feel so much better if the sun were shining." I remind the client that, in fact, the sun is shining. We know that if we were to board a plane, we'd fly through the clouds and witness the dazzling sunshine. But we still feel swayed by our senses and experience the gloom of the dark, rainy day. "You know the sun is shining, but you can't see it from where you are," I explain. I speak of the inner core as the part of us that can show us what we can't see from where we are, that has a perspective broad enough to see resources that are blocked from consciousness at the moment.

The client is likely to respond to this description of the inner core with some combination of hope and skepticism. I support both. During this first stage of treatment, both are expected and both are functional. The client's belief that she may have within a profound unity, previously unknown resources, and the capacity for self-guidance leads to hope that change is possible. The client begins to sense that deep inside she is whole, wise, and worthy.

But along with hope there is generally ambivalence or skepticism. It's important to reframe this reluctance as a valuable signal from within, often from an alter personality (after the DID diagnosis has been made and discussed with the client) or the inner wisdom, that things are moving too quickly and caution is in order. If the DID client says she trusts you but is feeling some discomfort or hearing some internal opposition, it's helpful to point out that another personality may be protecting her from getting her hopes up when, after all, she hardly knows you. By validating the client's reluctance, the therapist encourages the client to express discomfort appropriately. This has a powerful impact on the other personalities who are listening in on the host's interactions with the therapist. Most DID clients have difficulty expressing their needs assertively and effectively. By honoring the client's misgivings and actively affirming their validity, the therapist sends a potent message to the entire system of personalities. The message is that energy will no longer have to be spent almost exclusively doing damage control, because internal and external resources will now become available so that the client can begin creating a meaningful life based on her own needs.

The client's acceptance of the diagnosis may take time, but there is one point that should be clarified at the outset. If the client assumes that the diagnosis implies an abuse history, I assure her that this is not necessarily so. I explain that apparently something happened in childhood that exceeded her capacity to cope, but it's not clear what this might have been, and it was not necessarily something that one would label as child abuse. I tell her that I have worked with clients who developed this disorder after seeing something that frightened them, being in an accident, or experiencing other kinds of distressing events that were not abuse related. One client with dissociative disorder not otherwise specified (DDNOS), who reported having witnessed domestic violence in early childhood, expressed concern that a previous therapist suggested she read a book for survivors of sexual abuse. She asked if her diagnosis necessarily implied that she had been sexually abused. I assured her that it did not, adding that she had already reported a traumatic event—the witnessing of domestic violence—which could have overwhelmed her as a young child, causing her disorder. Note that I didn't reassure her that she hadn't been sexually abused or comment on the likelihood of a sexual abuse history, but merely informed her that there was no reason to assume that sexual abuse had occurred.

During the first stage of therapy the client is offered a series of tools to help her increase her sense of safety, improve internal communication, and utilize the guidance available within. I use L. S. Brown's (1994) notion of "empowered consent" to ensure that the client is fully informed about the nature and purpose of the interventions being offered and feels free to decline them without fear of aversive repercussions. Pope and Brown (1996) described the scope of empowered consent:

> Empowered consent clarifies that the client is the ultimate arbiter of what is helpful and has the right to refuse any intervention, seek a second opinion, request that the therapist get consultation, or terminate treatment at any time without punitive consequences or having that refusal labeled as a form of pathology. (pp. 165–166)

In addition to providing the client opportunities to speak freely in session and explore the feelings that her experiences evoke, I offer two types of interventions early in therapy. The first involves training in relaxation, visualization, and meditation. The relaxation and visualization training is offered during the assessment process and takes about 20 or 30 minutes. The meditation approach I offer clients is based on Tonglen, a form of ancient Tibetan meditation. It involves an image of inhaling light from the Great Light of the Universe and using the light to vaporize the clouds (symbolizing whatever is weighing heavily on the client) that surround the heart. Verbatim instructions for these relaxation, visualization, and meditation practices, any of which can be used by the client to enter a meditative state, are presented in chapter 5. Some clients prefer to use other techniques to help them enter a meditative state. These other techniques may be methods that have proved relaxing and facilitative in the past, or they may be approaches they discover independently in the course of therapy. An example of the latter is presented in chapter 8.

As altered states of consciousness, formal hypnotic and meditative states may be similar or even identical, but as clinical interventions they are quite distinct. The meditative state may be analogous to a formal hypnotic state in terms of brain-wave activity and narrowing of attention, but the role of the therapist in the former intervention is generally limited to teaching the client how to enter a meditative state independently, helping the client plan the meditative experience, and supporting the client in applying what is learned from it. If the therapist speaks to the client during the meditative work, this is usually done in response to the client's request for assistance or is preceded by the question, "May I make a suggestion?" These dissimilarities between hypnosis and meditation notwithstanding, it is important to note that no DID treatment can be said to be free of hypnotic elements. As the ISSD (1994) guidelines state, "DID experts . . . agree that DID patients will frequently enter trance states during treatment (and outside of treatment) even when the therapist has not performed any hypnotic procedure" (p. 7). It may be helpful to conceptualize the meditative state as a hypnotic state that has been purged of those elements felt to be risky in working with this particular population.

The second type of intervention offered early in therapy involves visualized internal structures (elaborated in chapter 5) that can be utilized by the client while in a meditative state. I communicate clearly to the client that these inner structures are being *suggested* (i.e., they do not exist objectively) because they can be useful in facilitating the therapeutic experiences of increasing feelings of safety and control, fostering internal communication, and accessing the guidance of the inner wisdom. The structures that facilitate these processes are the private rooms in the hall of safety, the conference or meeting room, and the theater, respectively. It's important to emphasize that the structures are only suggested so that the client is empowered to explore what appears useful, and the therapist is not perceived as having authority over the client's internal experience.

If and when the client chooses to utilize these internal structures, an abbreviated version of the relaxation exercise can be followed by the suggestion that the client allow the inner wisdom to guide her in doing the healing work she has chosen for that session. This is all the guidance I offer, and it gradually becomes unnecessary for me to provide any verbal guidance at all as the client becomes increasing adept at entering a meditative state. After the client has had several experiences of entering a meditative state, I simply suggest that whenever the client is ready she can "go inside" and begin the work she's decided to undertake.

The client who chooses to explore the *hall of safety* is told that each personality (including the host) can find a room there, as a way to experience comfort, privacy, safety, and control. As the consenting client relaxes, her inner wisdom will guide her to the hallway, and when she stands outside the door with her name (or, in the case of a preliterate child, her picture) on it, the door will open and she can explore it. Typically, clients continue to use the safe rooms on their own. The availability of an internal retreat site assures the various personalities that their needs are valid and deserve to be respected. These include the need for pleasant surroundings, enjoyable activities, safety, privacy, and control. A client's introduction to the hall of safety is illustrated in chapter 8.

The second visualized internal structure, the *conference room*, has been called the meeting room, group room, community room, and consultation room by various clients. (I simply tell the client that if she would like to experience an internal venue conducive to dialogue within the personality system, she can allow her inner wisdom to guide her and that she will recognize it when she arrives.) Typically, DID clients feel as if a war were being waged inside their heads. All parties welcome an opportunity for peaceful communication, but none believes it possible until they experience it. The client who chooses to explore the conference room will be guided by her inner wisdom to a room where the system of personalities (or subsystem thereof) can meet and learn to hear each other out for the first time. The alters should be encouraged to tell the host what kinds of music, exercise, literature, entertainment, food, and activities they enjoy. It's important to suggest this type of discussion, so that at this stage of therapy the focus is on improving the quality of daily life, rather than on the past. The alters need to know their suggestions are heard and valued, and the host needs to know that the alters are capable of constructive influence. Gradually, dialogue and mutual respect come to replace internal chaos. Clients are much encouraged as they quickly begin to realize that the various alters have valuable suggestions and contributions to make and are capable of mutual support once they are assured that their individual feelings and needs are valid. Chapter 8 illustrates the use of the conference room. I encourage my DID clients to use the conference room frequently throughout the first and second phases of therapy, and most choose to do so.

The third visualized structure, the *theater*, is also valuable during the first two phases of therapy and may be used occasionally during the final phase as well. Once the consenting client enters a meditative state, she will find herself guided to an empty room with a large blank screen on one wall. I explain that her inner wisdom uses the screen to display its guidance. She can ask questions and obtain answers in the form of visual images (either static or moving pictures) or verbal responses (either spoken words or words to be read off the screen). For example, she can ask how we might best use our time in session that day, what step she is ready to take in tackling a particular problem, whether or not it is in her best interest to remain in a given relationship, and so forth. She can ask her inner wisdom to show her a "film" depicting alternative ways to respond to a challenging situation and can then replay them, using the dial to amplify her emotional responses (see below). In this way, she can select the behavioral option that will prove most rewarding in the long run. This treatment model takes advantage of the client's innate capacity to use the altered state of consciousness to increase her perspective and expand her cognitive and behavioral range. Chapters 7 through 12 provide many illustrations of inner guidance sought and received by clients.

Each personality entering the theater is instructed to find individual remote controls for play, stop, pause, fast-forward, rewind, volume, zoom in or pan out, and so forth. Especially valuable on the control panel is a dial that can be turned down to decrease emotions and bodily sensations, and turned up to amplify them. Chapter 5 provides a brief history of screen techniques and outlines the contributions of this treatment model in extending the scope of interventions involving the use of the screen and manual controls.

The theater is utilized quite differently in the first and the second phases of therapy. During the first phase the client uses the theater to obtain guidance for solving problems in daily living, as discussed above, and also to mobilize hope for healing and increase intrasystemic understanding. The initial experience in the theater may well be an experience of seeking a vision of hope for the future. I first explain to the client that it's possible to go to the theater and see a "film," projected onto the screen by the inner wisdom, about something she can look forward to in the future. There are many ways hope can be mobilized. If the client is distressed by conflict in a current relationship or if she is afraid she will never have a healthy, intimate partnership, she can ask for a vision of what will be possible once she has resolved some of the problems that have brought her into therapy. If she is having difficulty functioning in an occupational, academic, or parenting role, she can ask for a vision of how she will be able to function in that role in the future when she is well under way with her healing process. If she is suicidal, she can ask for a vision of how her life will be different and better someday as a result of the work she is doing in therapy. If she has just had a first experience in the conference room and the various personalities were all speaking at once, she can ask for a vision of how they will be able to interact more harmoniously in the conference room within a few weeks or months. I suggest that the client turn up the dial for sensations and emotions to more fully experience the feelings of safety and harmony. Clinical case material illustrating each of these difficulties, and how the inner wisdom provides visions of hope for clients seeking to overcome them, is presented in chapters 7 through 12.

Sometimes a client needs an assessment of her general capacity to function that is more accurate than either her own conscious impression or the therapist's impression. For example, one DID client reported feeling quite fragile as she contemplated the challenges posed by a new job she had just accepted. An intelligent and competent professional, this client knew that certain aspects of the job would cause her to reflect on her childhood experiences. She spoke of feeling at the brink of emotional demise, as if her accommodations to the tasks of daily living were like a house of cards, in danger of collapse if a single card were removed. I suggested she ask her inner wisdom whether she was actually as fragile as she perceived herself to be. She accepted my suggestion, entered a meditative state in session, and emerged to share with me the guidance that she received. Her inner wisdom had told her: "If you had any idea what you have already passed through, you would know how far from fragile you really are."

DID clients also have difficulty understanding what will happen to their personality structure as therapy progresses. Typically, the alter personalities fear that they will be eliminated when the host becomes healthy and no longer needs them, and the host may fear "being alone" and not having anyone else to take over when the going gets rough. Many DID therapists aim for integration or fusion of the personality system. The Collective Heart model uses the notion of "being together as one" as a treatment goal in lieu of integration or fusion because it offers the client more latitude, acknowledging the client's comfort level. Early in therapy, the inner wisdom can be asked to provide images for how the system of personalities will someday be "together as one." The consenting client will experience a vision of future wholeness and continuity of experience. By suggesting that the client obtain this vision at the screen in the theater, the therapist indicates that it will be possible for the client to achieve some kind of harmonious state, but does not interfere by dictating whether the harmony will be achieved through fusion or through other means. This vision provides hope that future harmony is possible and reassurance that no part of the system will be discarded. It paves the way for some sort of joining process, varying across clients, which occurs naturally after the groundwork has been laid.

Clients may also choose to visit the theater, rather than the conference room, so that various personalities can communicate experiences nonverbally. In an intervention I call *shared videos of recent experience*, the screen in the theater can display (with mutual consent) the recent experience of a member of the personality system so that other members of the system can grasp it experientially. (The name of the intervention emphasizes the recency of the memories to distinguish them from early traumatic memories.) While watching a film about the recent experiences of another member of the system, viewers can use the dial to amplify sensations and emotions, thereby greatly enhancing intrasystemic empathy. This intervention, which is illustrated in chapter 8, can be quite helpful in dismantling dissociative barriers between personalities.

Before I discuss the second phase of treatment and how the theater is utilized somewhat differently at that time, I'd like to expand a bit on the way sessions are used during the first phase. After the initial evaluation (see chapter 4), I begin each session by encouraging the client to fill me in on recent developments in her life. Whenever possible, I link the introduction of the visualized internal structures and meditation training to specific concerns raised in session by the client. For example, a client may complain that life is hectic and stressful, both in her external life and internally. After exploring any ideas she may have about how to calm things down, I might offer her an opportunity to explore the private rooms on the hall of safety, in a meditative state, to increase her sense of safety, privacy, and control. In the following session she might allude to difficulties in a significant relationship. After discussing the problem and her desired outcome, I might describe the conference room and ask if she would like an opportunity to meet with the others inside and see what suggestions they might have for improving the relationship. If she expresses difficulty envisioning positive outcomes, either in terms of the near or distant future, I might describe the theater and suggest that she consider going to the screen to seek a vision of what might be possible for her as she begins to resolve the problems that have brought her to therapy. Because training in Tonglen takes about 20 minutes, I often describe it in one session and suggest we could try it in the following session if it appeals to her as a way of reducing her stress. The general rule is that the therapist offers tools that may be helpful, but the client decides how to use the time in session.

The therapist can help the client achieve increased stability by showing her how to differentiate past and present. During flashbacks, the sensory components of past experience so impinge on the present that the client may become disoriented to time. When the host describes a troubling incident in her current life, she can be offered an opportunity to consult the inner wisdom about what was happening internally at that time. If the inner wisdom informs her that an alter was confusing past and present, the therapist can offer to show the host how to train the alter to make the distinction. The consenting host is then told that she can instruct the alter to look around her and name aloud what she sees in the current physical environment. Emphasis is placed on observations that will help distinguish the current environment from the traumatic context, which is often the childhood environment. The alter can remind herself where she is, what year it is, how old the host is, that the host is learning to keep her safe, and so forth. After the alter has mastered this grounding technique, she can teach it (internally) to any other alter within the system who may be having difficulty distinguishing past and present. The technique is taught and rehearsed in a neutral context and then applied when the alter becomes disoriented to time.

It's helpful to be flexible about interacting with the alters. If they want to come out and spend some time with you, be receptive and welcoming of this opportunity to get to know them. But remember that what's most valuable to the client is the internal communication. An alter who participates in dialogues in the conference room may not feel the need to take control of the body and establish a personal relationship with the therapist early in therapy. Above all, it's important for the therapist to suppress curiosity about the system of personalities and the nature of the memories they hold. There are three reasons for this. First, this curiosity focuses the client away from resolving current concerns, the appropriate focus for the first stage of therapy. Second, after a straightforward history-taking during the assessment process, questions regarding memories may be suggestive. Finally, only a therapist who is able to tolerate ambiguity can assist a client in respecting the inner timetable. A therapist who is too eager to do uncovering work may be overtly telling the client to follow the inner guidance while actually overriding the guidance, the internally determined pace, by failing to suppress personal curiosity.

Remember that you are always "talking through" to the alters. Every time you say that our feelings make perfect sense in light of our perceptions, an alter is listening in and feels affirmed. Even though that alter may not have yet revealed her experience, if she feels blamed within the system for her rage or her fear, your words assure her that she is not wrong to feel as she does. When you say there's a universal human need to belong and to know that we have something of value to contribute, she becomes increasingly hopeful that some day she will be valued within the system for her strengths and gifts.

There are four different ways the therapist "talks through" to the alters. First, in virtually every interaction between the therapist and the host, at least some part of the system of alters can be assumed to be listening in, whether or not the therapist is aware of it. The second way is when the therapist's remarks are designed to be therapeutic to the alters, but the therapist does nothing to signal this to the host. The example used in the previous paragraph illustrates this second approach: "Our feelings make perfect sense in light of our perceptions." The statement is addressed to the host, but is subtly directed toward the entire system. The third approach is when the therapist alludes generally to the emotional responses of the alters, as in "I imagine some of the other personalities inside are proud of you for being able to tell me that you almost didn't come to therapy today. They know you tend to fear disapproval, so that was a pretty brave thing to admit." The fourth way is when the therapist clearly addresses remarks, delivered through the host personality, to specific alters or to the entire system. The therapist might say "I'd like everyone to listen to this" or "If any personality knows anything about how the body got bruised, I would like him or her to listen in and participate as we explore this in therapy today." In its many forms, "talking through" is an important technique throughout the first two phases of therapy.

A major theme of Stage 1 work is that childhood abuse is not only a life event but also a source of misinformation about the self and the world. Because of the developmental impact of early experiences, the child who is abused, neglected, maltreated, or abandoned naturally feels little self-worth. The therapist directs the client toward the inner wisdom, which consistently challenges the client's distorted beliefs about her self-worth. One DID client spoke of her struggle to correct her distorted beliefs: "It's a matter of not really succumbing to that old feeling of lacking value. . . .

I'm learning to tap into some of the other sources [of information] that are more accurate."

No introduction to the first treatment phase is complete without acknowledging that therapy often follows quite an intermittent course during this period. Significant progress in terms of visions for hope and increasing internal communication are often followed by despair, a desire on the part of the host to shut the alters out of awareness again, and even suicidal ideation. These challenges, and others typically encountered in Stage 1, are discussed in chapter 6, and illustrated in chapters 7 and 8.

By focusing initially on current problems of daily living and by learning meditative techniques to mobilize inner guidance and enhance internal cooperation, the client accomplishes a great deal during this first stage of treatment. She is able to take steps to protect herself and improve the quality of her daily life. She begins to successfully challenge false fixed beliefs and self-defeating thoughts. She experiences increased ability to inhibit impulsive and other unhealthy habitual responses by utilizing inner guidance to perceive alternative courses of action and compare their long-term consequences. As the contributions of each alter are acknowledged and appreciated, internal communication is improved. As the client learns that the therapist doesn't manipulate or seek to control her, but respects the expressed needs of each personality and defers to the inner guidance when appropriate, the therapeutic alliance is strengthened. As the client comes to trust both the therapist and the deepest aspect of herself, the inner wisdom, she becomes more hopeful and less depressed. Finally, as inner communication increases, the host personality experiences an increase in energy and this, in turn, permits greater progress. By the end of the first stage of treatment, the client experiences far fewer amnesic episodes and is often ready to make a major lifestyle change such as working full-time and relinquishing any disability benefits she may have been receiving.

I once treated an 8-year-old boy. During play therapy one day he carefully equipped his Lego figures with swords, shields, breastplates, and helmets. "The war's not starting until everyone's got their stuff to protect them," he explained. And so it is with phase-oriented DID treatment. We want to make sure every resource is in place before we undertake the challenges inherent in Stage 2.

Stage 2

The transition to the second stage of therapy is initiated when the inner wisdom begins to suggest that the time has come to explore painful memories that have been held by the alters. The stage doesn't start abruptly. After the client has made considerable progress toward attaining the goals of the first therapeutic phase, this new focus begins to emerge. One day a client may go to the theater and ask how she might best use her time in therapy that day, and be told that a specific alter needs to talk or, in the case of a young child alter, to draw. In some cases the alter may have already confided her pain to the therapist, indicating that the host was not yet strong enough to know about it. At this point, however, the host has sufficient resources to tolerate paced disclosure of painful memories: She has hope for a better future (which counteracts suicidal tendencies), she trusts that her personalities have common goals and increased mutual respect, she has a solid connection with the therapist, and she has the inner wisdom as a source of guidance and a reminder of her inherent worthiness. She is ready to begin to encounter the aspects of her self and her history that were previously intolerable.

Stage 2

The goals of the second stage of therapy are as follows:

* further dismantling of dissociative barriers between personalities through the sharing, and emotional processing, of previously withheld memories;
* increased collaboration between personalities as they internally (i.e., in the meditative state) challenge the perceived authority of abusers;
* continued progress in asserting needs and ongoing attention to safety and self-validation;
* increased feelings of mastery and control;
* spontaneous joining of alters as their separateness ceases to serve a useful function.

Despite the fact that Stage 2 involves processing and metabolizing traumatic material, the Collective Heart model emphasizes the recovery of personal authority rather than the recovery of memories. It is important that the therapist not initiate memory work. Both the initiation and the pacing of this process are determined by the inner wisdom. The remote controls in the theater, which have been suggested by the therapist, are used to tone down feelings and sensations, thereby empowering the client to pace whatever memory retrieval may be essential to her therapeutic progress. This is a complex process that takes months or years, depending on the extent of the past trauma. It is often the case that one alter takes weeks or months to share her memories before another alter begins her memory work. There are many ways an alter can share her memories with the host. Visual, verbal, and tactile techniques for sharing memories, as well as approaches to "controlling the dose" of shared memories, are described and illustrated in chapter 12.

While in some cases DID may result from exposure to nonabusive traumatization, the majority of DID clients were abused during childhood, and many experienced additional abuse in adolescence and adult-hood. In treating those DID clients who were abused, the therapist offers opportunities to challenge the perceived authority of the abuser after the relevant personalities have accessed traumatic memories and processed them according to the guidance of the inner wisdom. This internal chal-lenging process involves an act of solidarity among all relevant personali-ties: typically, all of those who were involved in the traumatic experience, including the host personality, as well as any other alters who are ready to participate. In introducing this intervention, the therapist reminds the client that she now has resources that were lacking at the time of the trauma, because the personalities have established a close working re-lationship and have learned how to mobilize the guidance of the inner wisdom, thereby creating a level playing field for the first time. It can be helpful to tell the client that long ago, when she was hurt, it was "the law of the jungle." The physically and socially powerful got their way. But now she'll have an opportunity to challenge the abuser inside her-self, where physical strength and social status have nothing to do with power. I tell the client that the most profound kind of power is the power of moral authority that flows through her collective heart. Although I cannot predict specifically what will happen inside when the personali-ties act together to challenge the perceived power of the abuser, I remind the client that she is acting on the authority of her inner wisdom. What's more, had the abuser been following inner wisdom, the abuse would not have occurred. Therefore, the client can rise to the challenge of this in-ner confrontation with the knowledge that the deck is no longer stacked against her and moral authority is on her side.

If the host and involved personalities choose to confront the abuser in this way and the inner wisdom confirms that they are ready to do so, I explain that they can go to the theater together. There they can watch the beginning of the abusive scene on the screen. When the time is right, they will be able to enter the image on the screen together and confront the abuser about the abuse. (Alternatively, when they enter a meditative state, they may report that they are at the scene of the original abuse, rather than viewing it on a screen. In either case, they are fully aware of the current context: They are not reliving a past experience, but are revisiting the scene with the intention of utilizing their current adult resources in confronting the abuser.) When the abuse has been corroborated, I always state clearly that they are not going to rewrite history. Confronting the abuser can't change what happened, but it can stop the feeling that the abuser continues to have power over them. The therapist does not coach the client on what to say in confronting the abuser. Typically clients tell their abusers that they had no right to do what they did, that the client was not bad and didn't deserve to be treated that way, that the abusers have no more power over the client, and so forth. Chapter 11 illustrates this remarkably potent intervention whereby the abused client reestablishes her own collective authority.

The internal confrontation scene is appropriate whether or not the abuse is corroborated. However, lack of corroboration does affect the wording of the intervention. Because the statement "You are not going to rewrite history" implies that the recalled event did occur, alternative wording is indicated. When abuse is uncorroborated, I simply tell the client that the suggested intervention isn't designed to alter her memory but is an opportunity to experientially revisit *with her current resources* the experience as she recalls it, because she is now ready to change her understanding of herself with regard to vulnerability and power.

There are a number of reasons why this particular therapeutic technique, the internal challenging of the abuser, is so effective. The most obvious is that the client is able to speak up, place the blame on the perpetrator, and shed the shame associated with having been abused. Another reason is that the experience of acting in solidarity, especially in a context requiring great courage, provides the participating personalities a glimpse of their fundamental unity. In addition, the client realizes that even though she cannot rewrite her history, she does have the power to modify her *experience* of remembering. Finally, the alters see that the host is much more capable than they had realized. The host is no longer in need of protection from the knowledge that the abuse occurred. What's more, she's able to act bravely in challenging the abuser and establishing her own authority and worth. For these reasons, this intervention is instrumental in reducing dissociative boundaries and preparing the alter who shared the memory to join the host as one. It assists considerably with what Kluft (1993c) called the restoration of the Shattered Basic Assumptions "that one is relatively invulnerable, that life is meaningful, and that one can see oneself in a positive light" (p. 96).

Now we understand the relevance to the treatment model of McGowan's statement about information being power, but only under certain circumstances. The very information that would have destabilized the host personality if presented prematurely—the traumatic memories—facilitate her self-empowerment when presented in a timely manner and in their most useful form.

The inner wisdom directs the alter to do all of the memory work that is necessary before the joining process can occur. It's important for the therapist to know that the alter may continue to hold some private memories at the time of joining and may not have provided the therapist with a full chronology of her traumatic memories. In other words, the therapist may not experience the sense of closure that's usually associated with the alter's resolution of her work. However, the inner wisdom knows when the alter no longer needs to exist as a separate entity and is ready to join the host personality. When the alter has done all of her necessary work associated with sharing and processing her memories, she realizes that she no longer needs to remain separate. She may speak of how much energy it takes to remain separate and how it would be easier to join the host. The actual experience of joining may happen in session or between sessions, and is a naturally occurring process requiring no direction from the therapist. It's understandable that the therapist may wish to witness the moment of joining. However, it's important to convey respect for the client by not trying to influence her in this regard.

Typically each alter joins the host when the requisite groundwork has been laid. However, sometimes one personality will choose to take another personality with her in joining, especially a personality she may have cared for during the years before therapy began. In these cases, the work of both alters must be completed before the joining occurs. (Chapter 12 illustrates this process.) After each experience of joining, attention should be devoted to the reactions of the remaining personalities and their reconfiguration within the system. Therapists who ignore the importance of the reconfiguration may inadvertently put pressure on the remaining personalities to decide who will be next to step forward and do their memory work. Even during the second stage of therapy, pressure to do memory work is countertherapeutic.

One feature of Stage 2 which should be mentioned here is discussion of whether the client wishes to take legal action. Although I in no way encourage clients to do so, there is an important ethical concern at issue here. If memories are retrieved regarding abuse by a perpetrator who is still alive, the client should be informed regarding any state laws governing the statute of limitations for pressing charges. From the time the abuse is discovered in the context of therapy with a psychotherapist whose credentials may be specified in the relevant state law, the client may have a limited window of opportunity in which to press charges. The client is once again disempowered when a therapist is negligent in this regard. An additional concern is that the client could later sue a therapist who didn't inform her of the state statute in a timely manner. Clients who consider taking legal action against an alleged abuser should be encouraged to explore the advantages and disadvantages of litigating. An argument against pressing charges is that litigation may undermine the success of the therapy because litigation involves investment in feeling damaged, while the therapy works to reveal the undamaged core and heal the damaged personality structure. However, the client may feel there is value in pressing charges, particularly if she has corroborating evidence to support her suit and has reason to fear for the safety of other children. In any case, a decision to confront or sue is not to be made hastily (see chapter 2). If a client is ambivalent about pressing charges, I suggest that she consult her inner wisdom for guidance. It's important that the therapist convey to the client that, whether or not the client chooses to litigate, she will have other means of establishing that the perpetrator no longer has power over her. To date, I have not had a single client elect to press charges, although, when the perpetrator is alive, many clients do eventually discuss the abuse with the alleged abuser and often receive a confession and an apology.

An important process, actually introduced during the first phase of treatment, becomes increasingly apparent during Stage 2: The therapist encourages the client to obtain inner guidance in ordinary states of consciousness. Instead of always entering a meditative state in order to seek guidance, the client becomes increasingly aware that her inner wisdom permeates both normal waking consciousness and the dream state. Quite naturally the client begins to express confidence that the time is right or not right to take a particular therapeutic step, or the client articulates a need with conviction. The client may report that the inner wisdom is offering guidance while the client and therapist are talking. One client reported that she asked her inner wisdom to help her make a housing decision while she was sleeping, and awoke knowing that it would not be in her best interest to live with the person she had been considering as a prospective roommate. The therapist takes advantage of these opportunities to observe that unconscious guidance appears to be flowing spontaneously into the conscious mind. This process is encouraged and the tendency to experience guidance in ordinary states of consciousness is amplified. Case illustrations provided in chapters 7 through 12 demonstrate some of the ways clients come to know what they need and when they need it. As we will see, one of the things clients sense intuitively (and the therapist affirms actively) is that being "together as one" will not resolve all the difficulties that brought the client into therapy. But it will put the client at a distinct advantage as she continues to work at creating a harmonious and rewarding life.

Stage 3

Stage 3 starts abruptly. As soon as the last alter has joined the host, the unified personality faces a number of challenges, which constitute the goals of this final stage of therapy:

- increased capacity to handle environmental and internal stress adaptively, including improved modulation of affect, increased reliance on nondissociative defenses, and resolution of maladaptive cognitive and behavioral patterns, some of which may have been inherited from the alters;

- mastery of any other developmental tasks that may have been disrupted by traumatization, dissociation, and multiplicity;
- resolution of anger and grief;
- development of a sense of identity as a unified whole;
- redirection of energy into personal, interpersonal, and occupational growth;
- renewed sense of reconnection, meaning, and purpose;
- expression and resolution of feelings regarding termination of therapy.

At this point in therapy, the client is no longer hearing voices, losing time, experiencing flashbacks, finding evidence of activities carried on outside of awareness, and so forth. That's the good news. However, she still has unresolved feelings of anger and grief and anxieties about the uncertain future, from which she can no longer escape via dissociation. She needs your help in finding new ways to tolerate emotional challenges.

During an earlier stage of therapy, one client's alter wondered what it would be like to join the host personality. I offered her an opportunity to experience a vision of being "together as one" while in a meditative state. In this symbolic vision, she saw herself being summoned to live "upstairs," meaning that she would join the host in being "out" all the time instead of spending most of her time in the inner world. Elated, she dashed up the stairs. Suddenly, she felt a bad memory impinging on her, emanating from another alter. She then discovered she had her remote control and was able to use the dial to tune down the emotions and sensations the memory would ordinarily evoke.

Tuning bad feelings down to make them manageable is a beautiful image for using higher order defenses. I was able to assure this alter that most people need to use strategies to cope with stress on a regular basis. When upset, they try to see things in perspective. They tell themselves to take things one step at a time. They ask themselves how they've dealt with similar problems successfully in the past. They consider how much of this problem is their own fault and how much is someone else's responsibility. They ask what would help them feel better. They contemplate what they can learn from the painful situation so as not to stay mired in it. They try to conduct themselves with dignity despite their feelings of vulnerability. All of these are healthy alternatives to being overwhelmed and destabilized. I assured this alter that her inner wisdom, in showing her how she could use the dial outside of the theater, was indicating that she will have the resources she needs to make painful emotions bearable without having to dissociate.

So the third stage of therapy is the time for the client to get into the habit, if she hasn't already done so, of symbolically carrying the remote control. I'm not suggesting that you introduce this image to the client, but rather that you allow the image to inform your own understanding of the work of this final stage of treatment. Encourage the client to control the "dose" and pace as she talks about the past, which is experienced as a continuous chronology for the first time. Offer empathy as you ordinarily would, but also highlight the compassion that is emanating from within her. Help her notice that the anger begins to feel differently now that she has reclaimed her own inner authority. When she felt permanently impaired by past trauma, she couldn't let go of anger because she was still suffering its effects acutely. Now that she has successfully challenged her abuser (or abusers) and knows that she has not been irreparably damaged, the anger has a different quality. She is no longer so much in its grip. She is also able for the first time to consistently distinguish between past and present. In one first-person account of multiplicity, Phillips (1995) described her startling discovery that "time divides" into past and future at the present moment.

The DID client finds that, instead of paralyzing her, her traumatic history now fuels her commitment to just, compassionate, and protective behavior. She will grieve the childhood losses and years of misery and reduced productivity. She will also come to redirect her energies into creating the life that she chooses to live, a life characterized by attunement with her inner wisdom and healthy relationships with other people. In following their inner wisdom, most clients choose to find ways of developing their talents and interests so that they can contribute to the well-being of others in some way, while experiencing their own worth and deriving much satisfaction from their efforts. They also find many new sources of pleasure in the social and natural world, now that their boundaries are clearer and they are able to keep themselves safe. One DID client had been so pained by the suffering in the world that she couldn't bear to watch the evening news. She decided, during her final stage of therapy, to volunteer with an adult literacy program one evening a week. "It will ease some of the ache in my heart," she explained, "and it won't overstep my boundaries."

The complexity of third stage work depends, in large part, on the extent to which the client's progress through the developmental stages of childhood and adolescence has been disrupted by traumatization, dissociation, and multiplicity (see chapter 2). It also depends on the extent to which the host needs to resolve maladaptive behavioral habits, some of which may have been inherited by the host when the alters joined. For example, one client acquired the "sharp tongue" of one of her alters during the joining process. She later utilized guidance from her collective heart in order to learn how to express herself in more constructive and loving ways. The resolution of maladaptive behavioral habits is illustrated in chapter 12.

There have been a few surprises for me in implementing this model. I was surprised to discover that in some cases alters are ready to join the host before significant emotional processing of the retrieved memories has occurred. The host learns what the alter has experienced, develops a close relationship with the alter, challenges the authority of the abuser in an act of solidarity with the alter, and demonstrates to the alter that she can take care of herself and advocate for her needs. Apparently this is all that is needed before some alters are ready to join. Part of the verbal and affective processing of the retrieved memories may be saved for the third phase of treatment.

I was also surprised to discover that the inner wisdom often guides alters to join the host before certain memories have been shared internally. These memories are happy or neutral ones, and the host experiences them for the first time after the joining has occurred. The host reports that they are retrieved from within. For example, one newly joined DID client reported having recalled for the first time that, as the winner of a school contest, she had been given the honor of marching in front of all the other students in a big school parade. She knew that the alter, who had just joined her, was the part of her who had experienced the honor, but the memory was experienced as having come from within herself.

Another surprise was that joined alters continue to have new experiences which they communicate from within to the host personality. For example, one of my DID clients reported having learned something from the subset of her personality system that had recently joined her. These joined personalities now knew for the first time what it was like for the host to lose time to those personalities who had not yet joined. As alter personalities, they had continuous awareness, either out in the body or in the inner world. Now that they had joined the host, they realized how confusing it was for her to lose time, to simply have gaps in her consciousness. I was fascinated to learn that, although these three personalities had joined the host, they still had "personal" experiences, which they shared with the host from within. Because they shared the host's consciousness and lost time when she did, we know that they had joined her as one. However, their discovery also affirms that, after joining, alters retain the capacity to compare fresh observations with their own past experience. This has important therapeutic implications. Since it indicates that alters remain *experiencing entities* even when they are no longer *distinct entities*, it can be used to ease alters' fears about ceasing to exist once they have joined the host.

These surprises underscore the importance of therapist humility. The therapist does not know when an alter is ready to join or what a joined alter's existence is like, and should not claim to have this knowledge or authority. The therapist's job is to develop competence and confidence in helping the client learn to utilize the internal resources that have always been and will always be available to her.

Some DID clients choose to engage in a cleansing ritual during the third stage of therapy. Clients who continue to experience shame, particularly shame about the body resulting from sexual or physical abuse, may welcome an opportunity to experience a ritual of purification. Other clients benefit from learning during the second stage of therapy that such rituals will be available during the final stage but do not feel the need for such symbolic cleansing by the time they reach this point.

Clients who opt to engage in a cleansing ritual may do so in a number of ways. The client may have some ideas about structuring the experience, the therapist may suggest ideas for the client's consideration, or the client can go to the theater to see a cleansing scene on the screen which she can enter. Many clients spontaneously speak of the light from the Tonglen meditation (see chapter 5) at various times during their therapy and report using Tonglen at home between sessions. These clients may respond well to the suggestion that they plan their purification ritual as an extension of Tonglen meditation. They can relax deeply, breathing the light into their lungs. Then, as they exhale, they can imagine sending "a warm stream of loving light" (Borysenko, 1995) to parts of the body still cloaked in darkness. As they inhale again they can imagine drawing some of the darkness through the light of the lungs and finally exhale it up to the Great Light of the Universe, where it is vaporized in a burst of light. They then repeat this sequence as many times as is necessary to dispel the darkness in vulnerable parts of the body and bathe the whole body in warm, cleansing light. Some clients prefer images involving water or choose to combine images of water with images of light. Whatever the specific imagery, the purification ritual can bring closure to a long sequence of interventions liberating the client from traumatic memories and associated self-perceptions.

What's missing from this treatment model? All mention of forgiveness! Forgiveness is a major theme in many therapies designed for abuse survivors. But there's a problem with the therapist raising the issue of forgiveness. The problem is that most of these clients come into therapy feeling inadequate. They have been traumatized, and many have been told they were hurt because they were bad or that no one would believe them if they disclosed the abuse. They've also been told that good people forgive, and their difficulty in forgiving often reinforces their sense of worthlessness. So it's better for the therapist not to mention forgiveness.

If the client asks about forgiveness, the therapist can suggest that she ask her inner wisdom whether she will someday forgive her abuser, and if so, whether something needs to happen before she will be ready to do so. Some clients never mention forgiveness, but speak of finally being able to put the abuse "in its place" after years of experiencing the traumatic memories poisoning every aspect of their lives.

Although all DID therapies are relatively long term and quite complex, with the Collective Heart model, termination issues tend to be fairly straightforward. A solid therapeutic alliance is formed, but dependency is minimal. Although my clients know that I have 24-hour answering service coverage, carry a pager, and expect them to call me if they need to, between-session phone calls are extremely rare for most DID clients. It's obvious why this is the case. Throughout the course of therapy, whenever the client presents with questions or emotional distress, I offer her an opportunity to check inside herself and see what it is that she needs. As the therapy progresses, "checking inside" becomes less literal. The result is that the client develops an appropriate level of independence and a respect for her intuition, which by this time is telling her that she no longer needs the therapist in order to continue to grow and enrich her life.

It is now clear that, for the most part, the goals of this treatment model are not unique. Both the three-phase structure and the goals of each phase are quite compatible with the clinical consensus that emerged during the last 5 to 10 years of the 20th century. The following are emphasized in this model and in the consensus model: safety and stability both inside and outside of the therapy, symptom reduction and enhanced daily functioning, improved internal communication and cooperation, modification of cognitive distortions secondary to traumatization, ego-strengthening, self-efficacy, responsible decision making, restoration of shattered assumptions, timely attention to traumatic memories, dismantling of dissociative barriers, promotion of internal harmony, and identity development.

What is distinctive about this model is the emphasis on attunement not only to the various members of the personality system, but also to the collective heart or inner wisdom shared by the full system. From this theoretical distinction flow a number of intervention strategies that are related to techniques appearing in the literature but that contain some novel features. As these strategies are elaborated in chapter 5, the contributions of others with regard to hypnotic screen techniques are noted. Chapter 13 further explores the extent to which the theoretical and procedural elements of this model are innovative.

CHAPTER

Assessment of Dissociative Identity Disorder

Mr. Oliver called the practice at 9:00 a.m. sharp. He was seeking treatment for his wife, who was in crisis. During our initial phone conversation, he reported that his wife was experiencing vivid images of her older brother breaking down her bedroom door in their childhood home and pinning her down on the bed. She was reportedly horrified by images of her brother's genitalia and struggled desperately to fight off the conclusion that he had sexually assaulted her. Her husband described her as being unable to care for their three young children, and so distraught that she had not been able to get out of bed in 12 days. This was in marked contrast to her previous level of functioning. We scheduled an appointment for later that day. I asked Mr. Oliver to call his wife to the phone. She sounded extremely timid and fragile. She required much encouragement before she was willing to even come in for an appointment.

I met with Mr. and Mrs. Oliver for the initial evaluation. My immediate task was to reassure her that she could feel safe in describing what she had been experiencing. My ultimate goal was to conceptualize her condition, arrive at the appropriate diagnosis, and provide the hope that together we could help her to move forward. The initial diagnostic session would permit me to begin this important process.

☐ Initial Evaluation

The fourth edition of the *Diagnostic and Statistical Manual of Mental Disorders* (*DSM-IV*; American Psychiatric Association, 1994) lists fewer diagnostic criteria for DID than for other serious forms of psychopathology. In diagnosing DID, the clinician must establish the presence of at least two "distinct identities or personality states" (p. 487), at least two of which "recurrently take control of the person's behavior" (p. 487). Furthermore, the person must display significant amnesia for important personal information, a criterion included in *DSM-III* (American Psychiatric Association, 1980) but deleted from *DSM-III-R* (American Psychiatric Association, 1987). Finally, the disturbance does not reflect merely the direct physiological effects of substance use or a general medical condition. The process by which these four relatively straightforward criteria are met, however, varies in complexity from case to case. This chapter addresses the assessment procedure.

Paper and Pencil Measures

Symptom Checklist

I ask the new client to fill out a symptom checklist comprising a variety of psychiatric symptoms reflecting anxiety, depression, substance abuse, eating disorders, dissociation, headaches, nightmares, suicidality, homicidality, PTSD, interpersonal difficulties, and impairment of sleep, attention, concentration, academic or occupational performance, and memory. Clinicians have been criticized for using checklists designed to indicate that individuals endorsing certain items are likely to have been abused, as such measures are suggestive (Spanos, 1996). It is important to avoid this type of checklist. Checklists are appropriate when comprising a variety of symptoms and used as a guide in pointing the clinician toward areas in need of further exploration.

Dissociative Experiences Scale

It is also useful to have the client complete a Dissociative Experiences Scale (DES; Bernstein & Putnam, 1986) if there is reason to suspect dissociation. The 28 items reflect dissociative amnesia, depersonalization and derealization, and absorption. The client responds by indicating whether, and how frequently, she has the type of experience described in each item. The DES has been used extensively as a measure in published studies and is a useful screening instrument, but it should never be used as the sole basis for a dissociative diagnosis (Carlson & Armstrong, 1994). It yields an unacceptably high false-positive rate due to the low base rate for the disorder in the psychiatric population, so high scorers on the DES (individuals obtaining scores of 30 and higher) should be viewed as only possibly having a dissociative disorder (Carlson & Armstrong, 1994). As with the checklist, the DES is most valuable clinically when used to guide the clinical interview. It is helpful to ask the client to provide examples of any experiences endorsed as familiar.

Diagnostic Instruments

Of the various structured interview instruments designed to diagnose dissociative disorders, Courtois (1999) recommended the Structured Clinical Interview for *DSM-IV* Dissociative Disorders (SCID-D; Steinberg, 1994) when a psychometrically tested diagnostic instrument for dissociation is required. While Carlson and Armstrong (1994) recommended utilizing a structured interview instrument, Zelikovsky and Lynn (1994) suggested that "it is ... imperative that the therapist or assessor cultivate a positive rapport and a robust working alliance" (p. 191) when working with trauma survivors, and carefully consider delaying test administration and data gathering until rapport has been well established. For this reason, I keep the client's paperwork at a minimum and conduct a rather unstructured interview that permits the client to discuss concerns in the context of life experiences and request the desired assistance.

Clinical Interview

History

In the course of the clinical interview, before conducting the mental status exam, various aspects of the client's personal and family history should be assessed. Encourage the client to provide a full life chronology, if possible, including academic, occupational, interpersonal, psychological/psychiatric, substance abuse, and general medical history. Family history of mental illness and substance abuse is also assessed. In addition, assess the client's legal history, with attention to whether any charges are currently pending and whether the client is involved in, or is contemplating, litigation. This information will help the clinician differentiate DID and PTSD from malingering and factitious disorder (see the section later in this chapter on "Differential Diagnosis").

It is appropriate to inquire whether the client has experienced traumatic or overwhelming life events, such as accidents, medical trauma, natural disasters, and abuse. These inquiries can be made in a neutral, straightforward manner. Having thoroughly researched concerns about the suggestiveness of this type of history-taking, Courtois (1999) concluded that "the present consensus on the subject is in accord with Lindsay's view that '... research does not support the notion that people are likely to develop illusory memories of traumatic events in response to a few straightforward questions' (Lindsay, 1997, p. 6)" (p. 220). Pope and Brown (1996) recommended alternative wording, so that the therapist asks the client about "experiences in childhood that they found sexually inappropriate, uncomfortable, or frightening" (p. 158), circumventing the need to use the term *sexual abuse*. Courtois (1999) recommended interspersing trauma-related questions with other questions, so that the assessment procedure is characterized by a stance of supportive neutrality and neither suppresses nor suggests a trauma history. The ISSD (1994) guidelines specify that the patient should be asked about such experiences as amnesia, fugue states, derealization, depersonalization, identity confusion, and "feeling compelled from within the psyche to behave in an uncharacteristic way" (p. 2).

Possible Indications of Dissociation

Throughout the clinical interview, I follow both the content and process of the client's presentation. Any of the following may reflect dissociation:

Reported Experiences

- hearing a clear and distinct voice, or voices, inside her head,
- an abuse history, particularly if memories of trauma were retrieved some time after the traumatic incident, or the client indicates that she suspects the abuse may be more extensive than she had realized,
- amnestic episodes, which are often experienced subjectively as "lost time,"
- evidence of activities carried on outside of awareness,
- discovery that she has knowledge or skills with no awareness of how they were acquired,
- passive influence experiences,
- co-consciousness,
- flashbacks,
- intrusive images,
- nightmares,
- frequent headaches,
- questioning whether terrible things actually happened to her, or if she only dreamed (or otherwise invented) them,

- high pain tolerance,
- the belief that if people knew what she was really like they might think she was crazy.

Behavioral Observations

- eye movements suggesting that she may be attending to internal stimuli,
- the absence, or relative absence, of childhood memories,
- inability to present a reasonable chronology of her childhood experience,
- unexplained affective shifts or episodes of uncharacteristically hostile, vulgar, or immature speech,
- extreme postural or vocal changes,
- indication that she may not have heard what was just said, particularly when combined with efforts to cover up her confusion,
- overly vague or distracted responses,
- unexplained bruising, lacerations, or other evidence of physical injury.

Exploring Possible Indications of Dissociation

In exploring any of the indications of dissociation, the general rule of thumb is to offer support without being suggestive. If the client's eye movements suggest that she may be attending to internal stimuli but she denies hallucinations, assess the presence of voices heard within the head. If you have ruled out psychosis, it can be helpful to tell the client that you are not asking about "crazy" voices that sound like they're coming from outside the head, and that many people who are not "crazy," or psychotic, do hear voices inside their head. Some DID clients will initially deny hearing voices, but will then admit to hearing their "own thoughts" spoken aloud inside the head. One DID client dismissed the notion that she was hearing voices, explaining that the only voice she heard was her conscience, manifested as a female voice attempting to guide her actions. It is useful to ask about any experience of voices inside the head that comment on her behavior or her self-worth.

If the client admits to hearing internal voices, I ask her to tell me more about this experience. As I listen to her description, I am careful to follow—not lead—her in exploring the nature of these voices: what they sound like, whether there is more than one distinct voice, whether there are familiar emotional tones associated with the voices, and whether there are genders or ages associated with them. I may ask if she is hearing a voice currently, and if so, what it is saying. Many DID clients report hearing a variety of voices that are deprecating, comforting, threatening, and frightened. Depending on the client's responses, I might ask whether the voice is commenting on the client's behavior, on me, or on how the session is going. If she admits to this and appears embarrassed or evasive, I inform her that she shouldn't be apologetic if the voice is critical or is using language about me or the session that she finds offensive. I reassure her that I'm not offended. (It is very common for DID clients to report during the initial sessions that they hear an internal debate as to whether or not the therapy will be productive.) If at this point in the assessment procedure the client has already presented an abuse history, I might explain that it's not unusual for people reporting this type of experience to have a protective aspect of themselves. I add that she can feel thankful for this cautious and protective aspect, even if it's embarrassing at the moment.

While many abuse survivors are nondissociative, dissociation should be assessed whenever there is a known or suspected abuse history, particularly when delayed memories are at issue or if the client suspects the abuse may have been more extensive than she had realized. In response to the question, "Have you ever been abused?" some clients offer a vague answer such as "Not really," "I don't think so," or "I don't know if you could call it abuse." Such responses always warrant further exploration. While working in a state mental hospital, I not infrequently encountered patients, particularly older patients, who had received forms of physical punishment for misbehavior in childhood that we would now consider abusive. Such patients explained that their parents weren't being cruel but just thought this was the right way to discipline children. While such a response doesn't rule out dissociation, it may account for an alternative basis for a vague response to "Have you been abused?", indicating that not all vague or equivocal responses to this question indicate that the client is dissociative. If the client presents an abuse history, I ask whether she has always known what she just reported. If not, I ask when and how she began to recall these events.

It's a good idea to inquire further whenever a client mentions wondering if terrible things happened to her or if she only dreamed them or otherwise invented them. There are a number of items on the DES relating to difficulty distinguishing reality from fantasy or imagination. If a client endorses any of these items, I ask for any examples she may be able to provide to help me understand her experience.

Memory disturbance in DID manifests in two ways: the contemporary experience of losing time and significant gaps in long-term memory. Some dissociative clients report losing time. More often they try to conceal the fact that they experience this difficulty. Putnam (1989) noted that the personality being questioned may lack access to the requested information, may be under pressure from other alters not to disclose it, or may realize that the gap in memory is unacceptable and may therefore confabulate a response. Inability to present a reasonable chronology of childhood experiences may suggest dissociative pathology. Similarly, the absence, or relative absence, of childhood memories is unusual and warrants further exploration. Typically, a nondissociative individual should be able to report where she lived at which ages, the names or at least a vague description of most of her teachers and friends in elementary school, and so forth. Occasionally a dissociative client will have early memories, but then have almost no memory for several consecutive years later in her childhood. One of my clients recalled school experiences, but was amnestic for her home life throughout her high school years. It later emerged that her one alter personality relied on the host to go to school, as the alter had no interest in academics, but dealt with the incest that permeated her home life for years, leaving the host amnestic for events within the home.

Evidence of activities carried on outside of awareness reflects amnesia. Several DES items assess evidence of this type of activity. They ask about unfamiliar clothes found in one's closet, unfamiliar writing or drawings found in one's home, and so forth. Other items assess this symptom less directly by asking whether the client has been approached by unfamiliar people claiming to know her or whether the client is frequently accused of lying when she does not believe she has lied. It's helpful to explore further, gently eliciting examples, whenever a client endorses of any of these items.

Some clients may be more willing to describe such evidence than to report the amnesia directly. When I was working in a state mental hospital, the first indication that a patient was dissociative was often the patient's inability to account for the events precipitating the admission. Typically, the patient reported seeing blood flowing from her wrists but had no memory for how the injury had come about, or she found herself in the emergency room having her stomach pumped but had no memory of ingesting the toxic substance. One hospital patient reported that strange and troubling things had been happening to her recently. For example, she found a speeding ticket in her apartment and concluded that someone who was speeding in her car obviously looked enough like her to get away with using her driver's license.

A DES item assesses whether the client has knowledge or skills without knowing how they were acquired. This may be viewed as a special case of evidence of activities carried on outside of awareness, in the sense that the learning experience is not recalled, with the result that the knowledge or skill seems to appear spontaneously. Musical or other artistic abilities, academic or job skills, and foreign language skills may be "discovered" by a client who has no idea when they might have been learned. One client reported that when she performed oral sex for what she thought was the first time, her partner asked her where she learned to do that. Other dissociative clients have reported having cognitive maps of places they believed they were visiting for the first time.

Intermittent loss of skills may also reflect dissociation. For example, one client reported that while working successfully for a large corporation several years previously, she would sometimes arrive at the office unable to recall how to turn on her computer. She later learned in therapy that she had been feeling the influence of one of her young alters who seldom emerged at work and was unfamiliar with the various office procedures.

Hospitalized DID patients frequently claim innocence and ignorance when confronted by ward staff with reports that they were seen behaving aggressively, seductively, or otherwise inappropriately. Such claims of ignorance and innocence are, of course, consistent with the DID diagnosis. During my early years treating the disorder, I was initially thrown off track by a hospitalized patient who appeared to be dissociative but acted tough when questioned about her reportedly aggressive behavior on the ward. Her response was essentially "Yeah, sure I did it. Wanna make something of it?" She later admitted that she felt more secure owning the antisocial behavior and being thought bad, than denying it and being thought crazy. She was the first of two DID patients I assessed in that unit who displayed this particular strategy for concealing their amnesia.

Some DID clients present with experiences of *co-consciousness*. In co-consciousness, the observing self experiences detachment from the observed self. This phenomenon is illustrated by West (1999), who, in the prologue to his first person account of multiplicity, reported watching a man cut himself on the forearm, as if he were viewing the man from across the street:

> He makes another pass with the knife, and fresh blood fills the wound, trailing down his arm, splattering in the sink. Suddenly, a familiar force seizes me; a silent vacuum pulls my viscous self through the window and across the street. I'm now behind the man with the bloody arm, watching him lean over the sink. He spots me in the mirror, and like a balloon filling with molasses, I slowly expand and fill his body. Now I am inside.... I realize that it's my face looking back at me, it's my hand holding the knife, my arm bleeding into the sink. *Oh my God!* (p. 1)

Of course, co-consciousness is not always terrifying. An adult host may watch as his child alter builds a tower with blocks while sitting on the floor with his young son or daughter. The host and an alter can also participate co-consciously in an activity where one is essentially mentoring or coaching the other.

Frequent headaches, flashbacks, intrusive images, and nightmares are all common in dissociative clients. The headache pattern is often described verbally as a tight band or cap around the head, but some clients report an asymmetrical pattern in which pain in a particular part of the head is associated with a specific alter personality. Putnam (1989) pointed out that most dissociative patients are less reluctant to admit to having nightmares than flashbacks or intrusive images (p. 81). They seem to feel that it is more acceptable to have terrifying experiences during sleep than during the waking hours. Barrett (1994) reported the results of a survey of dream characteristics in dissociative disorders. She identified 10 types of dream experiences reported by her subjects, the most common of which were dreams involving multiplicity metaphors (83%) and memory retrieval (65%). Also common were reports of alters appearing as characters in dreams (57%), personalities reporting different dreams (35%), and personalities reporting different roles in the same dream (26%). While Barrett makes no claims regarding the diagnostic utility of such reported dream content, the diagnostician familiar with her findings may glean more from listening to clients discuss their dream experiences during evaluation and throughout treatment.

In my experience, many dissociative survivors of sexual abuse admit to flashbacks during sex. One client reported violent nausea as soon as her boyfriend unbuttoned his shirt. Another client experienced intrusive imagery when she felt the weight of her husband's body on top of her but could tolerate sex as long as he supported his small frame on his arms. Another experienced gagging when she dated a man who was hirsute and also when she needed to dispose of hair that accumulated in her bathtub drain. Clients may be able to discuss what seems to precipitate the physical symptoms they report, such as nausea or the sensation of choking, while they may avoid talking about the more psychological aspects of flashbacks.

Dissociative clients report a range of passive influence phenomena. I explore any report of feeling the body being controlled as if by an outside force. This frequently takes the form of feeling irritable, angry, or enraged without knowing why. Some clients speak of "blind anger" or "blind rage." One of my clients described a "seething" feeling that seemed to come out of nowhere. A client with a corroborated history of early childhood abandonment reported feeling his child alter, who couldn't bear to be away from family members a moment longer than necessary, urging him to speed on the way home from work. In other cases, the client may also feel inexplicably drained of energy. It's helpful to ask, "Do you often find yourself having strong feelings that seem to come out of nowhere or urgent impulses to do something and you don't know why?" Lack of insight into the context of emotional responses does not necessarily reflect dissociation, of course. But adequate insight in other areas and confusion in this area warrants further exploration.

Putnam (1994) suggested that auditory hallucinations can be viewed as one of many passive influence phenomena, because one personality is influenced by the verbalized thoughts of another personality. Suicidal impulses may be experienced as passive influence phenomena.

A range of protective behaviors may be similarly prompted by means of passive influence. For example, one client described "the sense that there's someone inside who puts a cap on things to maintain stability." This client also reported a history of recurrent urges to drink shampoo. Years later, while in therapy, she recognized these impulses as the solution of sexually victimized young alters who wanted to get clean from the inside out after being forced to ingest semen. Once I noticed another client looking wistfully at the space under my desk where the chair would be tucked after the session. It emerged that a child alter was feeling a strong desire to hide away in a safe place. As that spot "called" to her, the host experienced both an unexplained urge to hide there and the sense that it would be ridiculous to do so. A third client had lost time after learning that her college financial aid, which had covered room and board as well as tuition, was discontinued. She later felt unexplained impulses to try to use her meal card at the dining hall again. Acting on the impulse, she was delighted to find that her card worked. It wasn't until the following year, after seeking therapy, that she solved the mystery. An alter had taken the matter into her own hands and had resolved the confusion at the financial aid office, and then influenced the host to verify that the card was working again.

High pain tolerance is another dissociative symptom that is assessed directly on the DES. If a client endorses this item, ask how she thinks she does it. Clients admitting to a high threshold for pain may or may not have a way of accounting for this ability. Some merely acknowledge that they can tolerate pain more easily than others. Others can describe a specific strategy, such as staring at an object in the environment until they lose themselves in it.

Sometimes a client denies evidence of dissociative phenomena, but shows behavioral signs of dissociation. I take note of any unexplained affective shifts or episodes of uncharacteristically hostile, vulgar, or immature speech. These shifts may include a change in posture, facial expression, voice quality, and so forth. For example, a client who draws into a fetal position after assuming an expansive, confident stance or a threatening posture may be a DID client. Some shifts may be very subtle or brief. Once during an initial evaluation, an alter emerged momentarily to mutter "Shut up, you bitch!" and then withdrew just as quickly, leaving the confused host to read surprise in my face and wonder what had just transpired. I'm also sensitive to any indication that a client may not have heard what was just said, combined with efforts to cover up her confusion. A nondissociative client will typically acknowledge her lapse in attention if she was temporarily distracted during the interview. DID clients, in contrast, have had years of experience in hiding their confusion and may handle the situation with apparent aplomb.

Another behavioral indicator of possible dissociation is a pattern of overly vague or distracted responses. Explore these responses gently, with prompts such as, "Can you help me understand that better?" and "Tell me more about that so I'll know what it's like for you."

If I observe bruises, scabs, scars, or other evidence of physical injury, I ask about the source. Although unexplained bruises may reflect amnestic episodes, clients with such bruises should also consult their physicians to rule out a physiological basis for this symptom if they have not already done so.

Often after rapport is established and the client begins to feel safe, a DID client will admit to believing that if people knew what she was really like they might think she was crazy. This disclosure is typically not made until she has reason to hope that the therapist accepts her experiences as legitimate, sensible, and meaningful, given her life history as she perceives it.

Assessment of Access to Unconscious Material

Traditionally, the administration of a hypnotic ability scale and hypnotherapeutic exploration have been commonly utilized in the assessment of dissociative disorders. However, in Ross et al.'s (1989) analysis of 236 cases of MPD, it was found that hypnosis was not required in diagnosing the disorder in the majority of cases. As discussed in chapter 2, concerns regarding the clinical and legal impact of hypnosis, emerging in the context of the delayed memory controversy, make alternatives to formal hypnotic work desirable in working with clients who are likely to report recovery of traumatic memories. The Collective Heart model's assessment procedure involves exploring the extent to which the client has access to unconscious material but does not involve formal hypnosis. (See chapter 3 for discussion of similarities and differences between hypnotic and meditative states.)

Following the clinical interview, the client who displays dissociative tendencies is offered the opportunity to learn some relaxation and visualization techniques. The therapist explains that the client, like other clients who report similar types of experiences, may have easy access to unconscious guidance. If this is the case, a simple relaxation exercise may facilitate the transfer of helpful and reassuring information from the unconscious mind to the conscious mind. The therapist suggests that the relaxation exercise be followed by an opportunity to receive a happy memory from the unconscious mind (Dolan, 1991), perhaps the memory of a time long ago, when the client was protected and safe. The transfer of the memory from the unconscious to the conscious mind can be likened to the experience of feeling a dream coming into awareness after awakening from sleep.

I first explain the plan to the client and seek consent to proceed. I explain that I'll provide two relaxation/visualization exercises to help her feel increased levels of comfort and well-being. It's important to explain the plan in advance and not proceed without the full consent of both the client and any "voices" that may be offering an opinion of the proposed intervention. (It is not yet appropriate to refer to them as alters since the diagnosis is not made until they have emerged, and they have typically not done so at this point in the assessment process.) I describe the imagery to be used in the relaxation and visualization exercises, so that the client understands exactly what she is being offered. It is also important to explain the scope of the intervention—relaxation and the attempt to retrieve a happy memory—and emphasize that you will not be extending the intervention in any way. Before informed consent is requested, the client must be assured that you will not inquire about anything of a potentially disturbing nature, or make any additional suggestions, while she is in a deeply relaxed state.

If the client consents to this relaxation and exploration process and has no further questions, I proceed as planned. (See the following section for a discussion of handling reluctance.) Chapter 5 contains a full description of the relaxation and visualization exercises, which are used for therapeutic as well as diagnostic purposes. Following the relaxation, I proceed to the retrieval of the happy memory as introduced to the client. I tell her that when she is ready, her conscious mind will receive any good memory that she is ready to welcome into awareness at this time. I advise her to take her time and ask her to let me know when the process has been completed. After she informs me that this has occurred, I tell her to slowly prepare to open her eyes and reorient to the office.

Afterwards I ask her if she would be willing to share her experience with me. If she reports having retrieved a memory and chooses to share it with me, I ask if she believes the memory is to be understood literally and to what extent it fits in with other memories she may have. I also listen to her description of the memory so that I understand whether this was a sensory experience or a more abstract experience. DID clients will typically describe their inner experiences in vivid sensory terms, although this does not always happen during the initial evaluation.

The retrieval of the happy memory is valuable for many reasons. The focus on retrieving a reassuring memory is an excellent reintroduction to the unconscious mind, which may have been known previously as a repository for images too terrible to be allowed into conscious awareness. It gives the client hope that there are more treasures within, encouraging interest in continuing therapy. The therapist's commitment to resisting further diagnostic exploration, and respect for the client's choices, encourages trust. Finally, some clients choose to share the happy memory with siblings or parents and obtain corroboration, which further increases the client's trust in the therapeutic process.

While most DID clients report retrieving a happy memory, it's important to be relaxed and accepting about whatever the client experiences. The client is encouraged to discuss what she liked and didn't like about the experience and to explore any modifications to the relaxation exercise that might increase feelings of comfort.

☐ Completing the Diagnostic Process

No matter how easily the client enters an altered state of consciousness, and no matter how strongly the client's history suggests the presence of alters who take executive control of the body, leaving the host amnestic for activities carried on by alters, the diagnosis is deferred until the therapist can document evidence of at least one alter's recurrent exercising of executive control and the host's associated amnesia. While the therapist is awaiting this evidence, it is appropriate to use a provisional diagnosis of DDNOS rather than DID, to indicate a lack of zealotry regarding the DID diagnosis.

In the sessions following the initial evaluation, the client is offered additional opportunities to relax and request more reassurance and guidance. I explain that I use the term "inner wisdom" to refer to that part of the unconscious mind that knows what the conscious mind needs at all times. I offer to help the client relax, using an abbreviated version of the relaxation exercise, until she is ready to do so without my help. She might want to ask her inner wisdom for a second happy memory, a vision of hope for what will be possible as she solves the problems that brought her to therapy, and so forth. She may also want to ask for guidance regarding how the session could be used most effectively. Each time, the intervention is planned before the client enters a relaxed or meditative state, with the client's full consent. Sooner or later, a DID client will receive inner guidance relating to the fragmentation of the personality system.

I tell the client that her many inner resources will become apparent as the therapy progresses and that I am open to discovering these resources along with her. This statement paves the way for any alters who may exist to perceive themselves as resources, but it does not suggest the existence of alters because all clients, including nondissociative clients, discover previously unknown inner resources in the course of therapy.

If the client reports that another personality exists, it is appropriate to invite him or her to meet with you. Encourage the host to describe her perception of the alter and use this information to shape your invitation. I tell the client that, in my experience, when alters do exist they want to help and protect the client, even if this isn't initially apparent, and it's best to encourage them to become involved in the therapy whenever they are ready to do so.

This invitation to the alter, which should be very low-key, may well be facilitated by suggesting that the alter, if one exists, may wish to speak with you during this or a subsequent session. During the interval between the invitation and the subsequent session, inner dynamics may work to mobilize the alter's hope for help and increase her readiness to engage with the therapist.

When the client expresses readiness to have the alter meet with me, I ask if she hears or senses anything that may suggest that the alter is similarly willing. If the alter appears willing, I tell the client that since they are both in agreement, if she simply closes her eyes, I'll just wait for the alter to come out. If she detects any resistance on the part of the alter, I affirm the resistance as valid and useful. I assure the client that even though she may be frustrated because she would like to proceed with therapy by letting me talk to the alter, it's important to try to understand that, if an alter exists, the alter may have good reason to be reluctant. I add that caution may be the best course. If the client feels I'm siding with the alter against her, I assure her that I need to respect both of them by making sure that there is mutual consent before proceeding.

During this type of dialogue, the client will often report that she begins to hear the voice agreeing with me about the need for caution. Although this is encouraging, I don't reissue the invitation to emerge at this point. I simply empathize with the host's frustration and assure her that this entire process is unfolding according to the inner timetable and that every element of the healing process will occur when the time is right.

This cautious and respectful approach generally leads to the emergence, within a few sessions, of an alter in adult DID clients. However, it is essential that the therapist proceed slowly with clients who are reluctant. It is helpful for the therapist to remember that by honoring the client's ability to express reluctance or ambivalence, and by willingness to establish a therapeutic relationship on the client's own terms, the therapy is off to an excellent start. It's not helpful for the therapist to view reluctance as resistance and to feel frustrated or angry that the client is sabotaging the assessment or treatment. The client's reluctance can be viewed as an unconscious test of the therapist's capacity to respect the client's needs and avoid abuse of authority. The therapist can be thankful for this opportunity to demonstrate at the outset that the client will receive respect and support and maintain control and dignity. Therapist and client alike benefit from recognizing that the client's reluctance, framed as inner guidance to avoid further destabilization, leads to an alternative, but equally healing, treatment path.

It is extremely important to be patient with the diagnostic process. The evidence permitting the completion of the diagnosis will emerge in due time. Courtois (1999) cautioned the less experienced clinician to arrange a consultation, before diagnostic determination is made, with a more senior colleague with expertise in the diagnosis and treatment of dissociative disorders. Whenever possible, the client should be referred to a psychiatrist well versed in dissociative disorders when psychopharmacological evaluation of depression and posttraumatic symptoms is indicated.

One important consideration to bear in mind while completing the diagnostic process is that you are diagnosing a disorder, not a history. You are not diagnosing the client as an abuse survivor. Unlike the PTSD diagnosis, where the identification of a traumatic stressor is essential, the DID diagnosis is purely descriptive and there is no reference to etiology. When a noncorroborated trauma history is provided by a client satisfying the diagnostic criteria for DID, it is noted as "reported" or "alleged," but it is not crucial to the diagnosis. Even a corroborated trauma history with intervening amnesia does not justify a casual approach to assessing the diagnostic criteria.

Differential Diagnosis

The differential diagnosis of DID involves comparing the client's symptoms with diagnostic criteria for other dissociative disorders, psychotic disorders, affective disorders, personality disorders, symptoms of substance use and general medical conditions, factitious disorder, and malingering. Because DID is still viewed with some skepticism, it is especially important to be cautious, conservative, and thorough in making the correct diagnosis or diagnoses.

DSM-III-R (American Psychiatric Association, 1987) stated that among the dissociative disorders, psychogenic fugue and psychogenic amnesia may be confused with DID. Amnesia is a central feature of all three disorders, but psychogenic fugue and psychogenic amnesia do not involve the repeated shifts in identity, nor do they involve identity disturbance since childhood. Rather, they are generally limited to a single episode, which resolves and does not recur. *DSM-IV* (American Psychiatric Association, 1994) introduced the directive that DID takes precedence over dissociative amnesia, dissociative fugue, and depersonalization disorder.

Sometimes clinicians, especially those who were treating dissociative disorders before the publication of *DSM-IV* (American Psychiatric Association, 1994), use the DID diagnosis to reflect the existence of alter personalities. No matter how numerous or distinct the personalities, however, the correct diagnosis is DDNOS if the host consistently experiences co-consciousness for the behaviors and emotional responses of the alters. Since the *DSM-IV* (American Psychiatric Association, 1994) criteria for DID include significant amnesia, the criteria are not met if the host doesn't experience loss of consciousness.

DID is often confused with schizoaffective disorder or psychosis when the diagnostician is unfamiliar with dissociative disorders. In fact, as Kluft (1984b, 1987) observed, many MPD patients present with Schneiderian first-rank symptoms for schizophrenia. Clinicians may associate the combination of auditory hallucinations, attentional difficulties, confusion, and chaotic behavior with psychosis and may make the diagnosis based on this subset of symptoms. Ross et al. (1989) found that, in their series of 236 cases of MPD, 40.8% of the patients had been previously misdiagnosed as schizophrenic. Increased familiarity with dissociative symptomatology allows the clinician to distinguish between the two types of disorders. For example, the voices heard in psychosis and DID are very different. The psychotic patient may hear a voice appearing to originate outside the head. The voice may be vague or otherwise indistinct and is rather primitive. The voice may issue commands. The voices in DID originate inside the head and are distinct and highly complex. The client is able to tell you what kind of personality this voice seems to come from. For example, if a client reports that she hears an angry male voice, a female who seems to be trying to keep the peace, and a little girl crying, she is more likely to have DID.

Among the affective disorders, bipolar disorder with rapid cycling may be confused with DID. The affective shifts between personalities in the latter disorder may be mistaken for the cyclical, frequent mood fluctuations in the former disorder. Thorough assessment is indicated in order to make this distinction. Comorbidity, which is discussed shortly, is also common. Many DID clients are chronically depressed as they struggle to maintain any kind of stability, given their inner fragmentation and the chaos it produces in their lives. In the case of situational unipolar depression, I feel that the DID subsumes the depression and give only the DID diagnosis. However, major depressive disorder or bipolar disorder, if present, should always be diagnosed.

DID is often mistaken for borderline personality disorder (BPD) in acute treatment wards of psychiatric hospitals. Staff who have not been trained in the diagnosis and treatment of dissociative disorders often believe that dissociative patients are manipulative because they may display aggressive or seductive behaviors which they later deny. (While I do not view denial of activities carried on outside of awareness as manipulative, I acknowledge that these clients do tend to be manipulative in trying to hide evidence of losing time, hearing voices, and resulting confusion.) Sudden affective shifts, identity disturbance, apparent impulsivity, substance abuse, and self-injurious behavior are all characteristic of both disorders. The diagnosing clinician may find that the nature of the countertransference helps distinguish between DID and BPD. While the client with BPD tends to push all your buttons, the DID client tends to mobilize your protective instincts (P. Dell, personal communication, 1990). (Comorbidity of DID and personality disorders is discussed in the following section.)

Some DID clients are thought to be borderline or histrionic due to interpretation of their responses to the Minnesota Multiphasic Personality Inventory (MMPI). DID clients tend to score high on the F scale, a validity scale that measures the conventionality of the test-taker's responses. Because the scale comprises items endorsed in the critical direction by no more than 10% of an early subsample of the Minnesota normative group, elevations reflect unconventional responses. Traditionally, a T-score of 70 or greater is interpreted as reflecting one of the following: severe psychopathology, such as a thought disorder; conscious or unconscious overreporting of symptomatology for purposes of primary or secondary gain; a deliberately random, all-true, or all-false mode of responding; or inability to perceive or comprehend the items due to visual impairment or reading comprehension difficulties (see review in Krakauer, 1991). Therefore, when no thought disorder, visual impairment, or reading comprehension problem is present, the test-taker is often assumed to be uncooperative or overreporting symptomatology. Unfortunately, the elevated F scores obtained by dissociative individuals have often been interpreted as reflecting a "fake-bad" or overreporting response set. In fact, DID clients generally "overreport" only in the sense that they frequently endorse items endorsed by no more that 10% of the early normative subsample. Since their disorder is shared with less than 10% of the population, it should not be surprising that they report having experiences unfamiliar to at least 90% of the population. The appropriate interpretation for an elevated F score obtained by a DID client is that it reflects severe psychopathology rather than manipulation. Clinically, these clients tend to minimize their symptoms rather than exaggerate them.

Distinguishing multiplicity from hysteria is especially interesting in light of the history of dissociation (see chapter 1). While multiplicity was once understood as a hysterical disorder, as in "the traumatic origins of hysteria," we now classify hysteria as characterological and multiplicity as dissociative. We consider a reaction hysterical when it is extreme and disproportionate to any objective threat posed. We would tolerate a great deal of emotionality in a person experiencing or witnessing a violent attack, for example, without labeling it as hysterical. With posttraumatic flashbacks, however, the reexperiencing of the terrifying situation is internal. The observer sees the reaction but not the overwhelming event and may label the reaction excessive or hysterical. Without an understanding of the inner experience, the outward behavior appears excessive. With advances in traumatology, we now differentiate dissociative, posttraumatic responses from characterological ones.

DSM-IV (American Psychiatric Association, 1994) introduced the necessity for distinguishing DID from the direct physiological effects of general medical conditions and substance use. Complex partial seizures, for example, produce amnestic episodes, but they generally last no more than 5 minutes and do not produce the gross identity and behavioral disturbances observed in DID. Substance abuse may involve activities carried on outside of awareness, as during an alcoholic blackout. These distinctions must be assessed carefully. Of course, in some cases DID and substance abuse or general medical conditions do coexist.

Like PTSD, DID must be distinguished from malingering whenever benefit eligibility or financial or forensic gain is a factor (American Psychiatric Association, 1994). In addition, DID must be distinguished from factitious disorder when a pattern of help-seeking behavior suggests that primary gain may be motivating the client (American Psychiatric Association, 1994). If the client has legal charges pending, exercise extreme caution in assessing dissociation. Not only do you want to avoid a false positive in making a diagnosis, but you want to avoid mentioning anything that could help a malingerer impress another clinician with her dissociative tendencies. In other words, avoid educating her in dissociative phenomena. Exercise this sort of caution whenever there appears to be primary or secondary gain from the diagnosis. Most individuals with DID resist the diagnosis initially. After all, this is a "disorder of hiddenness" (P. Dell, personal communication, 1989) and there is a very strong tendency to conceal, rather than reveal, dissociative pathology. If a client appears eager for the diagnosis, carefully assess the likelihood of primary and secondary gain.

During my 11 years of working with DID clients, I have only encountered two malingerers who tried to convince me of their multiplicity. One was an inpatient who told me about her other personalities. I was unconvinced. Not only was her character pathology striking, but her delight in having "other personalities" was uncharacteristic of DID, and I got no sense of the complex relationships between the personalities as I listened to her. I didn't challenge or confront her regarding my suspicions, but made the borderline diagnosis. I suspected that one day I would gain some insight into her presentation. A few weeks later, I overheard her telling a peer on the ward how she had been in another building where there was a patient who got a lot of attention because she had several personalities. She said that she had decided, "Hey, *I've* got other personalities, too!"

The other was an outpatient case, a man with a history of serving time for sexually abusing his stepdaughter. He tried to convince me he had "multiple personalities," telling me how it was so much fun to take his grandson to the amusement park because first he can be the grandfather, enjoying it as an adult, and then when he goes on the rides, he can become a little boy, and so forth. This ego-syntonic description of the switching did not ring true, and after assessing him cautiously, I had to disappoint him with the news that I could not give him the diagnosis he sought. During the subsequent therapy, I never doubted that I had made the right decision.

I have to admit that I have been excessively skeptical at times. Once I referred a dissociative inpatient to a colleague rather than make the MPD/DID diagnosis, because I felt insufficiently convinced of her multiplicity. The colleague later assured me that the client did have DID.

On another occasion I was eventually able to get beyond my own skepticism. Upon assessment, an outpatient appeared to have seven personalities. When I discussed my findings she appeared so pleased that I mistook her eagerness for an indication that primary or secondary gain might be a factor. I proceeded with caution and was not able to confirm the diagnosis of DID until the 11th session.

Comorbidity

Comorbidity rates are high for DID clients, particularly for eating disorders and substance abuse, although alters within a single client often differ with regard to eating disordered and substance abusing behaviors. These diagnoses should be given where criteria are met, as they are not subsumed by the DID diagnosis. Chu (1998) pointed out that eating disorders and substance abuse are common secondary symptoms in individuals who have experienced severe, persistent abuse. He observed that while these symptoms are not necessarily less important than the primary posttraumatic and dissociative symptoms, they may be considered secondary because they result from efforts to manage the primary symptoms rather than from the abuse itself.

Although significant anxiety and depression are often secondary to dissociative pathology and its impact on quality of life, and may be subsumed by DID, there are advantages in providing every diagnosis justifiable on the basis of the client's symptoms. If the client is hospitalized or comes to the attention of another clinician who does not understand or treat dissociative disorders, the diverse diagnoses will convey a range of difficulties to be addressed. Furthermore, disorders which are understood as endogenous rather than posttraumatic may increase the client's insurance benefits under parity laws, and should therefore be diagnosed whenever the diagnostic criteria are satisfied.

Characterological features are not uncommon in DID, with traits varying among the alters. Coons et al. (1988) reported that in their study of 50 cases of MPD, 86% met the diagnostic criteria for at least one personality disorder on the basis of their MMPI results. However, I feel that a conservative approach should be taken in assigning Axis II diagnoses to these clients, so that they are only used when clearly appropriate. For example, personality disorder not otherwise specified should not be used to reflect a dependent trait in one alter, an avoidant trait in another, a hysterical trait in a third, and so forth. Even in cases where specific personality disorder diagnoses are considered, these decisions should be made judiciously. This is especially true because of the possibility that the diagnoses might come to the attention of a clinician unfamiliar with DID, whose treatment plan may be affected by the Axis II diagnoses.

It could be argued that in diagnosing BPD, which involves satisfying five of nine criteria, at least four of the nine criteria be excluded from consideration if they are satisfied only on the basis of dissociative phenomena in DID clients. Specifically, I feel that "identity disturbance" (American Psychiatric Association, 1994, p. 654) resulting from the multiple identities of alters should not be counted toward the five requisite criteria. Similarly, "affective instability due to a marked reactivity of mood" (American Psychiatric Association, 1994, p. 654) should not be counted if it is displayed only when there is switching or passive influence experiences. Additionally, it could be argued that a caveat be introduced regarding "a pattern of unstable and intense interpersonal relationships characterized by alternating between extremes of idealization and devaluation" (American Psychiatric Association, 1994, p. 654). If these polarities emanate exclusively from the discrepant responses of alters who feel differently towards given individuals, the intention of the criteria is not satisfied. (For example, a client whose angry alter abhors the parent who molested the client in childhood and whose child alter longs for that parent's love, does not reflect the dynamic intended by the phrase "alternating between extremes of idealization and devaluation" [American Psychiatric Association, 1994, p. 654].) Finally, the ninth diagnostic criteria for BPD, "transient, stress-related paranoid ideation or severe dissociative symptoms," (American Psychiatric Association, 1994, p. 654), a criterion introduced in *DSM-IV* (American Psychiatric Association, 1994), should not be used in assessing comorbid BPD in a DID client when it reflects nothing more than pathological dissociation or fear directly associated with the experience of traumatization. The integrity of the DID and BPD diagnoses cannot be maintained when the diagnostic criteria for BPD are used to reflect the hallmark symptoms of DID. However, the current trend appears to be toward increased recognition of comorbid DID and BPD (Chu, 1998). The comorbidity of DID and BPD is a complex issue that should receive increasing professional attention in coming years.

As explained in chapter 1, DID can be conceptualized as a complex form of childhood-onset PTSD. Although PTSD is subsumed by the DID diagnosis, clients satisfying diagnostic criteria for both PTSD and DID can be given both diagnoses. However, clinicians should bear in mind that if they use the PTSD diagnosis to reflect posttraumatic symptomatology and alleged, but noncorroborated, abuse, they make themselves vulnerable to accusations that they are overly endorsing the accuracy of the client's reported memories.

☐ Evaluation of Safety Concerns

Of course, arriving at the appropriate diagnosis is only one goal of the assessment process, albeit a major one. You may want to assess coping resources, adequacy of social support, and so forth. But there are two important questions regarding safety that you will certainly want to address before the end of the initial evaluation session. Does the client pose a threat to the safety of self or others? And do others in the environment pose a threat to the safety of the client?

Let us assume that the diagnostic criteria for DID have been satisfied, and explore how this may impact evaluation of threats to safety. There are many reasons why asking a DID client whether she has ever made a suicide attempt or has any thoughts of harming herself or ending her life may not be an adequate approach to assessing suicidality. You may be questioning a host personality who is not herself suicidal, while others within the personality system may be chronically and/or acutely suicidal. You cannot feel too reassured by a denial of suicidality in a client who finds evidence of activities carried on outside of awareness! Her denial would constitute a "false negative," which is what you want to avoid in assessing suicidality. You may be able to circumvent this denial by inquiring about suicidality in terms of passive influence phenomena. You might ask, for example, "Do you sometimes have a feeling come over you of wanting to die, or harm yourself, even though you know it isn't what you want, or doesn't seem to make sense?"

Alternatively, the personality you are questioning may experience suicidal ideation, but may be hearing voices telling her not to reveal this. If you notice characteristic eye movements before she denies suicidality, you can counteract the probable internal censure by expressing your belief that people who have had a difficult time are sometimes comforted by the thought that they have some control over the amount of pain they will have to endure. The client or personalities may fear that you will hospitalize them if they admit to suicidal ideation. It can be helpful to assure them that many dissociative clients experience these thoughts and that the treatment of choice is outpatient therapy that helps the client find other ways to stop the emotional pain so that there are better alternatives than suicide.

It is also possible that there is guilt associated with suicidality. One client's adolescent personality, plagued by memories of sexual abuse and frantic efforts to shield the host from these memories, felt deeply ashamed of her chronic suicidality. In therapy, it emerged that her shame resulted from her mother's response to her statement "I could always die." Her mother, not knowing about the abuse and the fragmentation of her daughter's personality structure, had responded emphatically that suicide was not an option. The adolescent personality was encouraged by my validation that she had needed to know she had a "trump card" before the time had come to do her healing work in therapy.

With DID clients, it's important to assess the history of harm to the body. If the client has a history of psychiatric hospitalization or trips to the emergency room, assess precipitants carefully. As stated earlier, it's not unusual for DID clients to present in the ER poisoned or bleeding profusely, with no memory of how the poisoning or bleeding came about. It's also a good idea to inquire about unexplained bruises and lacerations. Alter personalities may not know they all share the same body. Putnam (1989) wrote about alters often exhibiting "a fixed belief that they are separate and can physically harm another personality without injury to themselves" (p. 64). Kluft (1984a) referred to this belief in physical separateness as a "pseudodelusion." When speaking with a client who has been diagnosed with DID, it can be helpful to acknowledge that you know it's confusing because they are separate inside but have to share the same body when they come out. This is more respectful and effective than confronting the false belief. By affirming that both perceptions are true (one in terms of inner, psychological experience and one in terms of outer, physical experience), the personalities no longer need to reconcile the two perceptions by insisting on physical separateness and are free to accept their own daily observations of coming out in a body that has been dressed and groomed by another personality.

The "suicide attempts" that are perpetrated by one personality and discovered by another may often be better described as "internal homicide" attempts (Putnam, 1989, p. 287). Certainly there are cases where one personality may be intending to take her own life, and another personality intervenes to prevent the tragedy. But in many cases one personality attempts to kill off another (often the host), believing that he or she will survive the death of the other personality and will then be free to take over. For this reason, it is essential to explore any experiences of unexplained damage to the body, even if the host has no wish to die.

Assessing a DID client's potential for harming other people is as complex as assessing suicidality. Again, the host personality may be utterly free of such ideation, but the enraged alters who hold the traumatic memories may be preoccupied with revenge. There may also be personalities who behave inappropriately with children, although I have rarely encountered this in my practice. Unfortunately, it's extremely difficult to evaluate this potential in the initial sessions of therapy, before rapport has been established with the alters. The clinician certainly wants to avoid a suspicious or accusatory stance. Initially, it is usually necessary to base the assessment of potential for harm to others on overt threats and what is known of past behavior (legal history, charges pending, and so forth). It's helpful to offer a great deal of empathy for the anger experienced by the alters, right from the beginning of the therapy. Talking through to them, you can express your belief that, while their feelings are valid, there may be some behavioral choices that are better than others, and that you will help them learn for themselves how they can express their feelings and meet their needs most effectively. This sort of validation supports angry alters in finding healthy expressions of their anger and helps defuse acting-out tendencies.

So suicidality and homicidality must be addressed. But why focus on whether others in the environment pose a threat to the safety of the client? After all, clinicians don't generally inquire about this, assuming quite appropriately that clients will let them know if threats to their safety exist. The DID client may be limited in her capacity to perceive threats to her own safety. There may be alters who engage in high-risk behaviors, such as sexual promiscuity, speeding while driving, substance abuse, impulsive spending, and so forth. The host frequently finds herself dealing with the aftermath of such behaviors and feels the need to cover up for her confusion. The process of "normalizing" this kind of instability desensitizes the client to danger.

Furthermore, the DID client's world may be so chaotic that she may not even know the identities of people she encounters on a daily basis in intimate settings. For example, one DID inpatient reported that she had just figured out that the man she had been seeing in her apartment for months was the fiancé of one of her other personalities! She had been calling him "Daddy" because she thought he was married to an adult female whom she assumed was living in the apartment with them, and she considered this woman a motherly presence in her life. This man apparently did not pose a threat to the client's safety, but the case illustrates the potential risk to the client who, due her personality fragmentation, may be grossly confused and unable to assess danger adequately.

With DID clients reporting an abuse history, it is helpful to inquire whether the alleged perpetrators are still alive and, if so, whether contact is maintained. Often contact with abusive parents is maintained in part by a host who is amnestic, and therefore uninformed, about the abuse. Such hosts may lose time when visiting the parents, when the "informed" alters come out to protect the host from further trauma. Contact with abusive parents may also be maintained by child personalities who either feel attached to the abuser or believe the abuser's threats about what will happen if contact is discontinued.

If the host alleges abuse and maintains contact with the alleged abuser, you can ask whether any members of the personality system believe the client is endangered by this continued contact. If the client has children, you can ask whether any personalities believe the children are similarly endangered. When the trauma history is uncorroborated, this assessment should be coupled with information regarding the vagaries of human memory. The client can be told that, regardless of what may have happened in the past, safety in the present and future can be enhanced. Talking through to the alters in this manner is helpful for two reasons. First, it helps you assess risks to safety and take steps to minimize them. Second, it demonstrates from the outset that you value input from the alters, who are by definition fundamentally protective, and it allows them to mobilize a quality that enhances their growing alliance with the therapist.

CHAPTER

Basic Therapeutic Techniques: Where to Go and How to Get There

During the first stage of therapy the client makes an important discovery: She has the power to change her life for the better, and since this is so, she must not be as damaged as she thought she was. In this chapter I introduce the tools that help her make this discovery. In the next chapter I describe the therapeutic relationship that supports the discovery process. And in the chapters that follow I use case material to illustrate the various interventions that characterize the treatment model.

This chapter describes in detail the formal therapeutic techniques introduced early in therapy. These techniques help the client achieve a meditative or autohypnotic state in lieu of the heterohypnotic trance state utilized in many other approaches to treating DID. (Similarities and differences between these states are discussed in chapter 3.) The visualized inner structures, described briefly in chapter 3, are offered to the consenting client as means of increasing safety and control, fostering internal communication, and bringing unconscious resources into consciousness.

As I present each technique and structure, I describe its origin or my introduction to it. I also describe my own modifications or elaborations so that it will be clear to what extent these methods are innovative and how this model can be understood in the context of the professional literature.

☐ Techniques Facilitating the Meditative State

There are three relaxation, visualization, and meditation techniques I use in assessing and treating dissociative clients. I also use them with many of my nondissociative clients. I present them here, before introducing a variety of other interventions, because they lay the foundation for much of the subsequent treatment and because many clients later describe them as among their most powerful therapeutic resources.

The first two techniques are generally used in sequence. They were alluded to in chapter 4, as they are first introduced during the assessment procedure when dissociation is suspected. The third technique is derived from the ancient Tibetan meditation practice of Tonglen, or The Art of Giving and Receiving Love. I usually introduce Tonglen during the first couple of months of therapy, but not within the first few weeks.

In teaching these techniques initially, I've found that it's important to tell clients that there is a lot of variability in the ways different people use visualization or meditation, and that there is no one right way to visualize. I explain that some people visualize quite vividly and experience things in a concrete, sensory manner, while others have a more vague and abstract experience as they just try to imagine things with their eyes closed. The visualization exercise needn't be vivid in order to be valuable. This explanation not only minimizes anxiety, but serves to mitigate against demand characteristics as well. I also explain that many people find their minds wandering when they attempt visualization or meditation. I suggest that instead of feeling anxious about "doing it wrong," they remember that the human mind has a natural tendency to wander, and gently bring their attention back to the suggested imagery whenever they notice the mind straying. These suggestions about focusing the mind are only necessary when the meditation and visualization techniques are first introduced.

Physical Relaxation Training

This relaxation exercise is based on a technique for which I am indebted to Richard Griffin, the supervisor who provided my early training in the diagnosis and treatment of dissociative disorders during my predoctoral internship year. I've made some minor changes in order to lay the groundwork for the second technique, the visualization exercise.

I would also like to acknowledge the contributions of Joan Borysenko (1995) and Yvonne Dolan (1991), which I incorporate into this and the subsequent exercises. I borrow Borysenko's phrases "flowing like water" and "cascading like a river of light" for the first exercise. This imagery is quite evocative and greatly aids relaxation. I borrow Dolan's wording in terms of "inviting the client to notice" the impact of the imagery and suggesting that the client "add or subtract" from the experience to maximize its personal utility.

As with any visualization experience, I first explain the imagery and procedure to the client and seek informed consent or informed refusal. The basic image is that a wave of warmth flows gradually from the top of the head down to the tips of the toes, releasing and relaxing the muscles as it flows. Although in practice I don't use a formal script for the relaxation exercise, I present sample language and imagery here so that the reader has a clear understanding of how the relaxation training progresses. Occasionally I offer alternative wording (in brackets) for use with clients who may have more limited verbal skills. I watch the client's breathing and coordinate the word "down" with the client's exhalation to enhance the client's relaxation.

I proceed as follows with the consenting client, speaking slowly and gently:

Find a comfortable position for yourself in the chair, so that your head and body feel well supported. Feel free to close your eyes if you wish. We begin with the image of warmth at the top of your head, just as if a light were shining down on you, warming your scalp. Feel the muscles releasing there in the warmth ... as the warmth expands and begins to flow down into the forehead ... flowing like water down into all the little muscles around the eyes, releasing and relaxing ... flowing down into the temples ... into the cheeks ... and jaws ... releasing and relaxing ... and you may even want to let your jaw drop open a little, your whole face becoming warm and soft. And now the wave of warmth flows down into the neck, relaxing all the muscles you use all day long ... flowing down into the shoulders ... cascading like a river of light down over the shoulders and deep into the large muscles of the upper arms, releasing and relaxing ... as the warmth flows through the elbows, down into the lower arms, relaxing and letting go, as the warmth flows like water down through the wrists, down into the hands ... and all the way down through the knuckles to the very tips of the fingers. And any residual [leftover] tension can simply flow out the tips of the fingers, leaving the whole length of the arm feeling loose ... and heavy ... and increasingly relaxed. Then flowing from the shoulders down into the torso, feel the warmth flowing deep into the muscles of the back and chest wall ... releasing and letting go. And it's so nice to know that without your even thinking about it, the lungs expand to take in the oxygen your body needs, and contract to release the carbon dioxide that's not useful to you. It's so good to know that without any conscious effort on your part [without even thinking about it], the lungs expand and contract, expand and contract ... the wisdom of the body unfolding day and night to keep you in life and in health. Feel the belly rising and falling, following the wisdom of the body . . . as the wave of warmth flows deeply into all the inner organs of the body, releasing and relaxing . . . the warmth flowing all the way down into the buttocks, resting heavily on the chair, and down through the hips and into the large muscles of the thighs . . . relaxing . . . letting go . . . as the warmth flows through the knees and into the calves . . . feeling the muscles release as the wave of warmth flows like a river of light down through the ankles, into the feet, through the insteps and all the way down into the toes. And any residual [leftover] tension can simply flow out the tips of the toes, leaving the whole length of the body feeling loose . . . and heavy . . . and deeply relaxed. [Pause] Now you may wish to take a moment to make any adjustments to enhance your experience of comfort and relaxation, adding anything that you'd find helpful, and subtracting anything I've said that you may have found distracting or disturbing in any way. [Pause] Now I invite you to notice the difference it makes throughout your body when you take the time, as you have today, to visualize warmth flowing through the body.

Incidentally, the portion of this exercise that I added to Dr. Griffin's imagery, in order to lay the groundwork for the following exercise, is the notion of the "wisdom of the body"—first introduced here to describe lung-function—which parallels the "inner wisdom of the unconscious mind" and anticipates the action of the mind in the following exercise.

Note that the image of light or warmth "flowing like water" is not introduced when focusing on the mouth, throat and neck, or on the pelvic area. A client who experienced sexual abuse, whether or not she has conscious memories for such trauma, may respond negatively to an image of liquid flowing in certain parts of the body. For this reason, it's wise to proceed with sensitivity in offering this imagery.

Visualization Training

This exercise is based on an image of mind drainage suggested by Norman Vincent Peale (1954) and first brought to my attention by one of my clients. Peale's intention was to help his reader shed anxiety and worry and replace them with faith. I've adapted this exercise in order to avoid religious references and allow each client to frame it in the most personally useful way. (Although some clients may assimilate these therapeutic experiences into a religious or spiritual perspective, I avoid leading the client in this regard. Not only do I want to be as cautious and respectful as possible, but I am aware that some clients' spiritual faith has been shaken by traumatization. As therapeutic healing restores meaning to their world and a sense of worthiness to their self-perceptions, trust and faith may be restored.)

I also wish to acknowledge another contribution of Dolan (1991) at this point, as I incorporate into the second exercise her suggestion that the client bring back a "souvenir," a gift derived from the meditative state. In addition, I use her "invitations" to the patient to observe and make adjustments in this exercise, as in the preceding one.

I generally explain both exercises, the warm wave relaxation exercise and this mind drainage exercise, and then offer both in succession to the consenting client. I explain that the client will have an opportunity to visualize a basin filled with dark and murky water, like dirty wash water, which is like a mind filled with cares and worries. The basin, and the mind, can then be drained imaginatively of their heavy contents. The client can then visualize the basin filling with fresh water and visualize the mind filling with everything needed in order to move forward with confidence.

Again, I don't use a formal script with clients, but offer language and imagery here so that the reader has a sense of how this exercise may be implemented. In listing the various emotions and experiences with which the mind may fill, you may find it helpful to coordinate your suggestions with the client's inhalation. After the warm wave exercise has been completed and the client has had an opportunity to make any adjustments to maximize comfort and relaxation, I pause and then proceed as follows with the consenting client, speaking slowly and gently:

> Now I invite you to visualize a basin of water ... dark and murky water, like dirty wash water. Sense the heaviness of the contents of that basin, like a mind filled with cares and worries, doubts and apprehensions, insecurities, anxieties, and misgivings ... and when you have a sense of the heaviness, the burden, of these contents, prepare to let them drain out ... visualize the dirty water draining out of the basin ... like a mind letting go of all its cares and worries. [Pause] But just as the lungs contract to release the carbon dioxide that's not useful to the body and then expand to take in the oxygen you need, so, too, the empty basin fills with clear and sparkly water ... like a mind filling with ... self-acceptance ... with compassion [kindness] ... with safety.... Let the mind fill with security, with trust.... Let it fill with patience and understanding ... with light ... and vitality [energy].... It fills with confidence ... with curiosity ... with hope.... Let it fill with insight, with intuition ... with wisdom.... Let it fill with comfort ... with balance and harmony ... with flexibility ... with spaciousness [openness] ... with freedom.... Let it fill with clarity ... with well-being.... Let it fill with love.... It fills with purity, with tranquility [peacefulness] ... with inspiration. [Pause] It fills with the knowledge that you are a deserving participant in life. [Pause] It fills with the understanding that you have what it takes and you know what you need. [Pause] Let

the mind fill with the sense that you are not alone, but are always in a protective and loving presence. [Pause] It fills with a sense of connectedness
and belonging ... with the knowledge that you have something of value to
give. [Pause] Let the mind fill with everything you need in order to have
the kind of relationships you choose for yourself. Let it fill with everything
you need in order to experience yourself in the way you wish to experience
yourself. Let it fill with everything you need in order to use your energies
in ways that are satisfying and rewarding ... with whatever you need in
order to use your talents creatively, constructively, and compassionately.
In fact, allow the mind to fill with everything you need in order to move
forward in life. [Pause] Now I invite you to make any adjustments to enhance this experience for yourself, adding anything that you'd find helpful,
and subtracting anything I've said that you may have found distracting or
disturbing in any way. [Pause] Now you may wish to take a moment to
notice the difference it makes in your body and in your mind to have let go
of everything that wasn't useful and to have invited into your mind everything that you need. [Pause] Without feeling the need to make a conscious
decision, you may wish to simply allow yourself to notice something ...
be it something you hear, see, feel, or otherwise experience ... that you
could take back in the corner of your mind as a souvenir of whatever aspect of this experience you find useful. [Pause] Like taking a photograph
of a happy time ... and then storing it safely in a photo album, knowing
that anytime you wish, you can simply take out the album and open it
up and you can remember ... you can keep this souvenir in the corner
of your mind, and then bring it to the center of your mind whenever you
wish to encourage yourself, to remind yourself that you have the power
to know what you need. [Pause] In a moment, we'll be getting ready to
reorient to the room, but in the meantime, you may wish to take a moment to express inwardly your sense of gratitude for the inner wisdom of
the body that keeps you in life and in health, and for the inner wisdom
of the unconscious mind that guides you through relaxation and through
feelings of well-being. [Pause] And now, take your time as you prepare to
reorient to the room, perhaps stretching or even yawning. And whenever
you're ready, allow your eyes to open.

In exploring the client's response to the exercise, I inquire about what
was useful and not useful. It's important to display comfort with hearing
that something was not useful, so as to encourage the client's ability to
provide feedback of all kinds. I also ask whether the client noticed a souvenir, and if so, what it was. This minimizes demand characteristics by
indicating that I don't expect the client to respond to every suggestion
I make. Finally, I ask if the client "added or subtracted" anything. My
verbal suggestions have evolved over the years in response to clients' additions. For example, both "patience and understanding" and "freedom"
were contributions of clients.

Tonglen and Tonglen-Derivative Meditation Techniques

I was introduced to Tonglen an ancient Tibetan meditation technique, by Joan Borysenko at a workshop in April 1995. I am much indebted to her for sharing this most useful and versatile technique. The basic imagery underlying Tonglen, as taught by Borysenko, is that we can breathe in light from the Great Light of the universe and use this light to dispel whatever it is that is weighing heavily on us, which is represented by smoke surrounding the heart and obscuring the light within, the light of our true nature, a microcosm of the Great Light of the universe. Borysenko suggests that as an alternative to smoke, the image of clouds may be less aversive and more useful. I always use the image of clouds rather than smoke. As water vapor, clouds lend themselves nicely to the image of "vaporizing instantly in a burst of light," a phrase I borrow from Borysenko.

I first explain the imagery and procedure to the client and seek informed consent or informed refusal. I'm careful not to limit the interpretation of the "Great Light of the universe" by elaborating the image. I have found that spiritually minded clients often later describe this as the light of Divine Love, while less spiritually minded clients may visualize this as a physical light, like the sun. Whatever understanding the client has regarding the Great Light, physical or nonphysical, the meditation is beneficial. The important point here is that it is best not to interfere with the client's interpretation by using suggestive language.

If the client wishes to proceed with this meditative experience, I offer the following guidance:

> When you are ready, gently close your eyes and direct your attention to the Great Light of the universe above you and slightly in front of you. Take as much time as you need to experience the warmth and energy radiating from the Great Light. [Pause] When you have taken all the time you need to experience this light, just give a little nod of your head so I'll know you're ready to move on. [After the nod:] Now direct your attention to your own heart, noticing to what extent the light within is obscured [blocked] by the things that weigh heavily on you, like a layer of clouds surrounding the heart. Take your time to observe the quality of those clouds, noticing whether they are light and wispy, dark or viscous [thick], and to what extent they obscure [block] the light within your own heart. Take as long as you need to get a sense of what that cloud barrier is like and to what extent the light within is hidden by it. [Pause] When you are ready to move on, just nod your head. [After the nod:] Now redirect your attention back to the Great Light of the universe and prepare to begin the work of Tonglen, inhaling the light on the in-breath and releasing a little wisp of cloud on the out-breath, whichever bit is ready to be released, and let it be vaporized in a burst of light in the Great Light of the universe. Then breathe

more light into your own heart, repeating this process as many times as you need in order to complete the healing work that you are ready to do today. [Pause] When you are ready to move on, just nod your head. [After the nod:] Please nod again if you now have an experience of the light within your heart.

When I first learned and taught Tonglen, the instruction was to continue this process until all the clouds were dispelled and the light within was shining strongly and clearly. I've learned from my clients, however, that it's not always possible to clear all of the clouds in a single session, although it is always possible for the client to make some inroads, or at least (in rare instances when no change is possible) for the client to gain insight into how she has been holding onto emotional pain, refusing to release it. For this reason, it is important to be respectful of the client by not predicting what can be accomplished, but simply stating that you will allow plenty of time for completion of the healing work that the client is ready to undertake at this time.

There are a number of ways the Tonglen meditation can be elaborated. The original intention of the Tonglen meditation, as I understand it, is the transmission of healing light to others and to the world after one's personal connection to the universal light has been experienced vividly. After the DID client has become aware of the existence of other personalities, the basic Tonglen experience can be extended to promote compassion within the system. For example, after completing the meditation as described above, the client can be invited to visualize one of the other personalities sitting or standing across from her. She can then inhale the light from the Great Light of the universe, pass it through the light of her own heart (which has been liberated to some extent by the meditation), and exhale the light toward the other personality. I like to use Borysenko's (1995) suggestion that the client "breathe a warm stream of loving light" to the other. When the client inhales again, she draws away a little bit of the cloud barrier surrounding the heart of the alter personality and then either vaporizes it in the light of her own heart or passes it through her heart, exhaling it for vaporization in the Great Light.

You may notice that I use the word "heart" in a slightly unconventional manner. One would ordinarily speak of using the lungs to inhale and exhale. Clients tend not to be bothered by this metaphoric language and usually respond quite well to this notion of heart-connection with the universe and with each part of the system. I would certainly adjust my language and imagery to maximize the utility of the meditation for any client who preferred to visualize lung-function in a more anatomically accurate manner.

One client found the Tonglen exercise so helpful that he decided to teach it to his alters. "It's amazing how, when you focus on that sun, everything seems so much brighter," he explained. "Inside your eyelids, everything seems orangey-bright. Everything seems to open up a little bit more." He described how he demonstrated the technique to one of his alters: "I did it first. I tried to show him how much brighter and more open everything feels."

☐ Visualized Structures Utilized in the Meditative State

The goals of increasing stability and improving internal communication are promoted through the use of three internal visualized structures (introduced in chapter 3) which can be experienced by the client in a meditative state. I describe the structures and how they may be used, and elicit informed consent or informed refusal. I communicate clearly to the client that these inner structures are being *suggested* (i.e., they do not exist objectively) because they may be useful tools for the client. I generally explain one structure at a time, in the session when I feel that particular structure would be most useful.

The Theater

I typically describe the theater first. I tell the client that if she would like, she can relax deeply and allow her inner wisdom to guide her to a place inside herself that looks like a private movie theater, with a screen on the wall that allows the inner wisdom to guide her by means of visual images (moving or still) or verbal suggestions (words written on the screen or spoken aloud). I explain that although the movie theater doesn't "exist" inside objectively, her inner wisdom creates it if she chooses to use it as a setting for healing work, because it can be a helpful mechanism for the inner wisdom to communicate with the conscious mind. I also explain that she will find a set of controls that allow the conscious mind to communicate with the unconscious. There are controls for play, stop, pause, fast-forward, rewind, speed control, volume control, zoom in, and pan out. Especially valuable on the control panel is a dial that can be turned down to decrease emotions and bodily sensations and turned up to amplify them.

When I first describe the theater early in the therapy process, I generally suggest that if the client wishes to, she can go to the theater to ask for a vision of what will be possible once she overcomes the difficulties that have caused her to seek therapy. I explain that this isn't a literal glimpse into the future, as if she were gazing into a crystal ball, but it is an opportunity for her inner wisdom to show her, using the images that are most meaningful to her at this time, what she can look forward to as a result of her participation in therapy.

If and when the client consents to a meditative visit to the theater to view a vision of hope for the future, an abbreviated version of the relaxation exercise can be followed by the suggestion that the client allow her inner wisdom to guide her in doing the healing work she has chosen for that session. It gradually becomes unnecessary for me to provide any verbal guidance at all as the client becomes increasing adept at entering a meditative state. After several sessions, I suggest that whenever the DID client is ready she can "go inside" and begin the work she's decided to undertake. If the host persists in relying on me to help her to go inside, an alter's assistance can be enlisted. I suggest that if an alter wishes to guide the host, and the host welcomes the alter's assistance, the alter can listen in as I speak, and the next time can guide the host to relax into the meditative state. This approach not only promotes the client's independence of me but also fosters internal cooperation and trust. Alters love to assume helpful roles, and the host needs indications that the alters genuinely want to help and are capable of doing so.

Chapters 7 through 12 provide illustrations of the visual guidance and encouragement that clients have received in the theater. Specific types of requests are summarized in chapter 7. The client can obtain guidance from the inner wisdom via the screen either by asking for a film that provides answers or by entering questions on a computer keyboard in the internal theater. If the latter method of inquiry is selected, the client sees her questions registered on the screen, followed by the inner wisdom's responses. I suggest at various times that the client request guidance for the future, both proximate and distant.

In addition to conveying inner guidance to the conscious mind, the screen can also be used to communicate experiential information held by one part of the conscious mind—one personality—to another. I have found that the members of the personality system can use the theater to increase mutual understanding and empathy by sharing recent experiences in a sensory manner. This intervention, shared videos of recent experiences, is described in chapter 3 and is illustrated in chapter 8.

Although these techniques don't involve formal hypnotic induction, they were derived from hypnotic techniques involving a screen or stage which have been described briefly in the literature on the treatment of dissociation. For example, Putnam (1989) described screen techniques that permit the client to maintain adequate psychological distance while retrieving and processing traumatic memories. He included an account of the various mechanical operations the patient can control while viewing the screen: slowing down and speeding up the action, freezing and reversing the film, zooming in and panning out, and even splitting or subdividing the screen to expand the patient's perspective.

Horevitz and Loewenstein (1994), in presenting their 3-phase model, described screen and stage techniques appropriate for use during Stage 2, the memory retrieval and integration phase. They recommended that the factual aspect of memory retrieval be facilitated by hypnotic screen techniques that permit a detached gathering of information, followed by nonhypnotic cognitive processing of the acquired historical data. Finally, they recommended additional hypnotic work to expedite an emotional reexperiencing of the traumatic memories after the requisite groundwork has been laid.

Paul Dell, who supervised outpatient treatment of dissociation during my predoctoral internship, introduced me to the use of perceived manual controls to be used by the client as part of the screen intervention. In addition to the functions described by Putnam (1989), Dell incorporated the dial (described above) to allow the client to reduce feelings and bodily sensations. This technique is useful in applying Braun's (1988) BASK (behavior, affect, sensation, knowledge) model of dissociation, permitting the K (knowledge) component to be isolated and processed in consciousness. By facilitating this isolation, the dial for sensations and emotions greatly enhances the client's capacity to tolerate traumatic information.

Few clinicians publish more than a sentence or two regarding their use of screen techniques in treating MPD/DID (R. P. Kluft, personal communication, September 9,1996). For this reason, it is not apparent whether others working in the field may attribute the images on the screen to a unitary unconscious rather than to the compartmentalized memories of specific alters. Similarly, it isn't clear to what extent screen techniques have been used for purposes other than the retrieval, exploration, and metabolism of traumatic memories.

The literature suggests that screen techniques have been used more extensively in a regressive rather than progressive manner. That is, these interventions tend to address past memories rather than future possibilities. There are, however, references to using a future orientation in the literature. Fine (1994), for example, presented a series of cognitive hypnotherapeutic interventions reflecting the tactical integrationalist approach to the treatment of MPD. She described a multiscreen approach in which "one screen is grounded in the past ... one screen is grounded in the present, and a third time-progressed screen pertains to the future" (p. 294). Many of the interventions she describes, like the ones characteristic of the Collective Heart model, utilize the dissociative client's natural autohypnotic ability and avoid formal hypnotic induction.

Interestingly, Fine (1994) also presented an intervention similar to the shared videos of recent experiences described here. She demonstrated how, without the use of formal hypnosis, she increases the empathic understanding between an angry alter and a fearful alter who had previously avoided each other. Fine asked the fearful one to mentally review an actual abuse scene, while the angry one "was asked to allow herself, on her own terms, to watch and feel in detail the experience of the scared one" (p. 295). One might borrow Fine's terms to describe the function of the dial when used for amplification during the shared videos intervention: It allows one, on one's own terms, to watch and feel the experience of another personality within the system.

Although I've eliminated abreactive work from my treatment, the use of the theater remains essential to my work. I have reframed the screen/ theater as a mechanism by which the inner wisdom conveys guidance to the conscious mind, and have shifted the focus away from memory retrieval. As I altered the focus of screen-based interventions, two additions to the client's use of the remote controls became necessary. On the basis of my training, I had been using the dial first to reduce sensations and emotions, and only secondarily to allow them to be experienced, as tolerable. When I found that the theater, with its client-operated controls, could be used to obtain guidance, including visions of hope for the future and guidance regarding possible modifications of maladaptive patterns, I began presenting the dial as primarily a mechanism for amplifying the guidance on the screen, to increase the emotions and sensations when watching soothing, reassuring, or inspiring images. By amplifying the experiential aspect of the images on the screen, the client can know in her "feeling self" and in her body, rather than just intellectually, what will be possible as a result of her therapeutic efforts.

A second change in the use of the client-operated controls became necessary when I began suggesting that more than one personality could visit the theater simultaneously to obtain inner guidance or view the shared videos of recent experiences. It became clear that each personality needed her own set of controls. During the second stage, when traumatic memories are shared, the need for individual controls is also apparent, as readiness to tolerate painful material varies considerably across personalities.

The Private Rooms on the Hall of Safety

Many clinicians find that their dissociative clients benefit from the use of a "safe place" of some kind. Putnam (1989), for example, recommended having the patient go, while in trance, to a safe and pleasant place, which can be experienced with increasing vividness (p. 224). Clients have responded so well to these rooms that I've done very little in terms of developing the intervention further.

The hall of safety is generally the second visualized structure that I describe and offer to DID clients. I explain that on this hall each personality can find a private, safe room. Again, I explain that it's not that the hall and rooms exist objectively, but that this can be an effective way for the inner wisdom to help the conscious mind experience comfort, privacy, safety, and control. I describe how, if the client chooses to try this visualization experience, she can relax and her inner wisdom will guide her to the hallway. When she finds herself standing outside the door with her name (or, in some cases, her picture or some symbol) on it, the door will open and she can explore it. I explain that no one can enter a room without the owner's permission. In the hallway, the host personality may also notice names on other doors. These are names of any other personalities she's ready to acknowledge. I emphasize that this readiness is determined by the inner wisdom. I explain that if she decides to visit her safe room on the hall of safety, I'll offer her an opportunity to spend some time there while I see if any other personalities are interested in finding and exploring their own safe rooms.

The consenting client can be assisted, by means of an abbreviated version of the relaxation exercise, as described above, to find and explore her own safe room. Typically she describes what she sees. Once she's become engaged in an activity there, such as reading, playing with a pet, looking at photographs, using art materials, or relaxing in a rocking chair, I ask if she'd like to spend some time there while I see if any of the others would like an opportunity to find their own safe rooms.

You may be wondering why, in a therapy that emphasizes overcoming fragmentation, I would suggest an intervention that heightens awareness of the distinctness of personalities and their need for privacy and separateness. The answer is that, as in most therapies, we begin where the client is now. Early in the treatment of DID, the personality structure is fragmented into distinct entities. We recall that Maslow's hierarchy of needs (1954) indicates that safety and survival needs must be met before higher order needs related to growth and self-actualization. Personalities within the system often feel quite threatened by each other's anger, depression, criticism, control tactics, suicidality, and so forth. Not only do the safe rooms provide a respite, but the very fact that such internal structures are available assures the various personalities that their needs are valid and deserve to be respected. These include the need for pleasant surroundings, enjoyable activities, safety, privacy, and control.

The Conference Room

The final visualized internal structure, the conference or group room, provides a setting conducive to fostering increased communication and cooperation between the various personalities. I describe it as a place the client can find, while in a meditative state, for meeting with some or all of the other personalities within the system. It provides a comfortable gathering place for becoming acquainted, discussing feelings and issues, negotiating, and planning.

The client who chooses to explore the meeting room will be guided by her inner wisdom to a room where the system of personalities (or subsystem thereof) can meet and learn to listen to each other nondefensively. Gradually, dialogue and mutual respect come to replace internal chaos. Clients are much encouraged as they quickly begin to realize that the various personalities have valuable suggestions and contributions to make and are capable of mutual support once they are assured that their individual feelings and needs are valid.

As therapy progresses, features of the theater and the conference room can be combined so that the client can quickly alternate between input from within the system of personalities and input from the inner wisdom. This combination of structures can be achieved through the suggestion that the personalities can look around the conference room for a small screen, perhaps a computer screen, that's like a small version of the screen in the movie theater. While the personalities are speaking with each other, they can glance at the screen and see if the inner wisdom has suggestions to guide their group process. At times clients have read discussion topics off the screen. At other times I have asked questions while the client is in the conference room (generally preceded by inquiring whether I may ask a question or make a suggestion). For example, I once asked a child alter how she deserves to be treated. She felt she deserved to be treated badly because she was a bad girl. I suggested that she look at the screen and see what the inner wisdom felt she deserved. She was too young to read, but as she looked at the screen she heard the message spoken: She deserved to be cherished, just as the client's little granddaughter was cherished.

The general notion of the conference room is not unique to this model. The goal of fostering internal communication and cooperation is common to nearly all psychological treatments of DID, and any venue supporting such interaction—be it a board room, group room, consultation room, or lounge—is essentially what I am calling a conference room. Allison and Schwartz (1998), for example, described a living room inside where the various personalities "could get together to talk about matters of mutual concern" (p. 125). Although it is possible that the incorporation of a screen into the conference room is unique to this model, it appears likely that many models for the treatment of DID include the use of an internal venue conducive to intrasystemic communication and enhanced empathy.

6

The Nature of the Therapeutic Relationship

I know that with you I don't feel crazy, and with you I have hope.

—One of my DID clients

As with all therapeutic relationships, the relationship between the therapist and the client with DID is built on a foundation of mutual trust and respect. The problem is that mutual trust and respect may be particularly difficult to establish with these clients for a variety of reasons. As survivors of trauma, these clients, or at least certain personalities within the system, have learned from their experiences to be deeply distrustful. If they were hurt during childhood by parents or by other adults in positions of authority (such as extended family members, other caregivers, teachers, or clergy), they may be especially likely to distrust someone who would normally be expected to look out for their best interests, such as a therapist.

If a client distrusts a therapist, might she still respect the therapist? She may attribute power to the therapist, and one might construe attribution of power as a kind of respect. But this is certainly not the kind of respect that promotes a functional therapeutic alliance. If a client doesn't trust the therapist to have her best interests at heart, but respects the "authority" of the therapist, the power differential is amplified. As we will see, the Collective Heart treatment model emphasizes the importance of reducing the power differential within the therapeutic relationship.

So one major hurdle in establishing an effective therapeutic alliance is engaging the client's capacity and willingness to trust the therapist. But there is a second, equally important reason why mutual trust and respect may be particularly difficult to establish with these clients, and this relates not to the client but to the therapist. The therapist may have a difficult time respecting a client who is leading a chaotic life and who may be so dysfunctional that she cannot maintain employment, meaningful relationships, continuous memory, sense of identity—in short, a client who may be so impaired that she cannot maintain any sort of stable existence. This is not to imply that all DID clients experience severe impairment in all of these realms, but in discussing challenges to the therapist in establishing an alliance with the DID client, it's important to consider how we could respect a client who appears to be quite severely damaged by early trauma and by the dissociative responses it mobilized. It's easy to understand how a therapist working with such a client might wish to rescue her. This desire, while it may be motivated by genuine caring, is fundamentally disrespectful of the client's own capability. I will try to convey in this chapter how, without in any way diminishing the importance of our professional training, our understanding of their disorder, and our personal capacity to live in a stable manner, we need to demonstrate to these clients that we don't claim to have all the answers and that our job is to use our skills to help them discover inner resources that will provide the answers. If we believe in their capacity to discover inner guidance, we can convey respect for these clients without underestimating their psychological difficulties.

We see how the therapist might need to overcome personal obstacles in terms of respecting the client. But what about trust? A therapist might have difficulty feeling secure in the presence of a client who may have hostile, potentially violent alter personalities. Or the therapist may feel threatened by seductive or otherwise manipulative personalities. It's important to recognize how difficulties with trust may not be the exclusive domain of the client.

It's also important to appreciate how the client's distrust and the therapist's distrust may interact. If a client perceives that on some level the therapist feels threatened by her or by some part of her personality system, the client senses that the therapist is looking out for himself—as we all do when threatened—and may conclude that the therapist isn't acting entirely in the best interest of the client. This dynamic may replicate the early trauma if it involved a powerful figure looking out for his or her own needs at the expense of the child's well-being. The potential for therapist distrust to exacerbate client distrust underscores the imperative that professional boundaries be established and maintained within the therapeutic relationship. Clear boundaries protect the client not only directly, but also indirectly by protecting the therapist whose comfort permits wholehearted commitment to the client's best interests.

The client's distrust may also evoke distrust on the part of the therapist. For example, if a therapist does everything possible to promote trust and the client is perceived as withholding it, the therapist may feel that the client is engaging in a power struggle, which the therapist is losing. If the therapist perceives the client not as withholding trust but as unable to feel it despite the therapist's best efforts, the therapist may feel inadequate, and may then distance from the client by exaggerating the client's psychopathology in order to explain the perceived therapeutic failure and restore a sense of professional competence.

This chapter addresses the fundamental issues of establishing a foundation of mutual trust and respect upon which the therapeutic alliance rests and explores a variety of challenges commonly encountered during the first phase of treatment. These challenges are introduced here because they can pose a threat to the therapeutic relationship and to the therapy. In addition, this chapter discusses the use of written contracts and other documents and addresses questions of legal accountability.

☐ Empowering the Client

I empower the DID client to function as a key agent in her own healing, without minimizing her impairment, by sharing with her my understanding about the effects of trauma and the process of healing. "Although your mind is fragmented," I may say, "deep in your heart at the very core of your being you are one harmonious whole. You were created as a harmonious whole, and no trauma or pain you've experienced had the power to destroy that. Now, in therapy, you'll have the opportunity to use the wisdom of that deep inner unity to heal that aspect of yourself that *has* been damaged by trauma: the personality system." In this way, I convey a deep trust and respect for the client at the most fundamental level.

Informed Consent or Refusal

I reinforce this trust and respect through careful attention to the client's consent to, or refusal of, suggested interventions, using L. S. Brown's (1994) "empowered consent" (see chapter 3). It's essential that the client be informed regarding the nature and purpose of any proposed intervention and freely provide or refuse consent. Supporting client refusal of consent is an especially potent intervention, as it initially appears to work against therapist self-interest and thereby reassures the client that the therapist is devoted to the interests of the client even when they don't coincide with the therapist's initiatives.

The therapist can encourage the client to consult the inner wisdom regarding the value of learning to speak up for herself. Angry alters are typically enthusiastic about pursuing this kind of meditative work. (See chapter 9, "Inner Lessons in Self-Advocacy.") One DID client agreed to "go inside" to see a film about the value of taking a stand. She described the film as follows: "It was about building a foundation. It was like we were a plant. In order to be strong you have to have lots of roots and they have to be planted deeply. Every time you take a stand you're digging deeper into the ground." We were able to draw on this image of a well-developed root system as we moved forward with our therapeutic collaboration.

Reducing the Power Differential Within the Therapeutic Relationship

Pope and Brown (1996) discussed the relevance of client empowerment to avoiding risks of creating false memories. They emphasized the importance of constructing "the therapy process as a cooperative venture taking place between two experts" (p. 172). Pope and Brown continued:

> When therapists see their clients as expert in themselves and expert in knowing aspects of their own experience, and see themselves as expert in the processes of creating safety and containment and facilitating change, then they have the parameters of a situation in which the risks of coercion and suggestions are greatly reduced. (p. 172)

When the power differential between therapist and client is reduced by viewing the therapy as a collaborative effort by two experts, each participant is enhanced, rather than diminished or threatened, by the contributions of the other. The therapist doesn't expect to be an expert on the client's experience any more than the client expects to be an expert on conducting psychotherapy, and a much-needed balance is created in one aspect of the client's interpersonal world.

Accurate Empathy

The therapist demonstrates respect for the client's expertise by means of accurate empathy. Often it's easy to be empathic, and good therapists are adept at conveying their empathic responses. However, there are times when the therapist may feel ambivalent about accepting the emotions a client expresses, and may respond by distorting or overriding the client's experience. In order to avoid doing so, it's helpful to remember that the therapist can empathize with the client's feelings without passively accepting the conclusions drawn by the client. For example, a host or alter personality may feel that suicide is a sensible step given the apparent evidence that continued misery lies ahead. The therapist's initial inner response may be one of anxiety regarding both the client's welfare and professional liability. However, a trusting empathic response involves acknowledging that you can understand that the client might consider suicide given her expectation that there is nothing to look forward to in life. The therapist can then suggest that the client needs more information about what will be possible for her once she resolves the difficulties that have brought her to therapy, so that she can make an informed decision as to whether life will be worth living. As illustrated in chapter 7, the consenting client can ask the inner wisdom of the unconscious mind for a vision of future possibilities, so that she can decide whether to continue living. In this way, the therapist empathizes with the client's suicidality, affirms the client's right to put a limit on how much she's willing to endure, but also helps the client utilize internal resources that serve as a basis for hope.

For example, one of my DID clients reported frequent suicidal impulses. This client was typical of complex cases in that she had dozens of alters and had a great deal of trouble maintaining stability. She entered treatment with me when she was in her late thirties and already had a long history of both outpatient and inpatient treatment. The host became aware that her suicidal impulses emanated from an enraged, destructive alter. This alter had been listening in one day when I suggested the host ask her inner wisdom for a vision of hope for the future. Some weeks later, the alter, encouraged by my reassurances that we would someday understand the protective intent underlying her angry and destructive behavior, told me that she had a different kind of hope, hope for escape into heaven. I offered the alter the opportunity to go inside to the theater and watch a film about which elements of heaven will be possible for her to experience on earth. She availed herself of the opportunity and later emerged to describe her experience. She had been amazed to see a lot of light and to hear peaceful music. She could see herself smiling, her face looking soft and youthful, and felt that her heart was so light that it could float. She was astounded to realize that her heart was free of anger and hurt, and that she was among others who shared her sense of well-being and no longer feared her, but accepted her with love. She experienced her heart, for the first time, as being whole and free. After relating her discoveries, she expressed skepticism about whether this vision could come true, whether it was really possible to be free of hurt and anger and experience inner peace in this world.

By empathizing with this angry alter's wish to escape from suffering, I had been able to motivate her to seek inner guidance that proved useful to her. Although the therapy continued to be difficult, the alter was able to begin challenging some of her fixed beliefs about the inevitability of continued anger and pain. In the aftermath of the session, the alter was able to understand what I had been saying about how we feel less angry when we discover that we are not damaged to the core. This experience had a significant impact on the host, who, for the first time, understood the pain underlying the alter's rage and suicidality. The host realized that she and her alter had common goals.

The case illustration found in chapter 8 provides another example of accurate empathy. During meditative-state work in session, another client's alter personality was unable to enter his room on the hall of safety because of an image of his abusive father apparently monitoring the hallway. (A simple, but ultimately disrespectful, solution might have been for the therapist to suggest that the father image be removed so that the hall of safety might function as it should.) Once the function of the threatening image was explored, it became clear that this particular alter used the image to rekindle his anger toward his abusive father so that he knew he'd have the courage to kill himself if necessary. Once this emerged, I was able to summarize the alter's dilemma: On the one hand, he needed this image so that he could be sure his feelings would remain strong enough to support his courage (his courage being the basis of his self-esteem), but on the other hand, the image was interfering with his ability to enter his room to experience the comfort, safety, and privacy he sought. He agreed with this summary. I suggested the alter discuss his dilemma with the other members of the personality system. He liked this suggestion and later reported that the host personality came up with a good solution: The alter could scan the image of his father onto a computer disk (in the inner world, of course) and put the disk in his shirt pocket. This way, he knew he could activate the image if ever he needed it, but he could also free himself from the intrusive presence of his father when it wasn't useful. By means of this intervention, he increased not only his sense of control but also cooperation within the personality system and confidence that future dilemmas could be resolved successfully. These successes in turn support the therapeutic alliance and the client's commitment to therapy.

Conveying accurate empathy can be challenging when a survivor of childhood abuse says that she deserved the maltreatment she received. Instead of contradicting the client's perception, the therapist can explore the client's feelings, assuring the client that our feelings grow out of our experiences and therefore make sense. However, the therapist can also ask the client whether any other child deserves to be treated in an abusive manner, even in the event that the child was badly behaved or did something to "invite" the abuse.

If the client feels that at some level she benefitted from the abuse because it may have involved certain kinds of gratifying attention, I often exaggerate by using an example in which the child is entirely responsible for initiating a behavior that no mature adult would permit, such as robbing a bank with the adult's participation, and encourage the client to consider whether even in this extreme case the child is responsible for the inappropriate behavior. This type of exploration generally serves to mobilize doubt over the assumption the client made about deserving maltreatment. By providing an example in which the child's responsibility is amplified, the therapist conveys empathy for the client's feelings of blameworthiness, while simultaneously engaging the client's knowledge that responsible adults set firm limits in protecting children from experiences that are likely to harm them. In addition to this exploration, of course, the client experiencing shame can ask her inner wisdom what it is that she's ready to understand about her self-worth.

Reframing "Resistance"

One of the most potent tools we can use in empowering the client is honoring what is commonly viewed as resistance. In this treatment model, resistance is understood as a sign of healthy vigilance against further destabilization, and the willingness to express it is felt to reflect the client's ability to take appropriate, self-protective action. For this reason, it's essential that the therapist not feel threatened by the client's resistance to the diagnosis or the therapy process. When the therapist reframes resistance as reluctance, ambivalence, or skepticism, the client's feelings are validated and the client can be encouraged to express them in a straightforward manner rather than indirectly or passive-aggressively.

If a host personality seems to be receiving warnings from within as to whether or not I am to be trusted, I urge that personality to listen to those concerns, explaining that they are appropriately focusing on safety issues, which are of utmost importance. If the client has received past therapy that has not helped her adequately, I may point out that in light of all the time, effort, and money she's invested in previous therapies, perhaps a self-protective voice within her doesn't want her to get her hopes up before there's some real evidence that this therapy is right for her. In this way, I join with the conservative, protective forces within and thereby promote the therapeutic alliance.

Client distrust or ambivalence is typical early in treatment. I never tell a client she should trust me. Instead, I remind her that she hardly knows me and is wise to go slowly. I tell her that over time she will form a reliable impression as to whether we can work productively together, and that trusting the inner impression that evolves over time is much more important than trusting me. Loewenstein (1993) urged protective alters to observe his behavior in therapy as much as possible, and to question him if they felt he failed to practice what he preached. "I state clearly," he wrote, "that I believe that trust is earned over time and should not be awarded without good reason" (p. 74).

Clients sometimes doubt the DID diagnosis. One client who admitted that she had a number of distinct personalities who took control at times nonetheless rejected the DID diagnosis. She reported that DID seemed so foreign to her, and she believed she had a simpler explanation for her difficulties: "I've always been a different person at home and everywhere else, so I guess what I'm feeling more and more these days is the 'divided' life I live." The solution for us was obvious: We started exploring the experience of being "divided" rather than dissociative.

The client may express reluctance about certain aspects of the therapy. Some clients are bothered by the term "the inner wisdom," and one client complained that it sounded like something spiritual to her. I ask these clients what they feel might be a better term. The client uncomfortable with spirituality preferred the "inner strength," which we then used consistently. Another client, who thought "wisdom" was too cerebral for someone like her who had trouble connecting her heart and her head, introduced the term "the collective heart," which I found so evocative that I later adopted it as the name of the emerging treatment model.

Occasionally a client expresses dislike for the hall of safety. Alters have complained that they fear being locked away there. This is related to the more global fear that the goal of therapy involves the demise of the alter personalities. Alters often feel conflicted: They want to continue therapy because it seems to promote stability, but they are afraid that they'll be done away with as therapy progresses. I explain that no part of the system will be done away with, that all parts of the system will work toward the goal of being together as one someday, with each part participating in the eventual experience of wholeness and harmony. If the client asks me to describe what this will be like, I tell her that I can only guess, but I'll look forward to hearing a fuller description from her someday, when she has achieved that state and can describe it from personal experience. I tell her that some clients have described it as a state where all of the alters can be out all the time, because their interrelationships have become so seamless that being out together enhances rather than compromises functioning. Chapters 7 and 8 provide illustrations of how the inner wisdom can also help convey the meaning of harmonious functioning. The visions provided by the inner wisdom can help the client understand how, at each stage of therapy, each alter can contribute in the way that is appropriate to that particular phase of treatment.

Early in one therapy an angry alter announced that she was the only alter who didn't want my help. I encouraged her to raise her concerns about my role while in conference with the other personalities because, I explained, her feelings are important even if she is outnumbered. I also encouraged her to share her concerns with me whenever she was ready. This type of therapeutic response is effective for two reasons. First, the message is that no one gets overpowered in this therapy. Second, the therapist's suggestion is more successful when it appears to run counter to self-interest. The alter might have expected me to try to talk her out of her feelings or at least shield the others from her disruptive influence. By encouraging internal communication rather than attempting to squelch dissension, the therapist communicates that what's best for the system is best for the therapy, and therefore best for the therapist.

Sometimes an alter comes out but expresses reluctance to talk. Once, when an adolescent personality told me she didn't want to talk, I asked her whether I should respect that, or whether she really needed some help and should overcome her avoidance of talking. Surprisingly, she chose the latter!

Take advantage of any expression of reluctance, ambivalence, or skepticism to affirm the client for speaking up and making her discomfort known. I've never treated a DID client who didn't have at least one alter who wished the host were more assertive. Some alters get angry and frustrated because the host is too nice, accommodating, passive, or forgiving. When the host expresses her discomfort, tell her you imagine that at least one of the others is proud of her for speaking up. This response is therapeutic on several different levels. It encourages future assertiveness. It shows the client that you are appreciative of, rather than threatened by, her growing capacity to make her needs known. It highlights the potential for positive responses (such as feeling proud and offering encouragement) on the part of personalities who may typically appear critical and impatient with the host. It helps the host to see how assertiveness is best not only for her personally but also for the system collectively. And it fosters my relationship with whichever alters value increased assertiveness, who begin to experience themselves in partnership with me. For all of these reasons, it's best not to praise the host yourself when she speaks up, but to allude to the appreciation within the system. Your approval is implicit. By not making it explicit, you focus quite appropriately on her approval of herself rather than on your approval of her. By validating and honoring expressions of reluctance and by avoiding focus on your approval of the client, you foster trust without encouraging excessive dependence. You facilitate the development of a strong collaborative alliance, but not an overly intense attachment.

☐ Forming a Relationship with the Personality System

In most therapies, the therapeutic relationship is established between a therapist and a client with a single personality. In treating DID, the therapist has a more complex task: the formation of a trusting alliance with each personality within the system. Since there is typically conflict and even animosity between personalities, the therapist may feel tempted to take sides. As long as you bear in mind the following, you'll find that it's surprisingly simple to avoid exclusive alliances: All personalities are potentially listening in to any discussion, all perspectives are based on experience (whether objective or subjective) and are therefore valid, ultimately what's best for one personality is best for all personalities, and internal resolution is possible and is supported by the inner wisdom.

When I was trained in the treatment of dissociative disorders, I was encouraged to spend a great deal of time in session with the various personalities, getting to know them, enlisting their support, and taking a fuller history than the host personality could provide. Over the years, I've spent less and less time in session talking directly with the alter personalities. My relationship with them consists largely in talking through to them and helping the host personality communicate with them. Occasionally they do come out in session and spend time with me directly, but in my current practice an alter emerges in fewer than 5% of sessions. In the great preponderance of sessions, the host speaks with me and typically spends some time in a meditative state in the theater or conference room doing "inside work."

Early in therapy, therapists sometimes make the mistake of allowing themselves to feel intimidated by angry alters; they then respond by becoming controlling or emotionally distant. In very rare circumstances, an alter may actually be dangerous, and this is best determined on the basis of history and the presence of actual threats rather than a threatening tone. (In my practice, I've encountered only one client with an alter who had actual assaultive or homicidal plans directed at someone who was perceived as having wronged the client, and I've never encountered an alter who planned or tried to harm me.) In the vast majority of cases, the DID client has at least one angry alter, and these personalities pose no threat to a respectful therapist. They are best understood as fiercely protective of a host who is perceived as vulnerable. Sometimes I tell clients

that such a personality is like a lioness protecting her cubs: Her threatening demeanor is directed exclusively toward ensuring that her charges
are not harmed.

These fiercely protective alters are easy to engage in the cooperative
venture of therapy for a number of reasons. They want an opportunity
to express their needs and concerns and are capable of doing so in
increasingly appropriate ways. They dislike being shut out of the host's
awareness and long to be valued and included. In general, they have a lot
of sound advice that has fallen on deaf ears because they tend to express
themselves in a heavy-handed manner. Therefore, they appreciate the
therapist's support for internal communication and cooperation. They
deeply desire safety and respect for the host and for the system, and
soon learn that you share this desire. They are easily affirmed by your
appreciation of their role and their efforts to convey their concerns. These
alters benefit enormously from glimpsing the possibility of change and
are soon willing to direct their considerable energy toward implementing
the guidance offered by the inner wisdom. Chapter 8 illustrates how
anger can mask overwhelming pain in these alters, who present initially
as intimidating to the personality system but who hold resources essential
to the healing process.

I like to tell the entire personality system that there's a universal human
need to feel worthwhile and to know you have something of value to
contribute. This conveys my confidence in their capacity to contribute
and to participate meaningfully in the healing process, without risking
the discomfort that praise can sometimes elicit. It also implies that all
alters within the system have more in common than they realize.

The various personalities are better able to believe that you view them
positively when you make statements that display your capacity to tolerate ambiguity and dual perspectives. For example, when you're unable
to determine the protective function of an alter's behavior, you can simply say that, while it's not yet clear how this behavior is intended to
protect the system, you're confident that over time you and the rest of
the personality system will come to understand its protective function.
When the host feels threatened by harsh or demeaning treatment by an
alter, you can observe aloud that both experiences make sense. "On the
one hand," you might tell the host, "it makes sense that you feel hurt by
frequent criticism and don't want to hear it. On the other hand, she feels
that she has some suggestions that would help you to function better and
gets frustrated that you don't listen to her. The more you don't listen, the
more likely she is to express herself with frustration and impatience, and
the more impatient she becomes, the more you try to block it out, which
makes her even angrier. It's a vicious cycle. Both responses make perfect
sense once you realize how the cycle operates." In the internal confer-

ence room, of course, you will encourage the personalities to discover that, when the expectation is that each will be heard, they can express themselves more calmly and effectively, inviting others to be open to their suggestions and more accepting of their needs. Chapter 8 elaborates this process of encouraging internal communication and teamwork, but here the important point is that your support of internal communication is essential to developing a therapeutic alliance with each member of the personality system.

☐ Responding to Backsliding

The two-steps-forward-one-step-backward pattern so characteristic of first-stage DID treatment can be disheartening for therapist and client alike. The client may leave one session quite encouraged, and return with suicidal ideation the following session. The client may be taking steps to improve internal communication, and then announce that she doesn't want to hear from any of the alters or has even decided that she's made the whole thing up and doesn't have any other personalities. Most DID clients wish that they could do away with their alters, or at least some of them, at times during the first stage of therapy. It's important that the therapist not feel discouraged by these developments, because the client's deepest fear may be that she's a "hopeless case," and she may interpret the therapist's discouragement as confirmation of this fear.

Another potentially discouraging development is that the client may begin expressing annoyance when the therapist responds to the client's question by affirming that it's an excellent question and then suggesting the client seek an answer from the inner wisdom. The therapist may wonder why, after obtaining such useful guidance from the inner wisdom, the client suddenly expects the therapist to provide the answers. I explained to one client that I don't want to influence her thinking regarding issues best addressed by her own inner wisdom. I also told her that the inner wisdom knows more than I do about what it is that she needs. She asked me how it's possible for the inner wisdom to know more than the therapist. I suggested she pose this important question to the inner wisdom. She consented. After emerging from her meditative state, she reported that she had seen an image of a house. Her inner wisdom told her that she is like the house, and each of the personalities is like a room in the house. The inner wisdom is the foundation. I am simply a person viewing the house from the outside.

Expect an intermittent course, especially during the first phase of treatment. When a client feels back at square one, you can offer her a chance to see a summary of what she has achieved in therapy to date via a film in the theater. This can be followed by guidance as to whether she's ready to take another step, and if so, what that step might be. The client can also ask for information regarding what caused the setback. The inner wisdom can provide this in the form of a film about the developments leading to feelings of depression and discouragement. It's important for the therapist to bear in mind that the client looks to the therapist, and to the therapeutic relationship, to sustain her hope before she has potentiated the inner resources to do so independently.

☐ Responding to Clinical Errors

From time to time, we make mistakes. Particularly in working with DID clients, who tend to confuse mistakes, regrets, and bad memories with poor self-worth, the therapist can model a more self-accepting and balanced response when a clinical error is detected. If the client brings the error to the therapist's attention, responding appreciatively to the client's assertiveness is a first step. Then convey your regret with an emphasis on learning from the experience and strengthening the therapeutic relationship by exploring interpersonal difficulties in a respectful manner. It's helpful to remember that angry alters are scrutinizing your response to your error, comparing you with authority figures from childhood. Courtois (1999) observed that patients are less likely to sue a therapist on the basis of clinical errors than on the basis of unsatisfactory responses when the patients bring these errors to the attention of the therapist.

☐ Preservation of Life Contracts

Written documents can concretize agreements made by the therapist and client and can serve as tangible reminders of mutual commitment. I developed Preservation of Life Contracts by adapting the Antisuicide Contract published by Fremouw, dePerczel, and Ellis (1990) to the special needs of the DID client. There are two varieties of the Preservation of Life Contract, one addressing suicidality and the other addressing homicidality and assaultiveness. I use the former frequently and the latter infrequently, as a significant percentage of my DID clients experience suicidality (see chapter 13) and, as noted above, very few experience homicidality. The Preservation of Life Contract pertaining to avoiding self-harm and the Preservation of Life Contract pertaining to avoiding harm to others appear in Appendices A and B, respectively. Note that the second Preservation of Life Contract doesn't refer to what Putnam (1989) called "internal homicide," in which one personality plans to kill another personality within the system. That concern is addressed in the first Preservation of Life Contract.

Because the contracts allude to alters and to specific types of guidance obtained from the inner wisdom, obviously the DID diagnosis must be made, and the relevant interventions must be offered to the client, before the signing of the contract. Before this is possible, a more generic safety contract is used. The danger in using a generic safety contract on an ongoing basis is that any contract that doesn't explicitly include the alters can be construed by the alters as relating exclusively to the host or whichever alter signed the contract.

Note that the central issue in each contract isn't behavioral control but the availability of inner guidance that will enable the client to avoid destructive behavior by finding more satisfying ways to meet needs. The principle of fairness within the system is also emphasized.

☐ The Use of Other Written Documents

Therapeutic Steps List

Dissociative clients tend to be forgetful and often benefit from lists compiled in session. These may be lists of suggestions emerging from an internal conference or from the inner wisdom, addressing steps the client can take to improve the quality of her daily life, current relationships, and so forth. They help the client to "carry the therapy" and the therapeutic relationship with her when she leaves the office.

The Alter List

I make and periodically update a list of all known personalities within the system. This list is an intervention as well as a documentation tool. I include information such as the alter's age, gender, race (when there is more than one race represented within the system), interests, and preferences. Whenever appropriate, I note the alter's relationships within the system, including mention of any alters who nurture, or are nurtured by, the alter. In addition, the list provides an opportunity to reframe the alter's behaviors in a way that supports the therapist's emerging alliance with each personality and conveys understanding for how the alter has faced the challenges inherent in therapy. For example, one alter was described as follows in the client's alter list:

> Her role has been to keep the peace at home by being obedient and doing what is expected of her by her parents. She began a lot of soul-searching

when other alters told her that her family had done some harm to the system earlier in life, and she began to wonder whether her loyalty to the family conflicts with her commitment to the system.

☐ Legal Accountability

No discussion of the nature of the therapeutic relationship is complete without mention of legal accountability. With this treatment model, where the client seeks inner guidance for help in determining her course of action, the therapist may develop such a deep trust of the client's inner guidance that legal accountability may be overlooked. Ultimately, the therapist is ethically, and in some cases legally, responsible for actions taken by the client on the basis of suggestions emerging from the therapy hour. It's important to remember that if you're sued, the jury isn't going to understand "but the inner wisdom said this was the right thing to do." If you're not comfortable with any inner guidance the client reports, tell the client you want some help from her inner wisdom in understanding the suggestion and why it is in her best interest. As the subsequent chapters reveal, the guidance is obviously sound and healthy almost all the time. However, if you need to make a decision regarding hospitalization of a suicidal client, for example, bear in mind that you will need to defend your clinical judgment without reference to the client's internal guidance.

☐ Acknowledging Appreciation for Your Role as the Client's Therapist

When I reflect on the nature of the therapeutic relationship characteristic of this treatment model, I'm struck by one final point: It is truly an awesome experience to play a facilitating role in the reconnection of each of these diverse personalities with their creative source, which I've called the inner wisdom or the collective heart. I tell my clients that I'm honored to have a role in such important transformative work. They seem to feel pleased that I'm honored to work with them. But I doubt that they can quite grasp what a profound experience it is for me personally, as well as professionally, to witness the power of their discoveries. For those of us who are nondissociative—who don't receive guidance from our inner wisdom so vividly, in such rich sensory detail—bearing witness to this remarkable "inside work" transforms us as well. It alerts us to the inner guidance that informs even nondissociatives continually, albeit in more subtle ways.

Seeking Guidance from the Inner Wisdom

This chapter describes and illustrates a broad range of interventions utilizing the internal theater introduced in chapter 3 and elaborated in chapter 5. A clinical vignette illustrates the use of these techniques in the first stage of therapy, when the focus is on the present and the future rather than the past. In the Collective Heart model, the therapist clarifies that the internal theater is a visualized structure that is used electively by clients who seek an effective vehicle by which the inner wisdom of the unconscious mind can communicate with the conscious mind. In this way, both the therapist's role and the nature of inner experience are demystified. The consenting client quickly learns to enter a self-induced meditative state in which the theater can be entered experientially.

Research on the effects of hypnosis on memory has had legal ramifications. Memories retrieved during hypnosis are no longer admissible as evidence in a court of law (Courtois, 1999). Under the circumstances, the techniques in this chapter may be particularly valuable, as they help clients learn to obtain information of a nontraumatic nature without the use of formal hypnosis.

☐ Types of Guidance Sought in the Theater

Although the possibilities are endless, there are five general categories of requests that a client may make in the theater. The responses to these requests may occur in either of two modalities: visual images and verbal guidance. The five categories are (a) help with decision making about life circumstances and self-care, (b) visions of hope for the future, (c) images of help received in the past, (d) assistance with treatment planning, and (e) increased insight and understanding. The following sections list, for each of the five categories, examples of questions a client might ask the inner wisdom in the theater during the first stage of therapy. Subsequently, I use a clinical case to illustrate the intervention by describing the guidance obtained in response to a number of these requests.

Help with Decision Making About Life Circumstances and Self-Care

For all of these requests for guidance, the client may wish to frame the question as, "What am I ready to understand today?" and/or "What step am I ready to take today in making my decision?"

- Is it in my best interest to initiate, continue, or end a specific living arrangement? Seek, maintain, or terminate employment? Make a geographic relocation? Tell a specific person about my diagnosis? End a specific relationship?
- How can I keep myself safe?
- How can I take better care of myself?
- How can I make my needs known more effectively?
- How can I function better as a parent? As a student? As an employee?
- How can I improve my marriage or other important relationship?
- How can I overcome my social isolation?
- How can I deal with my anger?
- How can I reclaim pleasures and abilities I used to enjoy?

Visions of Hope for the Future

When offered a vision of the future, some clients may think they will, in effect, be gazing into a crystal ball. For this reason, it's important to introduce this type of request by clarifying that the images are understood to convey emotional truth rather than to predict specific physical details of the client's future life. Typical requests for visions of hope include:

- What will be possible once I've resolved the problems that have brought me to therapy?

- What is the vision I need today in order to feel encouraged that I can move forward?
- What kind of role will I (or another personality) have within the system after we have learned to function more cooperatively?
- How will relationships within the system change during the course of therapy?
- In the future, how will I be able to experience a new kind of power (or authority, or protectiveness)?
- How will I use my energy differently after I resolve some of the problems I'm currently experiencing?
- What will it be like to be a harmonious whole someday? [This question is suggested only for clients who express concern about whether integration or fusion is a treatment goal.]
- How will the system be affected by the step I'm taking today?

Images of Help Received in the Past

It's important to specify that you're referring to help provided in a non-traumatic context when this question is asked in the first stage of therapy:

- What am I ready to know about how the inner wisdom helped me in the past before I learned to go to the theater to ask for guidance?
- What am I ready to know about how [a specific alter] has helped me in the past, perhaps even before I was aware of his or her existence?

Assistance with Treatment Planning

- How can we best use our time in session today?
- What is the source of my current distress? Is any alter in crisis? Suicidal?
- What can we do to help an alter who is having a particularly difficult time today?
- Who needs time and attention today, and who can wait for the next session?
- Would it be helpful for me to see a pie chart or other visual display so that I'll understand the relative importance of factors contributing to stress, depression, or suicidality?
- Is it in the best interest of the system to talk about certain painful memories or feelings? [This question is only asked when the host or an alter initiates discussion of painful memories or affects.]

Increased Insight and Understanding

- What am I ready to understand now that I misunderstood in the past when my resources were more limited? [This question is suggested when the host or an alter presents distorted thinking resulting from faulty learning, often regarding self-worth.]
- What am I ready to understand now about my disorder, dissociation, or depression?
- What am I ready to understand now about my true nature?
- How am I perceived by my inner wisdom?

☐ Introduction to Case Illustrations

The case illustrations in this and subsequent chapters aren't intended to summarize the course of treatment or convey a full range of interventions, even during a limited time period. The clinical vignette presented in this section addresses quite specifically the process of requesting and obtaining guidance from the inner wisdom. Efforts to ensure anonymity and preserve the integrity of the case material are described in the Preface.

Lynn

Lynn was at mid-life when she moved to Virginia and sought treatment for her dissociative disorder. Lynn and I spoke briefly on the phone when she called to schedule her appointment. She told me that she had MPD, had received extensive outpatient psychotherapy previously, and had had a single psychiatric hospitalization. She had been on antidepressants for years. She described her stability as quite tenuous and said she was looking for a therapist to help her maintain her treatment gains and "stay on an even keel." She hadn't considered the possibility that she might be able to improve her functional level and the quality of her daily life.

Lynn was able to provide a reasonably thorough life chronology in her initial session with me. A woman of superior intelligence with a professional work history, she reported abuse in early childhood, a great deal of weight gain, an extremely low energy level, and constant anxiety that she would never again be able to work more than a 4-hour workday. She was extremely isolated socially and was plagued by inner voices calling her "fat, stupid, and crazy." She was aware of six of her alters by name and sensed the existence of many others.

About 3 weeks into therapy, Lynn reported that her roommate was often inconsiderate and Lynn had difficulty speaking up to make her needs known. After we discussed strategies for gently asserting herself, Lynn accepted my suggestion that she enter a meditative state and then visit the internal theater so that the inner wisdom might show her what step she was ready to take in making her needs known. Lynn, who had several weeks of experience in consulting the inner wisdom at that time, was frustrated in her efforts to view the film. She became aware that one of the alters had put it "on pause." This alter was enraged and lacked the resources to express her anger except by disrupting the therapeutic process. I observed to Lynn that it was fortunate that the angry alter had access to a set of controls and was able to pause the film, because she certainly had some valid feelings to convey and needed to get Lynn's attention. I offered to speak with the alter.

Lynn could feel the angry alter trying to push forward to talk to me, with the rest of the system struggling inside to restrain her. The system felt this alter was destructive and could not be trusted to come out to talk with me. Speaking through to the angry alter, I offered her an opportunity for her own vision for hope:

> I understand that the rest of the system isn't comfortable with letting you come forward at this time, but I would like to offer you something that you can do inside that you may find helpful. You could go to that theater inside and watch a film about your own feelings. It might start with the anger you're feeling right now, and then go on to show how you'll be able to express yourself in the future. When it's over, you can ask for a souvenir of any part of it that makes you feel hopeful.

The alter agreed to consult the inner wisdom. Lynn later described the film that they had viewed together. Initially, the screen was filled with red and black, very primitive and chaotic, apparently representing uncontrollable rage. What followed was a contract not to use the body in risky ways, an agreement to avoid hurting the body, riding motorcycles, and speeding in cars. The final scene depicted this alter with a great deal of "good physical energy," swimming and running in a race. Her souvenir was a trophy: She had won the race!

Lynn remarked how different this was from her previous therapy, which she described as a trauma-retrieval therapy. She felt the earlier treatment had saved her life during the 5 years of thrice-weekly individual sessions, but reported: "All I could do was go to therapy and try to recover in between." She was delighted to discover that she had within herself the capability of visualizing a future of safety, vigor, and success. Moreover, she was greatly relieved to find that the source of hope had an impact on the most apparently distressed and potentially destructive member of the personality system. In subsequent sessions, this angry alter revealed her constructive potential, infusing the host with motivation to improve her physical health, take pride in her appearance, and take healthy risks in making her needs known.

It's interesting to note that perhaps the most essential element in the vision of hope emanated directly from the inner wisdom and not from my suggestion. What I suggested or implied was that it would be possible for the alter to receive guidance from the inner wisdom via the screen, that the film would show some evolution in her expression of emotion, that at least some element would provide hope, and that a sensory souvenir would be available to her. The inner wisdom added the core element that permitted the evolution: the agreement to protect the body. Once the angry alter could make a commitment to safeguard the body, she could be trusted to enjoy the use of the body as a vehicle for experiencing and expressing her passionate engagement with life.

Two months later, Lynn found that she had been reminiscing about some of the more enjoyable aspects of her childhood: her pleasure in creative, solitary activities. She recalled her delight in playing the piano, making up songs, and writing stories. I invited her to consult her inner wisdom for help with identifying the first step in reclaiming her creativity and sense of freedom. She entered a meditative state and, eyes closed, shared the verbal guidance she was receiving: "I'm supposed to keep moving. The weight is literally a weight, a glue. It's keeping me stuck." "Is it important for you to lose weight?" I asked. "Yes, but we can't think of it in those terms," she explained. "We need to think of it in terms of moving, getting more flexible and fit. Active. And we need to start writing." At this point Lynn, with her eyes still closed, began to experience disruption from alters who were afraid they would be forced to go away if Lynn solved her problems and had a satisfying life. I asked her if she'd like to see a vision of what it would be like to be together as one, a harmonious whole where no one is excluded or discarded. She consented, and later reported what she had seen: "I kept seeing this one on skates, skating, going really fast. And then like a dancer doing ballet. And then walking on a beach." I asked her to help me understand how this was related to being together as one. "It's the sense of *really being in the body*," she clarified, "instead of being only in the head."

Again it is apparent that Lynn received far more from her inner wisdom than I had suggested in framing the request for guidance. I hadn't considered that the mobilization of the body might be a first step to enjoying music and writing. The inner wisdom knew not only that this step was essential but also that focusing on weight loss per se would not be helpful. We see in this vignette how this deep, creative aspect of the unconscious mind, the inner wisdom, shares with the conscious mind the connection between physical immobility and emotional and artistic stagnation. In months to come, Lynn was to understand how the glue of her excessive body weight was also related to her social isolation, which in turn maintained her low self-esteem.

Lynn's vision of the system being together as one further illustrates my observation that the guidance of the inner wisdom far exceeds the suggestion of the therapist. Not only had I not anticipated the nature of the vision she would receive, but I had difficulty understanding how it reassured the system of the future state of connection and inclusion. Informed by the inner wisdom, Lynn's conscious mind was able to convey to me what the system most needed to appreciate about the future. Her alters needed to know that not only would they not be banished from the mind, but they would actually be more present than ever before. They would be right in the body, passionately engaged in the dance of life.

Two weeks later, Lynn's inner wisdom conveyed a most unwelcome message. Lynn's original plan had been to move in a few months' time, rejoining her family of origin in Wisconsin. I had avoided commenting on her plan, which obviously would have involved prematurely terminating what we both felt was a successful therapy. I believed her inner wisdom was the best source of guidance regarding geographic relocation, so I was careful not to introduce my concerns. One day in session, Lynn spoke of financial problems and then mentioned vague plans to seek therapy after her interstate move. Availing myself of the opportunity I had been awaiting, I suggested she consult her inner wisdom about resolving her financial difficulties and finding a therapist to assist her following her relocation. She accepted my suggestion and closed her eyes.

Very shortly Lynn opened her eyes, looking dismayed. She reported that she had used the technique of entering a question on a keyboard in the theater, a method of seeking inner guidance she'd found useful in previous sessions. No sooner had she inquired about resolving her financial problems than she saw an answer on the screen that shifted her attention to the second issue: "Therapy is more important." She proceeded to enter her second concern: "What can I do about therapy when I go back to Wisconsin to continue my healing?" Lynn was distressed by the response. "The answer," she reported, "was essentially that going back to Wisconsin will be a mistake. The screen said 'I think you'll be sorry.'" This was not what Lynn wanted to hear, and in my careful avoidance of advice, I had in no way prepared her for the shock of reconsidering her plans. She was too shaken to inquire further, but was to receive more inner guidance on this topic in subsequent sessions.

As distressing as this guidance was, it was useful in more ways than one. The obvious benefit was that it formed the basis for a series of decisions supporting Lynn's commitment to healing. But it had a hidden benefit as well: It convinced Lynn that messages transmitted via the screen weren't simply what her conscious mind wanted to see. As reassuring as previous visions and verbal guidance from the inner wisdom had been, Lynn harbored in the back of her mind fears that she was somehow projecting onto the screen what she wanted to see there, what she consciously hoped would be possible. In the months that followed, Lynn had many occasions to refer to this development, affirming for herself the genuine wisdom of her unconscious by reminiscing about how the advice to remain in Virginia couldn't have been the product of conscious wishes.

The aftermath of Lynn's "unwanted guidance" was interesting. In the following session, she reported that she'd awoken one morning knowing that if she returned to Wisconsin she would spend her energy doing what other people want, and trying to *avoid* doing what other people want. She could see one of her visions of hope for the future—an image of herself hiking confidently along a woodland trail—evaporating. She knew that her inner wisdom had been conveying something important while she slept: that once again making family pressures the centerpiece of her life meant relinquishing her dreams of competent selfhood. "There's kind of a scared feeling inside," she said, "but the other side of that is ... excitement, doing something for myself."

The decision to remain in Virginia naturally led to questions about the duration of therapy. Without the closure associated with an arbitrary termination date, Lynn explained, "somebody inside wanted to know how long the therapy would be." I suggested she ask inside. She quickly went in and entered her question on the keyboard. Using a technique developed by her system so that the host wouldn't be distracted while working inside, an unnamed alter who had volunteered to be a reporter kept me abreast of the inner developments, using the first person singular to convey Lynn's experiences. "I typed in 'How long?'" she reported. "Think in terms of semesters," the inner wisdom had responded. "And how many semesters will it be?" the second question read. "It depends on the progress," the screen read. "I asked: 'By thinking in terms of semesters, do you mean with breaks?'" the reporter continued. "It said 'Yes.'" After emerging from her meditative state, Lynn explained the guidance she had received by relating the anxiety she had felt in returning to college after a number of years out of school. She had been reassured that she just had to make it through the demands of each semester, and then could enjoy a break.

In subsequent sessions, Lynn's requests for inner guidance continued to focus on a range of important practical decisions regarding mobilizing the body, expressing her needs with increasing assertiveness, and making preparations for a local move, since she would not be able to remain in her apartment. A month after her question about coping with the prospect of a lengthy therapy, Lynn verbalized feelings of personal inadequacy. "I always feel that I have to do twice as well to be half as good as other people are," she confessed. I tried to assure her that she wouldn't always feel this way, that with the help of her inner wisdom she would come to accept more about her worth as a human being. She said she doubted that I was right. I said perhaps I was mistaken and that she could check inside for a more authoritative response. She was afraid of what the answer might be. I asked her how she could explain all of the encouragement she'd received inside if she's not worthy and deserving. She was reluctant to ask a general question about self-worth, but accepted my suggestion that she go inside and ask her inner wisdom what step she's ready to take in order to feel a little better about herself. To her surprise and mine, the inner wisdom told her she wasn't ready to ask this question. Instead of asking questions, the inner wisdom informed her, she needed to talk about feeling bad and she needed to cry. She needed to find words for the pain of social rejection she'd experienced, first in the schoolyard where she was teased as "two-ton," and later in an adult society fixated on slimness and insensitive to the feelings of overweight people. The inner wisdom conveyed what I had clearly failed to grasp: Lynn needed more than anything else at that moment to acknowledge and experience her pain and the connection between feelings about her body and her value as a human being. She needed to be exactly where she was before questions about moving forward could be productive.

There were other occasions when Lynn's inner wisdom told her to stop asking so many questions. She asked for much reassurance that the details of her life could be worked out in Virginia—housing, employment, and so forth—and the inner wisdom offered guidance addressing each of her concerns, while continuing to underscore the importance of keeping the body moving on a daily basis. However, Lynn's anxiety prompted her to ask inside what she should do if this or that didn't go according to plan, and once she reported having received the following response to her inquiries: "It told me to quit playing the 'What if?' game. If you just do what you're supposed to do every day it will work out. Just try to be flexible. It told me to go and enjoy my time and not worry."

About 7 months after Lynn began her therapy with me, she expressed curiosity about how the inner wisdom works. While in a meditative state, she spontaneously asked her inner wisdom, "Why do you know so much and I don't?" The inner wisdom responded:

> Because you're only a small part and there's so much more.... You can think of me as the father you never had, someone you can depend on and they'll always be there, no matter what.... I know what all the parts can do and how they can fit together, because I can see the whole.

Lynn reported seeing a beautiful yellow light inside after hearing about the nature of the inner wisdom. She elaborated:

That's the first time I saw that yellow. It was so pretty. It was just a really reassuring type of experience, like I'm not alone. A father is supposed to be the one who takes care of you.... I feel a real calmness, a sense of peace.

Even before discovering this yellow light, Lynn had found that after seeking guidance in the theater she could go to a place inside where she saw a purple light that was both calming and energizing. It was something she discovered completely on her own, and she frequently incorporated it into her meditative practices.

After about 11 months in therapy, Lynn realized that she was slipping into a depression and that this might explain why she was unable to accomplish more than one small task per day. She knew that recognizing her condition was a sign of progress because, as she said, "In the middle of a depression, I've never realized it before." She also knew she had made progress in terms of communication and cooperation within the personality system, which comprised over two dozen personalities. Furthermore, she had finally, after much encouragement from her inner wisdom, established a consistent practice of walking and was recording her mileage on a chart. After discussing her observation about her depression and the progress she had made, she decided to go inside to see whether her inner wisdom had any guidance for her. After emerging, she described her experience:

I kept seeing sunlight and waves. I'm supposed to walk in the sun. And I'm supposed to join a walking club because I need something to work for. And I'm supposed to get a map and mark my miles so I can see [the cumulative accomplishment] instead of just [seeing] numbers on paper. Oh, and what I'm supposed to learn from this depression is that I have a disease. I'm not just lazy. I'm not just making it up. And I'm supposed to remember that I always have the purple light inside. I thanked the inner wisdom for the purple light. I just felt like I was totally immersed in it. It was almost like being underwater, but without having to think about breathing.... I felt warm, safe, and alive.... The consistent feedback I got is that I'm okay, we're okay.

Two weeks later, I suggested Lynn might ask her inner wisdom for a film about her true nature, uncomplicated by the experiences that led to her disorder and to her need for therapy. "That might be good," she agreed, "because I don't know who I am." She later described the experience:

In all the images I saw, there was a continual bubbling up from below. Positive, confident, the bubbling up seemed like something, and no matter where I was, in these different phases, something bubbled through ... something of my true nature. The thing that joined all this [the many diverse images] was the confidence and the ability to do something even if it was different. And the laughing and the talking and the gesturing was so alive, almost effervescent. And now I see that there's a lot of good stuff in there [within her]. And if I look for it, I'll see it. There was nothing depressive about that being, just this lightness and joy and confidence. And coming back here [back to her normal state of consciousness] I feel so stifled, held back, guarded.

"Would you like to ask what step you're ready to take," I offered, "in liberating your innermost nature?" Lynn sought and received this guidance: "Enjoy things as they are happening. Look for something to enjoy."

As the internal communication continued to improve within the system, Lynn found herself picking up feelings of insecurity on the part of some of the child alters. Some were quite sensitive to interpersonal rejection and often felt that others disliked them, didn't want them around, and even suspected them of lying or stealing. One child personality was convinced that she was bad because of financial mismanagement. Lynn helped this alter consult the inner wisdom via verbal guidance on the screen. "You could have handled things better but you did the best you could at the time," the screen read. The message ended rather telegraphically: "Bad choices don't mean bad person."

Perhaps it was this discussion of interpersonal anxiety that prompted Lynn to verbalize her loneliness in the following session. She spoke of feeling very lonely and wanting a romantic relationship, but acknowledged that when she thought about being with other people she felt scared. She was frightened by the obligations that accompany relationships. "It almost seems impossible to meet anybody anymore," she added. After articulating her yearning and her fears about intimate connection, Lynn entered a meditative state to consult her inner wisdom about taking steps toward finding a partner. After emerging, she described what she had witnessed on the screen:

I saw myself taking my backpack and a lunch and water, going for a hike, stopping to have my lunch. Sitting in nice places and just enjoying the place. What I saw, heard, is that I have to find the things that I enjoy, and eventually someone else will be enjoying the same things.

☐ Discussion

This case illustrates the process by which the client learns to turn to her inner source of guidance and nurturance and receives the counsel she needs in making a full commitment to her own growth and healing. The positive focus of the model, with its present- and future-orientation, is evident. Lynn's experiences demonstrate the creative potential of the inner wisdom, which clearly transcends suggestions made by the therapist and information already within the client's conscious awareness. The case also illustrates a number of other features of the Collective Heart treatment model.

Fundamental Needs of the Alters and Their Capacity to Evolve

The behavior of Lynn's angry alter demonstrates that even the system's most apparently destructive alter is not difficult to engage in pursuing healthy alternatives to violence. The following chapter provides additional illustrations and elaborates the therapeutic progress made by one enraged alter with intense retaliatory impulses. Although alters have a need to share their painful memories and are invested in performing their habitual roles within the system, this treatment model asserts that all alters have even more fundamental needs than these. They experience universal human needs, including the need to know that they have something meaningful to contribute and that their needs and feelings are valid and worthy of attention. They need to know that they will have access to all the resources necessary for meeting their goals, which involve promoting and maintaining safety and integrity and creating a satisfying life. They need to know that they'll be appreciated for their contributions someday, that they'll be acknowledged as belonging. In short, they need to know that they are lovable, capable, and valuable.

The primacy of these needs puts the therapist at a tremendous advantage in working with challenging alters. Instead of working to persuade an alter to reject destructiveness, hopelessness, or otherwise counterproductive habits, the therapist can simply offer the alter tools to tap into the inner wisdom, that part of the unconscious mind that can guide them to achieve what they long for so profoundly. When the therapist trusts the most basic needs and motives of an alter, the therapeutic bond is greatly enhanced. The therapist is free to convey the most useful kind of empathy, the empathy inherent in wanting for the alter what she truly wants for herself, without denying the press of distorted beliefs and habitual behavioral responses. We find that what each alter yearns for at the most fundamental level is in the best interest of the system as a whole. For example, each member of the system needs to learn to appreciate a given alter as much as the alter needs to be appreciated.

Thus we have a most fortunate situation: It is in the best interest of the system as a whole for the deepest needs of each alter to be fulfilled, inner guidance is available in order to guide each part of the system toward need-fulfillment, and whatever is in the best interest of the system benefits the therapy and, thereby, the therapist. This frees the therapist of the need for any private agenda, which reassures the client that the therapist is trustworthy. The inherent harmony in this approach to treatment helps offset the chaos and internal conflict experienced by the DID client. While it by no means resolves the problem, it does introduce the new perspective that what's best for one, at the most profound level, is best for all. This new perspective only makes sense where there is attunement to the inner wisdom, so that the more superficial (though powerfully experienced) desires for control and revenge yield to the profound needs for safety and esteem.

The Relative Contributions of Therapist Suggestions and Inner Guidance in Promoting Health

The collaboration between the therapist and the client's inner wisdom is mediated by the conscious minds of the host and alters. The role of the therapist is threefold. First, the therapist must earn the trust of each personality so that each is willing to accept the therapist's suggestions that the inner wisdom be consulted. Second, the therapist must understand the nature of the disorder, the treatment model, and human memory processes so that appropriate suggestions are made and inappropriate suggestions are avoided. Finally, the therapist must genuinely accept the client's refusal of a suggestion to seek guidance, trusting that if the suggestion is beneficial for the client, she will accept it when the time is right. The therapist needs to maintain a therapeutic relationship in which it's easy and comfortable for both the client and the therapist when the therapist's suggestions are declined. The main focus is on the client's ability to tap into the inner guidance at will, and the therapist is merely a facilitator of that essential internal connection.

The inner wisdom takes it from there. The inner wisdom shows or tells the client's conscious mind what she is ready to know in terms or images that will make it most meaningful to her. I highlighted several contributions of Lynn's inner wisdom that clearly transcended what I suggested—or could have known consciously, for that matter. I couldn't have anticipated, for example, Lynn's reframing the long course of therapy as a series of semesters with breaks between them. She possessed the referent for this approach to therapy, the memory that she had made it through college by using the breaks to decompress and restore herself enough to face the demands of another semester. For this reason, her inner wisdom knew this image would be meaningful and useful to her conscious mind.

The inner wisdom not only responds to requests for guidance with answers I couldn't have anticipated, but also corrects me when I'm on the wrong track. For example, Lynn obtained guidance that she needed to acknowledge her emotional pain and allow herself to cry, rather than ask what she could do to help herself feel better.

Lest I give the impression that it doesn't matter what the therapist suggests because the inner wisdom will make all necessary adjustments, I'd like to reiterate the point made at the beginning of the chapter. Requests for inner guidance should be worded with emphasis on what the client is ready to understand currently, what step the client is ready to take currently, what is in the best interest of the system, and so forth. Within this general framework, the therapist can utilize clinical judgment and intuition flexibly in wording suggestions for requesting inner guidance.

The Course of Therapy

This clinical case illustrates several characteristics of the course of therapy. Although the first phase of therapy focuses on improved functioning and increased stability, it is apparent that during this phase painful emotions do emerge, and the inner wisdom guides the client to discuss them, acknowledge emotions, and cry. For the most part, alters need to contribute constructively in the present before focusing on the past, but we see that this isn't always possible. The safest course is for the therapist to approach distressed alters with empathy, assurance that their feelings are valid in light of their subjective experiences, encouragement to articulate their views regarding how to improve the quality of daily life, and help with expressing themselves so that the host and others within the system will listen. In alluding to traumatic memories by validating the alter's feelings as responses to past experiences, it is important to emphasize the alter's perceptions rather than to make assumptions regarding the historical reality of traumatic events, in the absence of corroboration. After acknowledging the validity of the alter's emotional experience, the therapist then shifts the focus to utilizing the alter's resources to improve daily life and to build cooperation within the system. The therapist carefully avoids talking about traumatic memories as a way of building a relationship with the alter. However, when the alter initiates discussion of painful memories and associated affects, the most respectful response is to suggest that the alter consult the inner wisdom as to whether it's in the best interest of the system to discuss these memories and feelings at that particular time.

Another characteristic of the course of therapy illustrated by this vignette is the need for plugging away. We would like to believe that insight is enough, that once we achieve awareness we are forever changed. Although insight is valuable, the long, slow process of change comes about through repetitive reworking over time. Lynn's inner wisdom reminded her repeatedly to walk on a daily basis, trust the guidance she was receiving, avoid worrying, and try to enjoy herself. The inner wisdom sometimes describes this need for repetition as essential to modifying the circuitry of the brain. We will see in chapter 8 how this process of gradually modifying the circuitry is essential to the healing process, and why it can't be accomplished via a flash of insight.

Finally, this case illustrates the most potentially frustrating feature of the course of therapy: Just when the client seems to have had a breakthrough or has received the most reassuring message of hope, she may appear to regress. We saw that Lynn discovered the experience of light within her and the associated feelings of well-being, only to find herself slipping into a depression. It's important for the therapist to understand why these frequent setbacks occur, so that the therapist doesn't become discouraged, thereby discouraging the client.

It appears that Lynn's therapeutic progress enabled her to recognize the symptoms of an endogenous depression and achieve insight and self-acceptance. But setbacks following therapeutic progress often occur for another reason. Since alters were created because they were needed to help the host survive aversive life circumstances, hope for a better life may have a paradoxical effect on them. Alters may fear that if life is too good, they'll be superfluous. They are, therefore, understandably ambivalent about the success of therapy. We saw that after Lynn received valuable guidance to get the body moving regularly and to start writing, her alters became anxious that they would no longer be needed. Because Lynn promptly identified the disruption her alters created, we were able to address their concerns. However, it is not uncommon for alters to precipitate a crisis early in therapy when they contemplate the consequences of change. It's helpful if the therapist responds to these fears with empathy and with suggestions that the inner wisdom show them what will be possible for them after they've resolved the difficulties that have brought them into therapy.

It's helpful to expect that therapy may follow a somewhat convoluted course. If the client doubts that she is making progress, she can be offered the opportunity to consult the inner wisdom regarding her doubts. I have found it helpful to speculate that the inner wisdom may show a two-part video, in which Part 1 shows the progress that has been made and Part 2 shows how the client has laid the groundwork for future progress.

Becoming a Team: Fostering Internal Communication and Cooperation

We're in a much safer life right now.

—Scott

This chapter illustrates how specific techniques can be used to promote systemic communication and cooperation during the first phase of treatment. Improved internal collaboration originating in the conference room, utilization of guidance obtained in the theater, combined with verbal processing in session of the developments experienced there, lead to significant cognitive and behavioral change and form the core of the first stage of therapy.

The task of internal team-building is a problematic one for the host personality. The diagnosis, with its implication that at least one alter personality exists, is rarely accepted readily. In order to enter into dialogue with the alters, the host must be able to acknowledge both the separateness of the alters as distinct personalities and the inevitable connection between all members of the system who share one body and, ultimately, one life story experienced by that body. The irony is that the host cannot really grasp the simultaneous fragmentation and unity of the self-structure before significant therapeutic work has been done, but the work is nearly impossible to do without acceptance of the paradoxical nature of the dissociative existence. Therefore, the guidance of the inner wisdom experienced via "film" becomes an integral part of the process of team-building. By entering the theater in a meditative state to ask for improved understanding, the client can see visions of how the system will one day function more cooperatively, how a currently disruptive or threatening alter will someday contribute constructively, and so forth. Armed with this insight, the host is able to initiate intrapersonal dialogue with a modicum of trust that wouldn't otherwise be easy to muster. Certainly the therapist's assurances about future internal cooperation aren't nearly as persuasive as internal guidance experienced in a multisensory manner.

The host personality faces another, more specific, obstacle in entering a dialogue with the alters: The host's initial assumption is that listening to his alters would mean relinquishing power to them. This assumption is borne of catastrophic loss of power during childhood trauma and is reinforced by awareness that alters may be suicidal, assaultive, promiscuous, or otherwise threatening to the safety and stability of the host. Again, the inner guidance obtained in the theater is invaluable in demonstrating how the alters will use their power to promote the best interests of the system as a whole.

The particular case I have chosen to illustrate the techniques used for fostering internal cooperation also elucidates an emotional disturbance common to DID clients. This client's inner wisdom told him that his "emotional paths" had been damaged by traumatic experiences and were in need of repair. This clinical vignette can be seen as a story of repairing emotional circuitry and building new pathways that permit the experiences of safety, self-esteem, harmony, and joy.

Scott presented with depression, anxiety, anger with violent impulses, suicidal ideation, and a broad range of dissociative symptoms, including flashbacks, nightmares, amnestic episodes, evidence of activities carried on outside of awareness, and voices heard inside the head. A married business executive with a school-age son and a preschool-age daughter, Scott had a long history of seeking outpatient therapy when in crisis and terminating abruptly once he experienced a little symptomatic relief. "I come back," he explained, "when I'm hanging on by a thread." Before seeking therapy with me, he made several suicide attempts via drug overdose when the thread threatened to give way.

Scott described a very painful childhood. He reported that his alcoholic father was physically and emotionally abusive to Scott and his siblings, and that his mother was dependent on his father and was unable to adequately protect her children. Scott had had continuous recollection of some traumatic childhood events and had experienced delayed recall of others. The latter had been recovered spontaneously, often following nightmares. Family members were able to corroborate many of Scott's memories of severe, chronic physical and emotional abuse. Scott's feelings of inadequacy were rooted not only in the abuse itself, but also in his inability to protect his siblings from their explosive father. Suicidality in adult life was generally related to regrets that he hadn't killed himself in childhood, thereby bringing the family to the attention of social services and saving his siblings from ongoing abuse. Scott's son was approaching the age at which Scott had experienced some particularly painful events, prompting Scott to seek therapy once again.

Scott elaborated his symptoms. "I can't eat without getting an upset stomach. I feel this blind rage, intense anger coming out of nowhere." Scott was especially distressed by not having memories for happy events. "I don't remember the births of my own children, but I vividly remember my dad saying the most crude, belittling, degrading things to me." He described the experience of dissociating:

> I zone out, disappear from my body. Sometimes it's more like floating. Sometimes it's more like swimming. It's almost like I'm standing right behind myself. It's not like I'm looking at the back of my head, but it's as if my head were a pair of binoculars.... I can carry out a conversation on auto-pilot. I only know I had the conversation because the other person alludes to it.... I just really have an uncanny ability to shut everything off.

Although Scott's previous therapists didn't diagnose and treat his DID, they did assist him with a number of stress reduction and anger management techniques that he continued to use successfully. His analytic cognitive style and his business training dovetailed nicely with therapeutic techniques addressing well-defined problems with systematic solutions. He had learned to use deep breathing to calm himself and to avoid responding impulsively. He found it helpful to list details about his current life circumstances—how old he was, where he lived and worked, who his spouse was, and how many children they had—to ground himself in current reality when he found himself lost in past pain. He practiced techniques to defuse the stress of others in his environment by lowering his voice tone and listening empathically. He used the visualization of a "safe place" inside his mind for self-soothing and stabilization.

The successful use of these coping strategies acquired in previous therapies stood Scott in good stead as I introduced the techniques and internal structures associated with the Collective Heart model. He drew on his extensive professional managerial experience in approaching the novelty of the internal conference room. He conceptualized the conference room as a board room with a "power seat." He set aside time at the beginning of each conference to review the goals of the meeting, encourage each participant to "put issues on the table," and agree on an agenda. Because he was able to adapt his management skills and previously learned therapeutic techniques, the intervention strategies I offered him felt natural and comfortable for Scott. He later shared a business principle that came to mind as he gained perspective by means of internal communication and receptivity to inner wisdom: "When you back up, the problem becomes clear, and when you back up even more, the solution becomes clear."

As Scott elaborated his complaints, two major themes emerged. The first was his restricted affective range and the inauthenticity of his emotional life:

> I've been trying to focus on emotion and why I can't feel emotion. Why I kind of fake happy and sad. . . . I don't seem to feel the emotion at the time, like really feel it. And I can't seem to get in touch with the sad or sorrowful part of me. I can't touch that part. I mean, I can't find it in my head. . . . That may be what's getting me so angry. . . . Growing up, I kind of responded to everything with anger, so I could be having all sorts of emotions going on and they're just coming out as anger.

Note the change in tense as Scott spoke. When he thought about the past or spoke of it, he tended to relive it, as evidenced by the shift in tense while describing his emotional responses in childhood. This tendency to re-inhabit the affective world of his childhood made it very difficult for Scott to believe he had the power to bring about significant changes in his emotional life.

The second theme that emerged early in Scott's treatment was his inability to speak up for himself, set limits on the demands others made on his time and energy, and make his own comfort and enjoyment a priority. As therapy progressed, he realized how his failure to self-advocate fueled conflict within the personality system. This dynamic is nearly universal in DID clients: At least one alter typically faces the consequences and/or absorbs the anger when the host fails to act in an appropriately self-protective manner. As a result, the alter may berate the host for being a "wimp" or being "too nice" to others. The host, depleted by the criticism, typically tries to ignore the accusations, thereby further infuriating the alters, who in turn may escalate the verbal attack.

☐ Scott's Progress with Utilizing Systemic Cooperation and Inner Wisdom

During Scott's third therapy session, I offered him the opportunity to enter a meditative state and experience a happy childhood memory. He did so with my assistance (see chapter 5), and found the happy memory to be so rewarding that he spontaneously retrieved several additional "neutral-to-good" memories at home before his next session. Within a session or two, it had become clear that he had at least two alter personalities, one of whom reported that it was his job to keep the other alter from committing suicide. Scott displayed surprisingly little resistance to the discovery of alter personalities within himself. He apparently put his managerial skills right to work in assimilating the personal data: He wondered aloud whether negotiation and compromise would be important in working with his alters.

I offered Scott the opportunity to enter a meditative state and visit the internal theater for a vision of hope for the future, a vision of what would be possible once he had resolved the difficulties that had brought him into therapy. He accepted, asking that I help him by providing verbal guidance for relaxation. Following the relaxation, he found himself in the internal theater with an alter seated on each side of him. One alter was the one who had communicated with me, and the other was described by Scott as a "dark presence." The vision involved images of Scott playing with his children and sitting on his sofa at home, watching television, feeling at ease with himself and experientially present in the moment. Using the controls (see chapter 5), he was able to amplify the sensation of comfort and emotional openness. It provided a tremendous amount of hope. Scott was also responsive to my offer to teach him Tonglen (see chapter 5). He was pleased to learn another technique he could use independently to reduce stress and increase feelings of well-being.

Similarly, Scott was eager to meditatively enter his private room on the hall of safety (see chapter 5). While he was spending time there alone, I spoke through to the alter who offered protection against suicide. He, too, readily accepted the opportunity to explore his own safe room. Leaving him there to enjoy the hospitable surroundings, I asked whether the one who had been described as a "dark presence" would like to find his room as well. "I don't see why," the latter answered sullenly. I explained that the choice was his, but that there might be something fun or interesting in his room and I just wanted him to have the same opportunity I'd offered the others. "I'll go look at it," he conceded guardedly. Standing in front of the open door, he reported that he could see the room, but he saw his father sitting nearby in the hallway and didn't know if he wanted to be alone at that moment. Rather than inquiring about his father, I decided to take advantage of his apparent receptivity to my companionship and asked him about himself. He told me that he was 18 years old and that he got very angry because Scott "never did anything" when his father hurt him. "He was chicken," he elaborated. "He could have left, he could have hit back." I empathized with his frustration and asked if he'd seen the film about how it can be different in the future. "Yeah," he replied,

"I don't think it's gonna happen, though. I saw Scott's kids. I saw him being happy, not being worried. I don't understand why he thinks he deserves this now."

It soon became apparent that part of the alter's skepticism about the future related to his own future status. He wanted to know what would happen to him. I explained how Scott needed him and always would, but how his role would change over time so that he could be of the most use to Scott. I explained that someday Scott would no longer need him to be a separate part within him, and they would be ready to be together as one. I told him that being together as one would be like being out all the time, but that his being out would no longer mean that Scott would lose time. I also explained how the inner wisdom is a very deep aspect of who they are and that the inner wisdom can see how all the personalities are connected and can help them all work towards a state of wholeness and harmony.

Despite the early therapeutic focus on emotional safety and increased control, it wasn't long before Scott became concerned about potential losses that might result from therapeutic progress. He was afraid he would lose his wife and his children. I encouraged him to consult the inner wisdom about his concerns, explaining that he would find a keyboard in the theater and could enter questions and watch the screen for verbal responses from the inner wisdom. He consented, visited the theater in a meditative state, and entered a question about whether he would lose anything as a result of being in therapy. The inner wisdom responded that the question was too general! Scott then inquired specifically whether he would lose his wife and children. He was told that he loves his family and would not lose them, but that he would have to give up certain ways of interacting with them in order to become healthy. Specifically, he would have to communicate his feelings and needs more openly with his family members, and he would have to let them know when their actions hurt him. In essence, he would "lose" the apparent protection of retreating from authentic participation in his most treasured relationships. It was for this reason that the inner wisdom couldn't provide a simple response to the question, "Will I lose anything?"

I observed aloud that Scott's alters probably felt proud of him for voicing his doubts about therapy. I let him know that it's normal to be ambivalent, especially about any process involving change, and that it's a healthy sign that he was able to articulate his concerns. Apparently encouraged by my affirmation, Scott confessed in the following session that he was experiencing the old familiar urge to terminate therapy because he was feeling better. But, he quickly added, he was upset by a recent dream in which he was charged with a murder committed while he was "blacked out." He knew we had a lot to talk about.

He was particularly interested in talking about the associations he had with the 18-year-old alter. Scott recalled that, when he was 18, his father blamed the children for his unhappiness and said he wished none of them had ever been born. Overwhelmed by emotional pain, Scott had cried that night. In therapy, Scott recalled that he had felt strong suicidal impulses following that incident and wondered whether they might have been related to the alter who had been described as being prone to suicidal ideation. Scott later reported that he had not cried since that night when he was 18.

I told Scott that the 18-year-old alter (who later identified himself as Charles) had seen his father in the hall of safety and we had not yet clarified what this meant and how they might proceed. I introduced the conference room as an internal venue for meeting with alters to discuss problems, express feelings and needs, and make plans for change. Scott accepted my suggestion that he meditatively enter the conference room to discuss with his alters anything Charles might wish to share about seeing his father in the hall of safety, and then ask the inner wisdom to help them determine which step to take in therapy at that time. He required very little assistance from me as he entered a meditative state. Once inside, however, he became mildly agitated as conflict arose between the two alters. With Scott's consent, I intervened in the conference, asking Charles if he recalled his father sitting outside his private room in the hallway. He reported that he kept that image of his father intentionally, to make himself angry enough that he would be able to kill himself. I articulated the logic of this practice: He didn't want to be a chicken and lose his nerve, and he knew if he kept this image before him he'd always be able to be angry enough to end his life if he chose to do so. After all, a person needs to know that there's a limit to how much maltreatment he's willing to accept and that he has the power to put an end to it. However, I continued, he had a dilemma: On the one hand, it was reassuring to know that he'd found a way to make sure he'd never lose his nerve, but on the other hand, the image of his father undermined the comfort of the hall of safety. I suggested that he discuss this dilemma with the inner wisdom.

Charles had a better idea. He discussed the problem with Scott and liked Scott's proposed solution! "Scott has an idea," he reported, "and I think it will work: I can put the image of my father on a computer disk and put the disk in my pocket." With this announcement, he conveyed to me that the important process of internal collaboration had begun.

When Scott emerged after the completion of the meditative work (which we simply called "inside work"), he confessed that he had initially tried to convince Charles to rid the system of the image of their father. Realizing that his approach wasn't going to work, he had the idea of "scanning him into the computer." The collaborative resolution of this problem was one of two therapeutic developments that helped Charles realize that he had the power to increase his sense of emotional safety. The other therapeutic development was a trip to the Anger Rock.

The Anger Rock (Watkins, 1980) is an intervention designed to be used hypnotically, but equally well suited to autohypnotic or meditative work. I was originally introduced to the Anger Rock by Richard Griffin, who trained me in the treatment of dissociative disorders, and I have been struck by the potency of the intervention, which I have modified somewhat over time. The host or alter is offered an opportunity to go inside to a clearing in the woods, where he sees a rock that reflects his degree of anger. If the client is a little bit angry, he'll find a small rock. If he's angrier, the rock is larger. If he's enraged, he finds a huge boulder. He then proceeds to smash the rock to smithereens, knowing that he's venting his anger without doing any harm to anyone. Incorporating an element added spontaneously by one of my clients, I augment the intervention with the suggestion that a small piece of rock can be found in the resulting rubble that can be sanded down to produce a smooth pebble. The pebble can be kept as a means of self-soothing and as a symbol of transformation.

I explained to Scott (talking through to Charles) that I felt Charles and the entire system might benefit from an opportunity for Charles to visit the Anger Rock. I clarified that the purpose of a visit was not to rid Charles of his anger but to calm him enough so that he could use his anger as an indication of what was not acceptable to him and in need of change. By venting some anger without hurting anyone, and by calming himself by stoking his smooth pebble, Charles could use his anger to promote growth rather than fuel suicidality. With this understanding, Scott agreed to enter a meditative state and offer Charles a trip to the Anger Rock. (Readers familiar with the treatment of DID may be struck by how relatively rarely I invite alters out to speak with me directly. As explained in chapter 6, my relationship with alters consists largely in talking through to them and fostering communication within the personality system.)

Scott expressed readiness to enter a meditative state without my assistance (6 weeks after beginning treatment), closed his eyes, and went deeply within himself. Having accepted Scott's proposal, Charles found the Anger Rock—a rock of massive proportions—and smashed it with a mallet he found nearby. He found a piece of rubble and sanded it into a smooth pebble. I suggested that he stroke it with his hand, noticing the sensations in his body as he did so. I could see him stroking it rhythmically in his right hand while he sat quietly in his chair, eyes closed, softly describing his observations:

When you rub on it, it just feels soft all over. It kind of tingles up your arm and into your body. It's soft. . . . I'm scared. Usually when I start feeling this good something bad happens. I just don't want anyone to hit me right now. I don't want anyone to yell at me, be mean to me.

It was a poignant moment. I could see how Charles' anger had protected him from experiencing his own vulnerability and how relinquishing some of the anger required a considerable degree of faith that it was safe to let his guard down. I reminded him that he had the computer disk with the scanned image of his father in one pocket, and pointed out that he could keep his smooth pebble in the other. He could control whether to get himself worked up or calmed down.

Charles liked my idea that he could go to the theater and ask the inner wisdom's guidance regarding his fears of being hurt. Charles described the guidance he was receiving via the screen there, in response to his question about what he should do if someone yelled at him or was mean to him:

See if they have a valid point. Try to make some sense of it. Find a way to . . . try not to let the emotion stick with us. . . . I'm asking how to do that. I have a mental picture, kind of like a sieve or a colander. I don't know if that'll work. Kind of take everything from people and put it in a filter and let all the emotion flow through. If they made a good point, it would stick up in the colander. . . . All the emotion and the mean-spirited part just flows through.

I recommended that Charles consider bringing this potent image of the sieve or colander back in the corner of his mind as a souvenir of that moment of guidance and encouragement, and restore it to the center of his awareness when he needed to use it to process emotions (a technique introduced by Dolan, 1991). "We could try that," he responded. After suggesting that he might want to express gratitude to his inner wisdom for the guidance he received, and affirming the importance of the work he had done in session, I told Charles that I wanted to spend a few minutes with Scott, who had expressed interest earlier in consulting the inner wisdom himself.

Scott went into the theater and asked what step he was ready to take towards a more authentic emotional life. He described what he saw: "It's just a screen saying that a lot of the emotional paths are blocked and that I can turn them on if I want. . . . It just says I have to ask. . . . Some were more damaged and need to be repaired."

I asked if the work Charles did that day was helping to repair the damage, and Scott nodded. He added that the inner wisdom also recommended writing down the emotions so that they could discuss them. After emerging from his meditative state, Scott reported that he had felt more "there," more emotionally engaged, than he had during previous meditative work. "In the past," he explained, "I was clearly not allowed to see certain parts. Today ... I saw more of a picture of the three of us talking. I feel a whole lot better inside."

During the following week, Scott noticed that Charles no longer seemed so "dark and angry," but more alert and present. Charles was able to express, in conference, concerns about how he could have fun—going to dances, meeting girls, and so forth—when Scott was already a grownup with a wife and children. Although Scott didn't know how the dilemma would be resolved, he was pleased that Charles was able to voice his concerns in an appropriate manner, and focus on the present and how they would manage daily living. As Charles spoke, Scott knew why for years he'd been finding unfamiliar charge receipts from "nights on the town" following amnestic episodes. I encouraged Scott to listen to Charles without judgment and articulate the two perspectives even-handedly. ("On the one hand, I don't like losing time and worrying whether I'm being a good husband, but on the other hand, you like to go out and have fun, and after all, you're not the one with the wife and kids.") In this way, they learned to minimize conflict and free their emotional energies for the pursuit of creative solutions.

However, within 2 weeks Scott was experiencing strong urges to kill himself and he didn't know why. He also wondered why he had been hearing the name "Dad" coming from the back of his head all week long. He admitted that he was afraid he'd make a successful suicide attempt if the means, the impulse, and freedom from interpersonal responsibilities all coincided. (He had a history of attempted suicide.) He volunteered that he had tried to go inside at home and have a conference to discuss where the suicidal urges originated, but, he reported, "no one was owning up to anything." I affirmed his independent and active approach and suggested we continue his exploratory efforts in session.

Scott asked me if I could remind him about the Tonglen meditation, so he could use it as a way of going inside. I was happy to support his initiative. When Scott entered a meditative state to ask his inner wisdom for help in understanding his suicidality, it became clear that Charles was troubled by images of mean things he had done during Scott's childhood and adolescence. I suggested that perhaps while feeling intense anger, his retaliatory impulses seemed justified, but with the recent decrease in anger, he was viewing his own behavior in a new light. Relieved by the possibility that his difficulty might reflect growth rather than inherent badness, Charles accepted my proposal that he watch a film in the theater about how he could come to terms with past behavior. Via the film, the inner wisdom told Charles that nothing he or Scott did had caused any permanent damage. Scott reported that Charles was relieved, but Scott himself remained skeptical.

I then suggested Charles watch a film about the things he'd done that had enduring positive effects. While trying to watch the film, Scott and Charles were distracted by the presence of "someone taunting [them] from behind." Whenever Scott turned his head to see what was going on behind him, he felt his head being smacked. (The reader will recall that, while in a meditative state, the DID client experiences a physical manifestation of his inner reality. While "inside," he sees his alters as having separate bodies because his inner reality, or psychological reality, is that they are distinct from him. Here, when Scott felt himself being smacked on the head, he was describing his experience while in a meditative state, where he and his alters perceived themselves as physically distinct and capable of inflicting "bodily harm" on one another.)

Charles encouraged the one behind him to join him and Scott in watching the film about the good things they had done, but the taunting presence refused to watch and continued to jeopardize their enjoyment of the film content. I suggested that perhaps their experience indicated that Scott and Charles would only be able to have a limited appreciation of the good things they'd done unless they came to terms with the part of them that they sensed behind them. Scott felt that this was right. He spontaneously asked the inner wisdom for help in feeling emotion. The inner wisdom recommended that they visualize a figure-8 as they breathed: up in front of the face, over the top of the head and down behind the head on the in-breath, curving forward and down in front of the heart and up in back of the heart on the out-breath. Through images of the alters joylessly engaging in otherwise pleasurable activities, the inner wisdom conveyed to Scott that until he learned to connect his heart with his head, no member of the system would be really happy. Even as the inner wisdom was communicating with them, Scott and Charles felt the taunting presence behind them. I suggested Scott ask the inner wisdom whether this taunting presence was a personality. Although Scott experienced interference and was unable to receive an answer to his query, he felt strongly that this was another member of the personality system. Furthermore, Scott reflected, "It seems that the part behind me is in control of the emotions."

Talking through to the taunting presence, I observed aloud that he obviously had something important to convey and seemed to be having a difficult time. I pointed out how much better Charles felt after scanning the image of Dad onto the computer disk and visiting the Anger Rock, and offered this apparent alter the opportunity to see a film about what would be possible for him after he'd resolved some of his current difficulties.

Scott reported that my suggestion wasn't favorably received. Scott sensed that this alter wanted to get rid of Scott and the other alters and take over the body. Acting on my recommendation that he ask the inner wisdom what he could do to complete the session (as we were nearing the end of the hour) and ensure safety until the next session, Scott saw the screen displaying images of how, in childhood, he and his siblings would call a truce when their rough-housing got out of control. He consulted the system about calling a truce. The only member of the system who wouldn't commit to the truce was the taunting alter. "But," Scott observed hopefully, "at least he didn't smack me on the head." Speaking through to the entire system, I reminded them that whenever any part of the system requested assistance from the inner wisdom, it had been provided. I likened this abundant source of help, emanating from the deepest part of their collective being, to the never-ending light source in the Tonglen meditation. After emerging from his meditative state, Scott revealed that the alter who had been taunting them from behind was the one the other alters had been calling "Dad." He had figured out why he had been hearing the name "Dad" inside his head.

Scott returned for his next session with a lot on his mind. He had been seeing "really bad images" and hearing "vulgar, degrading language ... trying to tell me I'm not a good person." He was troubled by memories of having deliberately injured neighborhood children when he was young and having damaged their property. He wanted to know how he could put these troubling images behind him and move on. I suggested he could ask the inner wisdom's help with seeing these incidents in light of the previous session's message about not having done any permanent damage. He added that he also wanted to ask the inner wisdom how this tied in with the present and the future. "It's so weird to always feel one step away from having to go back and live with my parents," he explained. "I need to see more of a permanent future." He accepted my suggestion that he experiment with using the figure-8 breathing as a way of going inside.

While in a meditative state, Scott described the questions he was asking and the answers he was receiving:

> The first thing I asked was: How can I be sure I didn't cause any permanent damage? And the answer I got was: Keep on thinking of these images as a flash.... I have to realize that after that event happened, [the other person's] life continued on.... They got past that, and the consequences of the things that I did were not permanent. Not to say that it didn't affect that person, but they're not still there at that spot. It's like a movie, where their life continued past [the incident]. Yeah, there may be some memories or some resentment towards me on their part, but that doesn't mean that I have to look at that as a permanent thing.

While receiving this inner guidance, Scott was aware of active involvement on the part of the alter who had been taunting him and smacking his head in the previous session. The alter challenged the message provided by the inner wisdom, telling Scott that if he and his siblings hadn't been born, his father wouldn't have been under so much stress and wouldn't have had some many health problems. Scott *had* caused permanent damage, the alter argued, evidenced by his father's health problems.

I offered the alter the opportunity to see a film about how he personally would come to understand, as therapy progresses, whether Scott was to blame for his father's behavior. Scott reported that the alter declined my offer. Scott tried to persuade him to watch the film. I told Scott that if the alter didn't want to watch the film, he didn't have to. I suggested that Scott might want to ask his inner wisdom to help him identify the next step he could take in handling the conflict between this alter and himself. Scott described the guidance he received:

> It's come up with some ideas to ... get more of a longer truce with him. [We need to] understand that to resolve anything ... you have to all sit down somewhere, you have to start a dialogue. That doesn't mean giving in or agreeing to just go away or anything. You just have to start somewhere.

Still in his meditative state, Scott asked me how he could take away the alter's power so that the alter couldn't hurt him. I explained that it was important for Scott to convey that he wouldn't try to make any alter go away. I also emphasized that, as hard as it was to imagine having common goals given the amount of overt conflict they were experiencing, ultimately what was in the best interest of one part of the personality system was in the best interest of every other part of the system and in the best interest of the system as a whole. For this reason, he would discover that he didn't need to take away the alter's power in order to be safe, and the alter would find that he wouldn't benefit from hurting Scott. I explained to Scott that, although this alter appeared to be quite threatening, basically he wanted the same things that everyone wants: to be safe, respected, loved, and confident that his contributions are valued. I assured Scott that when he became better acquainted with the alter, it would become clear that he was angry because he was in emotional pain himself. Once he had other means of processing and conveying his pain, the others in the system would no longer feel victimized.

Scott was particularly disturbed by the alter's refusal to commit to "a longer truce," and his insistence on "hanging onto suicide as a solution." Talking through to the alter, I told Scott that suicidality may have been a necessary trump card in the past when resources appeared to be more limited. At that time, they needed to know that they could put an end to the abuse. Now that they'd learned to consult the inner wisdom and confer with each other internally, I explained, they could find better ways to protect themselves from abuse. "That's making sense to him," Scott observed. I asked Scott to consider the impact it would have on this alter if Scott learned to speak up for himself more effectively. "If I just agree not to take abuse," Scott realized, "he'll be willing to cooperate more."

Scott had good news to share when he arrived for his next session: He had had a productive internal conference at home and, as a result, had experienced co-consciousness with two alters at various times during the week. Davy, a child personality, had used the conference as an opportunity to ask if he could use Scott's children's Lego set. Scott agreed to do it co-consciously with Davy after his daughter and son had gone to bed for the night.

Similarly, Charles had expressed interest in assisting Scott by leading a business meeting at work. After Scott assured himself that Charles understood the content of the meeting and knew what kind of professionalism would be required of him, they reached an agreement. Charles led the meeting successfully, with Scott observing everything from the inside. They both enjoyed feedback from coworkers regarding the lively presentation. Scott was surprised when he saw Charles in a subsequent internal conference: Instead of being dressed in his habitual jeans and t-shirt, Charles was wearing an elegant business suit. He explained to Scott that he was no longer 18. He had turned 22! His experience of aging was clearly a reflection of the significant strides he had made developmentally as a personality and as a member of an increasingly cooperative system.

However, Scott was concerned about the alter they'd been calling "Dad." Scott described the emotional hold that "Dad" seemed to be exerting over the system:

> It's almost like that part of me is controlling the emotions. All I can feel is depression or anger. It's very hard for me now to feel happy or sad, or even indifferent. It's almost like he's letting me go through therapy, and then he'll be back [to resume control]. I had a real disturbing dream about my son dying and I wasn't allowed to have any emotions. It was horrible, almost like torturing me.

Scott liked my idea that he meditatively enter the theater to ask for a film about how "Dad" would contribute to the system after he'd resolved the difficulties with which he was contending. Developing the intervention further, Scott decided to first visit the conference room so that he could set the stage for viewing the film collectively. He entered a meditative state independently and then described the developments in the conference room and theater as they unfolded:

> First thing ... conference room ... we're all talking about what we want to get out of being here, kind of setting the stage for going over to watch the movie. We're all kind of talking about different objectives. Each has his own agenda. Talking about how we can compromise if we need to.... Now we're going to see the movie about what it will be like and what the other parts will be able to contribute. [Pause] Okay, we're in the movie theater. It's kind of showing all the things that each part will do. The part of me I call "Dad" is being so mean. I keep telling him: "Just look at it!" All he wants to do is.... We can all see that part of me [in the movie]. He can kind of be my drive, the desire part of me, to keep me losing weight and spending more time with the family, playing racquetball, spending time with my friends. All he keeps saying [while viewing the movie] is that I always say I'll do these things, but I won't. All he has to do is just look at it [the movie]. We're not going to figure this out today. The 18-year-old is real mad. He doesn't understand why this part won't even look at the screen.

Although Scott felt it was unfair for "Dad" to refuse to look at the screen while the rest of the system participated in the viewing, he accepted my observation that perhaps, unlike the rest of the system, "Dad" simply wasn't ready to do so. Scott then reported that he was trying to get some closure for the day to keep the truce going, but that "Dad" responded to the suggestion by smacking Scott on the head. I raised the possibility that "Dad" was angry because he felt that we were going to dismiss everything that needed to happen before the developments in the film would be possible, before "Dad" manifested as the drive, the desire, and the motivation to make things happen in his life. I asked Scott to check if my hunch was right, and he confirmed that it was. I then suggested that just as Scott had wanted "Dad" to set aside his objections and watch the movie, it might be helpful for Scott to just listen to what "Dad" had to say.

As Scott listened to "Dad," he had to admit that some of the things "Dad" said made a lot of sense:

> He's saying ... I can't have any secrets, I have to tell everything. I need to share it with the other parts. We need to be willing to say everything that's ever happened, not just what I think we need to hear. We'll keep talking back and forth. He's throwing some images at me [of things "Dad" feels they should do more of]. I've agreed to that. He doesn't believe me.

I spoke of the inner timetable that governs the healing process. I explained that they may need to find a compromise between "Dad's" goal of telling all their secrets and Scott's desire not to be overwhelmed by opening up everything all at once. This appeared to help, as Scott could now admit that he wasn't ready to agree to immediate implementation of all of "Dad's" suggestions, and "Dad," in turn, could accept Scott's modified commitment as credible. "He believes I'll try," Scott announced. "He's agreed to keep a truce."

Upon emerging from his meditative state, Scott was struck by the incredible amount of tension in his body. "Almost like I've been in a car wreck," he elaborated. And so it was that "Dad" became more than a presence taunting Scott from behind and assumed his rightful place as a recognized member of the system, beginning to participate in plans for a collective future and leaving a residue of his tension throughout Scott's body.

I decided to take advantage of the increased internal cooperation to introduce the Preservation of Life Contract that I developed for use with DID clients (see Appendix A). Before adequate cooperation has been established, I use a more conventional safety contract with my DID clients. Once the host has recognized the existence of the alters and there is some preliminary commitment to work together toward mutual goals, I introduce the Preservation of Life Contract.

I reviewed the terms of the contract with Scott, talking through to the alters. As Scott signed the contract, he reported "getting real positive feedback from the other ones." He confessed, however, that he was experiencing "resistance from 'Dad'." I pointed to the clause referring to the commitment on the part of each member of the personality system in terms of voicing concerns about the contract, and framed this "resistance" as a sign that "Dad" was willing to express his discomfort rather than keep his objections to himself and then quietly sabotage the contract. "Dad" was reassured that his input was valued.

Because the signatures on the contract were all variations of Scott's name, and because Charles was, at that point, still referred to as "the 18-year-old" despite his recent growth spurt, I tossed out the general suggestion that the alters might want to give some thought to their names. When Scott arrived for his next therapy session, he was pleased to share the news that the 22-year-old had announced that his name was Charles.

Although Scott was enjoying the increasing openness and ease between Charles and himself, he was concerned about tensions in his relationship with "Dad." Scott reported an increasing sense that "Dad" would demand a confrontation with Scott's father regarding childhood maltreatment. Although he felt a confrontation was inevitable, Scott insisted that he would do anything for his parents and couldn't bear to accuse them of anything. While the very emergence of this conflict reflects increasing internal communication, it was hardly reassuring to Scott. I explained that if a family confrontation should prove to be essential to the healing process, he would have the resources to do it when the time was right. I likened this to the process of contemplating swimming in deep water before one has acquired swimming skills. What is originally an overwhelming prospect becomes manageable once the basic skills are in place. By the same token, if Scott continued to progress therapeutically in a stepwise manner, he would always be adequately equipped to take the next step. He didn't require much of a reminder that the inner wisdom would guide him in knowing which steps he needed to take and when he was ready to take them.

Scott reported that the muscle tension he had experienced at the end of the previous session had persisted, and he was "in a constant state of flex." I asked if he thought it might be productive to offer "Dad" a visit to the Anger Rock, as this intervention had proved so useful to Charles. Scott liked this idea, adding that Charles might want to help by orienting "Dad." As Scott entered a meditative state, he reported hearing "Dad" advising him to "take a pill, take a drink" to alleviate stress. Talking through to "Dad," I agreed that sometimes there are good short-term solutions to stress and anger, but that when you're feeling so angry that you could almost explode, it can be helpful to find a solution that has a longer lasting impact. Scott asked to go to his safe room and excused himself from observation of the Anger Rock experience.

"Dad" chose to have Charles, rather than me, describe the Anger Rock to him. After listening internally to Charles' introduction, "Dad" confessed: "I didn't realize that Charles and I shared a lot of the same experiences." In explaining the use of the Anger Rock, Charles had apparently spoken of the roots, or at least the experience, of his own anger. Not yet ready to commit, "Dad" asked me if he could just go and see the Anger Rock. I told him that sounded like a good idea.

As soon as "Dad" saw the Anger Rock, he knew that he couldn't possibly smash it to smithereens as Charles had. Charles objected vehemently that this wasn't fair, that he had smashed his Anger Rock and "Dad" should do likewise. But "Dad" knew he couldn't smash this rock: *His Anger Rock was a dam, holding back the water.* They would all be drowned if he were to break the dam. I explained to Charles that it wasn't a question of fairness, that what "Dad" saw perfectly matched his emotional experiences, just as what Charles had seen perfectly matched his. I suggested to "Dad" that he could go to the theater and ask the inner wisdom what to do about the Anger Rock, since he certainly didn't want to have a flood. I explained that he could enter questions on the screen using the computer keyboard, as Scott had done. He agreed, but encountered more frustration. He reported that he wanted to shout at the screen, but that Charles was telling him that he couldn't. I told him that he wouldn't need to shout, because he could say or ask whatever he wished, and the inner wisdom would answer.

The inner wisdom told "Dad," via the screen, that he should start to write down things he wanted to tell Scott, as if he were writing a letter. Communicating to Scott, the inner wisdom explained, was "kind of going to let the water out [gradually] behind the dam." "Dad" was also told that he was "confusing time" and that he had caused no permanent damage through any of his actions. Because he was confusing time, he was carrying past behavior into the present moment, as if it had enduring consequences. He described what he was seeing on the screen:

> I'm seeing different things that were resolved. I'm seeing times when I lied to my parents. I'm seeing back when I was in Chicago, I broke this window and lied to my parents about it. I think I should just be able to be this way [continue reliving his past mistakes], but Charles keeps telling me I have an excuse for everything.

I told "Dad" that he had a choice. He could continue as he had or he could let the inner wisdom help him find an alternative. In order to decide which to choose, I suggested that he might want to see a two-part film on the screen. Part 1 would show how he could continue as he was, and Part 2 would show what would happen if he followed the guidance the inner wisdom had been providing. I emphasized observing the consequences in the two scenarios, so that he'd be in a good position to compare and to choose how he wanted to live. I reminded him about the controls, encouraging him to increase or decrease the emotions and bodily sensations by using the dial. He agreed to watch the two-part film.

While viewing it, he reported realizing that a lot of what he had been feeling was guilt. "The picture I see," he explained, "is how much more light-hearted I would be" as a result of following the guidance of the inner wisdom. I asked if he had used the dial to amplify the emotions and sensations. As he had not, I suggested that he replay the film using the dial. He did so, reporting: "It feels good, but I feel a lot more vulnerable when I feel like that. When Scott is vulnerable, I take over. He needs to learn to take care of himself." I suggested that he ask the inner wisdom whether Scott will learn to take care of himself, with all of the parts of the personality system working to help him. He reported that the inner wisdom affirmed that this can happen. "I'm not sure I believe it," he continued, "but it *is* the inner wisdom."

In response to my suggestion that he could watch a film about how the system will one day function more harmoniously as a team, "Dad" saw footage of them being "kind of like a well-run business, where you're all doing your job, and everyone is getting along. You might have disagreements, but you work it out." I asked if he could see what his role would be. "I'm the emotional part," he replied, "but I'm also real analytic. The inner wisdom told me that Scott doesn't know I'm the one who puts the puzzles together."

I told him that it didn't sound like the name "Dad" suited the role he envisioned for himself and wondered if he'd given any thought to what might be a more appropriate name. He admitted that he'd been mulling it over since our previous session and had chosen a name. He was reluctant to share his choice, because he was afraid I'd think it was silly. Reassured that I was genuinely interested in his decision, he told me that he'd picked the name Thorin after a mythical character who was the son of a king. In the myth, Thorin didn't want to inherit the kingdom as a birthright but wanted to establish his legitimate sovereignty by means of compassionate and heroic acts.

I shared my delight that Thorin had found such a perfectly appropriate name. He, like the mythological Thorin, would find a way to claim his own power, not by emulating his father and seizing power just because he could get away with it, but by being true to himself and acting in ways that felt constructive and rewarding to him.

I wondered aloud whether Thorin was ready to share his new name with the rest of the system. Thorin was concerned that the others, eager to get back at him for all the mean things he'd done to them, would make fun of him because of his name. I suggested he consult the inner wisdom. He shared the guidance he received: "It says they won't. They all agree if I pick a name, they'll stick with it. They all have their own quirks."

Thorin decided to call a conference so that he could share his news. While still in a meditative state, he described the developments in the conference room:

> I told them they each had to tell me one quirky thing about themselves, and then I'd tell them my name. Charles said he likes spaghetti with scrambled eggs. Davy said he likes oreo cookies with beer. Scott said sometimes he likes to eat breakfast for dinner. I told them my name and we all chuckled together.... We reaffirmed the truce. It doesn't mean that we won't talk about suicidal feelings, but it means we won't act on them.

I congratulated Thorin on his excellent therapeutic work. Scott emerged from his meditative state, announcing "I feel like my mind is really open." He asked if it was normal that Thorin had moved to the back of his head again. I assured him that it was, adding that it will take time for Thorin to know he can trust them, just as it will take some time for them to know they can trust Thorin. Before ending the session, Scott and I discussed the symbolism of the name Thorin and agreed that it had been a powerful session.

☐ Stepping Out of the Narrative

Perhaps this is a good point to step out of the narrative, summarize the important developments, and then shift from a detailed chronology to somewhat broader strokes. The narrative to this point covers the first 11 weeks of therapy (14 individual sessions and two group therapy sessions) and has been presented in considerable detail. Scott's unusual readiness to accept the diagnosis, his high functional level, his relatively small personality system, his facility with adapting organizational management skills to the task of internal negotiation, and his initiative in conducting conferences at home all facilitated the rapid progress of therapy. A great deal happened in a relatively short period of time.

As we have seen, by the end of the first 11 weeks of therapy, Scott had made significant progress with enlisting the cooperation of the full system. His alters had all committed to the therapy process, had confidence in the inner wisdom (as Thorin said, "I'm not sure I believe it, but it *is* the inner wisdom"), and had participated in a detailed written safety contract. Scott had shared a state of co-consciousness with two alters. Charles and Thorin had both made significant strides in following inner guidance to address cognitive distortions and expand their emotional range. Charles used the Anger Rock, the smooth pebble, and the image of the sieve to begin to free himself of excessive negative affect and promote well-being. Having discovered that his anger was serving as a dam to prevent an overwhelming explosion of pain, Thorin learned that he could decrease his reliance on anger by gradually communicating with Scott. He was starting to understand that he didn't have to choose between creating a flood and living with the burden of holding back all the pain.

However, much work remained to be done. Although Scott, Charles, and Thorin had taken important first steps toward repairing the emotional pathways that had been damaged in childhood, a great deal of repairing and rebuilding work lay ahead. In addition, the system had not yet begun to address Scott's inability to speak up for himself, set limits on accommodations to the demands of others, and make his own needs a priority. Until this concern was explored, Scott couldn't have understood how central it was to the conflict within the system and how it was related to the overarching theme of restoring emotional paths to self-esteem and well-being.

We now turn to the developments of the next 13 months of Scott's therapy to summarize his gradual process of reclaiming and creating happy memories, a rich emotional repertoire, and a capacity to value himself.

☐ Overview of the Next 13 Months of Therapy

Of the many interwoven strands that formed the fabric of the next 13 months of therapy, we now follow three: changes in the conference structure and process; Scott's progress in experiencing positive emotions, happy memories, and self-esteem; and Thorin's evolution and its special contributions to the well-being of the system.

Changes in the Conference Room

After his 4th month of psychotherapy, Scott made a number of changes in the way the system conducted their conferences. One change was based on a suggestion I made. I proposed that Scott might streamline his "inside work" by incorporating a screen in the conference room so that they wouldn't have to walk between the conference room and the theater in order to obtain guidance from the inner wisdom while discussing concerns and making plans as a group. Scott found this helpful and was soon speaking of the inner wisdom "chiming in" with guidance on the screen during conferences.

The other modifications were made at Scott's own initiative. After Thorin displayed willingness to cooperate with the system, Scott decided to abandon the use of the "power seat" in conference. He felt that a more egalitarian approach was appropriate under the circumstances. Another innovation was Scott's proposal that his system try figure-8 breathing as a group, as well as using the Tonglen meditation collectively. He also introduced the practice of recognizing the contributions of each member of the system before launching into discussion of problems and concerns. Scott himself was often the recipient of welcome compliments, as the alters provided affirmation when he acted in an assertive manner with coworkers and family members. Scott found himself becoming more sensitive to this affirmation from the alters between conferences, as their feelings of satisfaction with his behavior bubbled up into his awareness.

Over time, Scott increased the frequency of at-home conferences. He found it helpful to convene inside on a nightly basis, even if just to touch base quickly on busy evenings. By the time he had been in therapy for about 4 months, Scott reported that the conference room had become the base from which he and his alters operated, the place where they set the stage for whatever they did. Scott reported that holding regular conferences allowed his alters to communicate without becoming suicidal.

Scott's Progress in Experiencing Positive Emotions, Happy Memories, and Self-Esteem

During Scott's first year of therapy, he was unable to significantly alter his pattern of acquiescing to the demands of coworkers and family members. This was a source of great frustration to the alters, who even threatened to boycott therapy at one point because they felt they were making healthy changes while Scott was refusing to do his part by saying "no" to excessive external demands. Furthermore, they felt Scott was merely paying lip-service to the importance of setting aside time for recreational activities. Although he said he would join a basketball league and call friends to play golf and racquetball, Scott was always too tired after working long hours to follow through with his commitments to his system. In conference, the alters frequently raised the issue of Scott "not saying 'no' to others" and "saying 'yes' to us, but not meaning it."

Although Scott was persuaded by the arguments of the alters, it was many, many months before he was able to understand his difficulty in implementing plans to set reasonable limits with others and be more generous with himself. He came to realize that the only value he saw in himself was in being useful to others, so he felt worthless when he wasn't performing this function. Actually, he felt worse than worthless. He realized that he was afraid of displeasing others because of the emotional linkage between doing so and being at risk for abuse. He had intrusive memories of his father's cruelty whenever Scott displeased him in any small way.

Before Scott was able to act more assertively, he needed to understand what the inner wisdom had been referring to as his damaged "emotional paths." Just as Scott had formed an emotional linkage between displeasing someone and being hurt, he had also formed an unconscious association between being hurt and feeling worthless. Because of the authority a child attributes to his parents, Scott believed his father's abusive behavior was evidence of Scott's worthlessness.

When Scott asked his inner wisdom why he was unable to feel positive emotions, his inner wisdom told him "the good emotions are there, but the connections aren't." Scott needed to work hard to build the connections. The inner wisdom assured him that when he had done this work, he would be able to feel the good emotions. Similarly, Scott asked his inner wisdom why he only had painful memories and couldn't remember happy times, like his wedding day and the births of his children. His inner wisdom responded that the happy memories were there, even happy memories from childhood, but that Scott didn't allow himself to feel them.

Although this work was painstaking, Scott gradually learned that his self-image was keyed to a particular subset of his life experiences, experiences involving terror and pain. It was extremely difficult for him to understand that he had the power to draw on another subset of experiences, but that, in order to do so, he had to work hard to access them, to build a pathway to them. His inner wisdom also told him that he had the power to forge new, happy memories in his current life. For example, instead of preserving the emotional associations between Christmas and childhood trauma, he could form new associations with the holidays by attending to the look of anticipation on his children's faces, noticing how pleased his wife was when he went gift-shopping with her, and so forth. In addition, the inner wisdom guided each alter to choose a special role to perform co-consciously with Scott as the holidays approached: selecting and wrapping gifts, trimming the tree, taking photographs, cooking, and so forth. In this way, internal cooperation became part of his new set of holiday associations.

Although this work was time-consuming, there were many rewards for Scott and his alters along the way. By the end of the 4th month of therapy, discussion in conference had produced the insight that if Scott stayed more present—avoided "zoning out"—and behaved more assertively, his alters absorbed less anger and were able to cooperate with him better. He rarely experienced impulses to harm himself after the Preservation of Life Contract was signed. By the time he had been in therapy for 5 months, he reported that he was no longer losing time and no longer experiencing indigestion. Around that time, he also observed that, although he still experienced mood swings, he no longer felt "blind rage" that appeared to come out of nowhere. After 9 months in therapy, Scott realized how much more present he was and how often he used to zone out. About this time, he also noticed how beautiful his wife was, almost as if he were seeing her with new eyes. About 11 months into therapy, during an at-home conference, the system suggested updating their mental image of their father. Scott had finally realized that whenever he thought of his father, he saw his father as he was during Scott's childhood, and that he had the power to modify this association. The alters told Scott that instead of reliving images of his father from decades past, they could *make them a memory*. In the following session, Scott reported that he had "actually had a memory of Dad in his present-day appearance. The inner wisdom reminded me that this is a big deal."

Within a year of starting therapy, Scott was attending individual psychotherapy only twice a month. The decrease in the frequency of his individual sessions was made possible in large part by his strong commitment to regular conferences between sessions and by efforts to implement the resulting recommendations. By the time he'd been working in therapy for about 16 months, he had finally made good on his promise to the system: He began saying "no" to excessive demands on his time and energy, and joined a basketball league. He enjoyed all the good feedback the alters provided.

Between months 14 and 17, Scott received a number of potent messages from the inner wisdom. One involved Scott's assumption that his failure to please his father was a reflection of his own inadequacy. The context in which this concern surfaced at that particular time is significant: Scott and his wife had been providing foster care to an infant, Chris, who remained in their care for nearly 6 months before an adoptive home was found. By that time, Scott had become quite emotionally attached to the little boy. As the adoption date approached, Scott found himself experiencing vertigo with associated emotional numbness. Sensing that part of his difficulty might have been related to ambivalence about having remained in his father's care during childhood, I suggested that the system confer about whether feelings about custody issues in Scott's childhood were affecting their emotional responses as Chris's departure date approached. It emerged that Thorin was defending Scott's father's behavior and trying to convince Scott that he should have been a better son. The inner wisdom "chimed in" to observe that Thorin was making a false connection between getting his father's approval and being a better son. The inner wisdom said that the two were not connected. I asked if Scott thought his inner wisdom could show them a film that would help explain why Scott could never get his father's approval. After viewing the film, Scott described what he had seen and how he had responded:

> It kind of makes me have pity for him [his father]. He was so disconnected from his own inner wisdom and his own heart. When he acted out towards us, it was really the only way he knew how to react and act. In reality, no matter what I had done, there wasn't anything I could have done that would have opened those pathways back up that were closed.... But it does help me understand that I wasn't a bad son.

After emerging from his meditative state, Scott added that while watching the end of the film, Thorin experienced something novel: "a flash of ... feeling the emotion of Chris leaving, without connecting it to the past. It's like it's coming into his mind and being processed by a different path."

About 6 weeks later, when Chris actually left their care, Scott was convinced that his recurring vertigo was related to his difficulty experiencing the emotion associated with the loss. By this point in his therapy, he and his alters had spent a great deal of time processing memories in conference so that they wouldn't keep experiencing them in the same primitive manner, with the same erroneous linkages to worthlessness, vulnerability, and despair. Scott decided to consult his inner wisdom about how he could handle his emotions following Chris' departure, so that he could remain "more level." He went inside and was told by the inner wisdom that he was experiencing vertigo because he was essentially packing a lot of emotion into a small part of his mind and that he needed to learn not to do this. Scott described his continuing interactions with the inner wisdom while in a meditative state:

> So I asked the inner wisdom: What do you do with that [emotion], then? Because we don't want to pack it in until it gets to be too much. The inner wisdom is saying that we've experienced a loss, and it's okay to feel sad. It's okay to be upset. But the difference is that I need to learn to process it and let it go, kind of like what we talked about with the memories. You need to process emotion like you process memories. You kind of clear out some emotions that have kind of piled up here recently. I'm . . . feeling on edge lately. I need to focus even more on—not on the emotion—but on processing, allowing it to go. We're watching a little film of it. The example in the film is, I have a safe place in the top of my head where I go when I don't feel too safe. If you take some emotion and put it there, it's just filling up and filling up. Instead, talk about it in the conference room. Let the emotion go. Just let it happen. That's okay, that's normal. . . . What I've been feeling lately is that there's so much emotion in my head, I keep bumping into it. . . . It's also showing that it's okay to feel a little bit happy that Chris is gone. I can devote more time to our kids and me. Also, it's saying that it's not selfish to want to focus on other things for a while. What we're kind of talking about is going back in the bedroom tonight, instead of turning on the TV, to have a nice, long conference time, and process it [feelings about Chris' departure] like we used to do the memories. And not put a time limit on it, because some of the things that are harder to deal with are going to take time. I do enough at work. I need to focus on me and the family at home. . . . If I can process the emotion like I do the memories, everything else will take care of itself. I just kind of asked the inner wisdom to give me an example. What flashed in was an image of Chris when he'd just learned to sit up. He was sitting on the floor, kicking his legs, smiling at us. I'm feeling the emotion. It's amazing how when you let it go right through you, it goes right down the chest and into your hands. [Letting it go] doesn't mean we'll forget the memory, that I wouldn't be able to remember it if I needed to, but it's been recognized how much it's impacted us. This whole time [while viewing the image on the screen] it's been bouncing around inside, working it through, letting go of that one place. The inner wisdom kind of assures me that if we keep working on this, I'll be more true to my emotions, and the vertigo issue will be better. If you don't process the emotions, they're all up in your head. The more we process them, the better we'll get at expressing them. We're just kind of trying to talk about a schedule. Someone wanted to decide how long

it will take. But we might spend the whole night just thinking about one memory or one emotion. You can't rush it. We're just talking about a couple of things: dealing with other family members. We're all dealing with a lot. It's inevitable that tensions will get high. It's best to just be understanding about that at home. Charles and Thorin are really appreciating the way they feel when the emotions run through [and don't want to stop], but I told them we'd continue this in the evening. We'll just shut the door and turn the TV off. They were saying that if I could spend as much time working on our own emotions as I do at work, I'd be fine.

After emerging from his meditative state, Scott added: "It's really intense, when the inner wisdom showed the emotion flowing through you, when Chris learned to sit up. You feel how happy you were then and how sad you are that he's gone." Scott had been able to experience, for the first time, the poignancy of the emotional spectrum associated with human attachment, the experiences of love and loss, without questioning his personal adequacy.

In order to more fully understand how Scott was able to successfully repair his emotional circuitry after the psychological devastation of childhood abuse, we need to return and pick up an important strand that has been left dangling. We need to attend to Thorin's experiences between the 4th and 17th months of therapy so that we can understand his contributions to Scott's healing process.

Thorin's Emotional Evolution

After signing the Preservation of Life Contract and choosing the name Thorin in the 11th week of therapy, Thorin continued to express a strong desire to be abrasive and to intimidate others, as Scott's father had. He had formed a very rigid linkage between intimidation and power and was afraid he'd lose his power if he didn't behave in an abusive manner. His impulse was to use intimidation in dealing with others within the personality system, and he also tried to influence Scott to use it in his dealings with other people at work and at home. Despite his desire to cooperate with the system, the association between intimidation and power was so entrenched that it took a long time to build a new pathway to the experience of power. In this final section of the case history, we explore Thorin's remarkable internal renovation process.

Thorin experienced strong impulses to act out in a variety of ways. Not only was he inclined to vent anger towards others both inside and outside the system, but he felt powerful urges to drink, gamble, and flirt with women. Scott handled his responses to Thorin's acting out tendencies in a healthy manner: He conveyed his concerns about the potential consequences of this type of behavior, but he viewed Thorin's destructive tendencies with compassion and encouraged Thorin to consult the inner wisdom for guidance in rebuilding emotional paths.

Between the 4th and 17th months of therapy, the inner wisdom responded to Thorin's requests for guidance with a powerful sequence of images and messages supporting Thorin's emotional development. The inner wisdom told Thorin that the acting out behavior was destructive in the long run, but that Thorin couldn't see this at that time. In the meantime, the inner wisdom counseled, Thorin should just continue to share with Scott, via writing and in conference, whatever feelings Thorin was ready to share and Scott was able to handle. Thorin should also continue to encourage Scott to make time for recreational and athletic activities, which provided important physical outlets for releasing tension. In addition, the inner wisdom provided a vision of how Thorin would someday be able to genuinely enjoy constructive activities. Thorin was able to amplify the emotions and sensations while watching the film and experience the pleasure of constructive activities. However, the experience of pleasure was accompanied by pain and anxiety. He and Scott realized that, while growing up, positive feelings always set them up for victimization. "No matter how much fun we had growing up," Scott explained, "it always ended up with me hiding from my dad. I always ended up hurt." Whenever Scott had felt proud of his accomplishments in childhood, his father exploited his state of emotional openness by finding something to harshly criticize. In therapy, Thorin was finally able to articulate his fear that if he allowed himself to feel positive emotions, Scott's father or wife could hurt them, and that they could lose everything they'd built in adult life. In response to a request for help in feeling positive emotions without setting himself up to be hurt, the inner wisdom provided the following guidance to Thorin, which Scott reported:

> It's hard to believe, but it just keeps saying that I have to trust. If I act in the right way, and don't act out of anger, everything will work out. My children will always be my children. . . . I need to be true to myself, act out of the true or real feeling side of me. Things will take care of themselves.

A few weeks later Thorin reported continued strong urges to vent anger at others. I suggested that, in a meditative state, Thorin ask the inner wisdom whether the personal rewards of acting in constructive ways exceed the personal rewards of being vindictive and retaliatory, and if not, why the inner wisdom was guiding him to abandon the latter strategy. In response, the inner wisdom told him the most important thing to remember was not to be violent, and that if he were to hurt anyone he really loved, the remorse would be overwhelming. Scott summed up the message that Thorin had received: "There's nothing good that can come out of hurting other people. The only caveat was self-defense."

After Scott reported having been plagued by vicious dreams which he felt were "abuse-related and guilt-related," Thorin asked Scott if he could speak with me privately in session. Scott had been in therapy with me for over 6 months and Thorin had not yet come out to speak with me in my office. Of course, he had communicated with me while in a meditative state, but this time he wanted to speak with me without the others listening in. He asked them to go to their private rooms inside so that he could speak with me in confidence. After they did so, Thorin came out and reported: "I'm so angry right now. I have some major pain from all these memories. No one expects me to show any emotion. I told Scott I come out when he's asleep. I control the dreams. I show them some of the stuff that happened."

After conveying empathy, I suggested that Thorin go inside to the theater to consult the inner wisdom. He agreed, entered a meditative state, and described his interactions with the inner wisdom:

> Okay. I typed in the question: What do I do with all this anger? [The inner wisdom is recommending] some things I've already asked Scott to do . . . exercise more. . . . talk to my brother and sisters, but I said I just can't do that. The inner wisdom came back: How about if you just write a letter and don't send it? It's telling me that taking over [acting out, causing Scott to dissociate] is worse in the long run. . . . I don't want to be like my father. He used to go out drinking. The inner wisdom is telling me that deep down inside I want to be more like the images I'm seeing that Scott shows me. . . . The reason I want to take over and have fun and find a woman or get wild and crazy or beat someone up . . . *I came up with those ideas when I was being beaten up* [Italics added]. And if I could figure out a way to get past it, I don't really want to be that way. . . . I don't feel any better afterwards, I feel guilty about what I've done. The picture [on the screen] is saying that I somehow need to figure out a way to bring this up in the conference room and not just do it through the dreams. But I don't want to be made fun of. I always seem to be on the losing end. [The inner wisdom] is just saying I need to express to everyone how concerned I am about being made fun of.

Thorin was not yet ready to act on the guidance he'd received. The following month, he urged Scott to respond violently to an isolated episode of misbehavior on the part of Scott's son. After meditatively watching a two-part film in which Thorin's approach and its consequences were followed by an alternative suggested by the inner wisdom, Thorin acknowledged that the consequences of a violent response would be that his son would no longer trust him and Scott wouldn't be able to look his wife in the eye. By remaining emotionally steady and holding the child accountable for his poor judgment, as the inner wisdom suggested, the child would learn to be more responsible and would continue to respect and trust his father.

At that time, Scott had just undergone surgery to repair an injured tendon in the elbow. I offered Thorin the job of assisting with the healing process. He eagerly accepted the challenge. He became adept at giving Scott subtle cues to keep the joint relaxed and to ice it after exertion. He was evidently pleased to perform a nurturing function for the system.

Despite Thorin's pride in his new role, his affective life remained quite restricted. Expressing his anger appropriately in conference, as the inner wisdom had recommended, was extremely difficult for Thorin. He came to see that he had always felt it was his job to protect the system from anger and pain (hence the dam), and he was afraid that if he confided his feelings, the system would think less of him.

The possibility of an expanded affective range presented a real dilemma for Thorin. In the 8th month of therapy, Thorin described his predicament: Whereas in the past he could just shut down and turn off emotion and walk away from relationships, now that he was starting to feel some emotions, he didn't know if he could just walk away. He was experiencing genuine attachment to the system and to his current family (Scott's wife and children). He didn't know if it was important to his emotional safety that he preserve the old belief that he could "walk away." I encouraged him to consult his inner wisdom about whether it's wise to be committed to the family, and if so, how he could feel safe doing so. I observed that he was trembling and his breathing was very shallow and constricted as he entered a meditative state and described his interactions with the inner wisdom:

> I know that my dad is not here. I know he doesn't even live in this town. I'm just so scared of everything.... The inner wisdom showed me some pictures of long-term: The family is what we want. It seems like there's gonna be some steps in getting to feel safe. One of them is that I need to try and share with Scott and the others what I'm feeling in terms of being afraid. I don't know how to do that because I've never shown them any weakness. And I need to find some way to go to my safe place [his private room on the hall of safety] when it's too much. But I don't know if I can do that either. Somehow they'll notify me if they need me [while he's in his room].

I asked Thorin if he'd like to propose to the system that they agree to respect and support any personality who says he's feeling vulnerable. He found this difficult because he'd been the worst offender in terms of preying on the vulnerabilities of others within the system. He agreed with my recommendation that he begin the group discussion with an apology for past behavior, go on to make the commitment himself, and then make the request for system-wide support. He described how he proceeded while inside:

> I'll go ahead and invite them into the conference room. It's funny: Just being in the conference room calms me down. My initial thought is that I'm calmer because I just don't want to let them see me scared, but I think it's because they calm me down. [Pause] What I did was I apologized. I talked a little about what we talked about.... We've all agreed that if anyone's saying that they're vulnerable, we won't take advantage of that. They won't think less of me for that, and it's okay for me to go into my room if I need to be there. That's okay. We're in a much safer life right now. We'll all work together on the emotion part. Thank you. I'm saying thank you for taking me seriously and for forgiving me. Okay. We're just gonna leave it at that for now. If anyone says they feel vulnerable, everyone else won't make fun of them for saying so, and they appreciate me for being there for them, and I can go to my safe place when I need to. We'll talk about emotions we've experienced in our conferences—what they are and what they mean. I want to go to my safe place now.

After Thorin went to his private room inside, Scott emerged and reported being amazed by two things. First, he was extremely surprised by how uncomfortable, worried, and frightened Thorin was, and how undeserving Thorin felt. "I never would have thought of him as being that vulnerable," Scott explained. "And the second thing," Scott continued, "that is still just flat amazing me is not feeling him here! It's like he's gone. I know he was going into his room.... He must just have so much stress bottled up."

Scott described some of the interactions that had occurred in conference that Thorin had omitted from his account.

> I told him I loved him. Charles did, too. Thorin kind of questioned it a little bit. I said he knows me well enough to know I wouldn't say it if I didn't mean it. He was barely holding on. I tried to let him know that he's safe with us emotionally. First we'll work on getting him to feel safe in the conference room with us, and then later we'll work on doing it outside of the conference room, with other people.... I feel real unusual. I still can't get over the fact that he's not around.

I asked Scott how he decided to tell Thorin that he loved him. "He was not understanding how I could just forgive him," Scott explained. "The reason I can," he elaborated, "is because I honestly do love him. I wouldn't be here today if it wasn't for what he did for me."

Thorin's willingness to acknowledge his vulnerability, to apologize for having intimidated the others in the past, and to initiate a contract of mutual support reflected enormous growth on his part. It also promoted a significant growth spurt for the system as a whole, with Scott and Charles verbalizing their love for Thorin and the entire system facilitating, by means of the commitment not to take advantage of anyone's vulnerability, a more authentic emotional experience than had ever been possible for them previously.

During the months that followed, Thorin was able to utilize the system's support in confronting a number of entrenched emotional patterns. One such pattern was the habit of reminding the system of humiliating experiences because he thought it would help them to be a better person. With guidance from the inner wisdom, Thorin was able to make a commitment to the system to stop using images to belittle the system. They decided to focus on the present: "Who we are as a person today, and what will help us move forward together," Scott explained.

However, it was not until Scott had been in therapy for a full year that Thorin was willing to abandon his preference for abrasiveness in dealing with people outside the system. The pivotal experience occurred in session, after Scott reported that Thorin had been encouraging him to be harsh with coworkers and clients. Talking through to Thorin, I told Scott that if anger is a warning sign that something isn't acceptable, the question is how best to promote change. I told him that abrasive behavior is rarely effective in promoting the desired change, because the other person is likely to withdraw, respond defensively, or counterattack, but will rarely perceive the valid point behind the abrasiveness. Scott agreed with me, but reported that he heard Thorin saying that when Scott's father yelled, everyone did everything they could to keep him happy, so Thorin had concluded that intimidation is effective. This important insight prompted me to propose that Thorin might want to go inside and watch a two-part film: the best of Strategy A, Dad's strategy for controlling people through intimidation, and Strategy B, using the broader vision of the inner wisdom, which addresses the best for all concerned in the long run. I suggested he amplify the emotions and sensations that the consequences of both strategies produced in him while viewing them and then compare the two inner experiences so that he could make an informed choice. What Thorin learned from watching the film inside was that although the former strategy worked in the short run, in the long run it was inferior for three reasons. First, he had to keep escalating the ferocity of his behavior to maintain control over people. Second, this strategy led to more internal conflict, as the host and other alters weren't comfortable with it. And finally, Thorin could see that the second strategy actually gave him more power. He could feel it in his body as he amplified his responses via the dial. He was convinced that the nonintimidating expressive style endorsed by the inner wisdom gave him more power and reduced the internal stress.

Once Thorin stopped advocating caustic behavior, Scott made significant strides in self-assertion and was able to place more reasonable limits on accommodating the needs of others. By learning not to overextend himself at work, he was also able to make time for recreational activities, as described above. However, it was another 5 months before Thorin was ready to tackle the next major hurdle in liberating himself from the emotional constriction engendered by childhood abuse.

Scott reported in session that Thorin had, for some time, been wanting to have a happy memory. Thorin finally thought he might be deserving of remembering something good. In an at-home conference, they had asked the inner wisdom for suggestions of what such a memory might be. The inner wisdom had provided a list, and Thorin found that two memories on the list caught his eye: the wedding day and the births of the children. While in a meditative state in session, Thorin proposed that he create a "Memory Room" inside, so that he could lock the door and watch a film about one of these happy occasions without fear of being hurt. Despite the fact that for months he had been practicing feeling safe in acknowledging his vulnerability in the conference room, he felt that the experience of a happy memory might be so powerful that he could be hurt while in a state of emotional openness. He even confided to me that the inner wisdom was encouraging him to tell me that he was afraid I would hurt him. I affirmed his courage in sharing his concerns and assured him that I wouldn't hurt him. I told him that if I ever inadvertently hurt his feelings, he could tell me how he felt and I would take responsibility for my behavior, rather than take advantage of his vulnerability.

While in a meditative state, Thorin felt considerable anxiety as he prepared to enter his internal Memory Room. "I don't know why I'm so afraid to watch something happy," Thorin said. "The inner wisdom says I can just turn the knob down and watch it once without any emotion." Encouraged by this suggestion, Thorin watched and rewatched a film about his wedding day. "It's weird, seeing my wedding through my eyes and realizing I was there and *we were all there*." He described how he had felt as he looked out at the assembled congregation, how the little flower girl had gone back to retrieve some of the strewn petals, afraid that she was using them up too quickly. "When they played the music for my wife to come down the aisle, I saw how beautiful she was, how happy I was." Finally, Thorin remembered. "And I remember," he added, "seeing all my friends there, so many people. It's funny, it actually makes me miss seeing those people."

Thorin found that the experience of watching a memory made him feel sad about all the happy occasions he had "missed." While in his meditative state, he explained:

I was kind of upset there because all the things—getting married and having kids and having the kids go to school—I was feeling sad about all the good things I missed. The inner wisdom reminds me that the kids are going to graduate high school and get their Learner's Permits and get married. And there's plenty of opportunity for me to learn more about how to feel emotions and then experience them. I have missed some of the things, but I have them in here and when I'm ready I can see them.... I'm back in the conference room and everybody's here. I don't understand why I get so scared. I think it's because something kind of touched a part of me that I don't normally let show. Charles seems to feel it's because I won't be able to take care of Scott if I feel good emotion. Scott is trying to reassure me that if I can figure out when it's appropriate to be happy and when it's appropriate to be more protective, then I'll be able to switch between the two and not be afraid of feeling happiness. The inner wisdom is saying that when I was younger, I had to protect myself from physical harm, and now the threat of physical harm is not really there and that I need to learn to feel other emotions so I can protect us. Being true to our emotions and being more integrated. I can feel happy emotions and I can feel sad, and that would actually help me take better care of all of us because the threat of physical harm just isn't there now.

In the aftermath of this session, Thorin showed the internal movie of the wedding to the others during their evening conference time.

Several weeks later, Scott reported that he had been quite flooded with positive emotion one day while he was helping his children with a project. His son told him how much he appreciated Scott's help, and his daughter threw her little arms around his neck and exclaimed "I love you, Daddy!" Ordinarily, his pleasure would have been very short-lived, because, he explained, "usually when I feel proud of myself I get negative feedback." In session, he went inside to ask the inner wisdom why this experience had been so powerful for him. While inside, he shared his answer:

It was because it was unexpected.... This was something that caught me off guard, so I wasn't prepared to push it away. What the inner wisdom was saying about that was that I'm a good person, and I'm allowed to be loved. And it's okay for someone to say that and for it to really touch me. I don't need to push it away.... We're just talking about doing some figure-8 breathing, and when I'm ready to experience some more of the times I've been loved, when I'm ready to experience them, I can have them.

Scott had been in therapy for nearly 18 months before he had established a path through happy memories and positive experiences that enabled him to feel worthy of being loved and assured that it was safe to do so. Due in large part to Thorin's willingness to grow and change, the system had gained experience in moving back and forth over what the inner wisdom called "the emotional spectrum," so that they could feel confident that they didn't have to worry about setting themselves up for a crash by feeling happy. They learned, as Scott explained, "When I'm upset I'm not going to run out and kill myself. It's okay to be happy, because if something happens to make you sad, you'll know how to deal with it." They had succeeded in repairing a damaged emotional pathway. Sadness, loss, and frustration were no longer synonymous with inadequacy, shame, and despair. Scott had made tremendous strides towards achieving the goals of the first phase of therapy.

About 21 months into the therapy process, Thorin had achieved enough affective flexibility that he was willing to participate in the shared videos of recent experience intervention. This intervention uses the screen in the theater or conference room to project the recent experience of a member of the personality system so that other members of the system can grasp it experientially. In this way, it complements the verbal communication occurring in conference. While watching a film about the recent experiences of another member of the system, viewers can use the dial to amplify sensations and emotions, thereby greatly enhancing empathy. The recency of the experience is emphasized because this intervention is distinguished from transmission of early traumatic memories.

I introduced this intervention strategy to Scott when he reported concerns about where his alters were during his intimate moments with his wife. He reported that during a recent moment in bed with his wife, he had stroked her cheek and suddenly noticed a reaction of "Wow! This is really soft," as if one of his alters was touching his wife's skin for the first time. He readily accepted my suggestion that any consenting alters who observed or participated in that intimate moment could share their experience via video, so that others members of the system would really understand what they had felt. Scott entered a meditative state and described his inner experience:

> It's just the weirdest feeling, watching the video from Charles' point of view. Watching my hand coming up over her back ... palms sweaty ... so much apprehension. It kind of makes my hand tingle. He's got a lot of fear.... He's afraid what he's doing is going to hurt her. It's kind of like he's getting aroused, but he doesn't know how to handle it or what to do. Now we're going to watch it from Thorin's point of view. It's weird how Charles was so wanting to be tender, rubbing her cheek and her hair, but Thorin is more like ... control, wanting to hold her tight. It's weird how he's more attuned to having that control. Charles was more touchy-feely. With Charles, I felt more sensation. Thorin is much more cold, more lack of emotion. It's almost as if he just wanted to feel safe. Holding her was like holding a teddy bear: It keeps you safe.

While still inside, Scott reported that Thorin felt badly that his experience was all about trying to be safe, whereas Charles had felt so much more tender emotion and sensory engagement. I asked how Thorin would be able to feel safe enough to experience the tenderness. Scott reported that Thorin had several suggestions:

> He came up with locking the bedroom door so no one could come in, making sure the phone won't ring, and talking to [Scott's wife] ahead of time so she'd know it was him. He also just wants those bad memories to stop.

After emerging from his meditative state, Scott spoke of how intense the experience had been for him: " I *felt* it. I *really felt* it. It was like I was there, brushing her cheek again, but through *his* eyes. I'm getting really good feedback inside about this session."

☐ **Discussion**

Before highlighting the various intervention strategies that have been illustrated by this case, it's helpful to consider how representative Scott's case may be. As stated above, Scott made unusually rapid progress for a number of reasons. Relative to many (but by no means all) other DID clients, Scott displayed a high functional level, accepted the diagnosis readily, and had a small personality system. (In the interest of preserving anonymity, I have devoted much attention to some alters while merely alluding to the existence of others in this narrative, but the size of the system has not been misrepresented.) Also noted above are Scott's facility with adapting organizational management skills to the task of internal negotiation and his unusual initiative in conducting conferences at home. Scott displayed exceptional initiative in experimenting with various ways of entering a meditative state, structuring conferences, and so forth. This case is also rather unusual in that Scott experienced no technical difficulties in his early meditative state work. While my DID clients typically learn to enter a meditative state independently within the first few months of therapy, their initial experiences in the theater and conference room vary. Many clients have difficulty seeing films or verbal messages on the screen initially and need assurance that if they are patient and accept what they receive, additional guidance will be forthcoming in good time.

Scott's case is somewhat atypical in that he did a lot of reporting to me while in a meditative state. This practice certainly enhanced this narrative, as I have been able to convey what he experienced, as he experienced it. Clients display a broad range of responses to the challenge of sharing their "inside work." Some go inside, do their work, come out, and summarize the process for me, sometimes elaborating later in their journals. Some clients, like Scott, provide a running account of inner developments. In other cases, an alter may accept my invitation to serve as a reporter (as in the case presented in chapter 7) so that I can record developments during the meditative state without distracting the host.

Atypical features notwithstanding, Scott's case is representative of DID in many important ways. He presented with dysphoria, anxiety, "blind rage" with violent impulses, suicidal ideation (sometimes coming out of the blue), and a broad range of dissociative symptoms, including flash-backs, nightmares, amnestic episodes, evidence of activities carried on outside of awareness, and voices heard inside the head. All of these are classic DID symptoms. His difficulties with self-advocacy and his chronic feelings of inadequacy and shame are also highly characteristic of DID. His abuse history, while it reflects only some of the types of abuse experienced by DID clients, is nonetheless consistent with the etiological role of overwhelming childhood trauma in DID.

The role of Scott's alters is typical as well. For example, at least one child alter and at least one angry alter who pushes the host to self-advocate, are almost universal in the systems of DID clients. (Scott's child alter was alluded to but not described, in the interest of preserving confidentiality.) Also typical is the alters' encouragement of physical and recreational activities. The sense of remorse experienced by Charles is typical of alters who have engaged in acting-out behavior as part of their posttraumatic response. As Charles learned to defuse some of his anger, he regretted having indulged his retaliatory impulses. Alters sometimes experience remorse when they learn, in the internal theater, that all actions have consequences for self and others, as Thorin did when he could see that punishing his child violently would have caused distrust on the part of the child and shame on the part of the client. Another pattern, which sometimes emerges in the second stage of therapy, is that an alter feels remorse when it becomes clear that the host will someday absorb the history of the alter's actions and may feel degraded by them.

The nature of the guidance conveyed by the inner wisdom is also quite representative. Although the specific issues vary from client to client, the nurturing inner presence is available and accessible to all the DID clients I have treated. A striking feature is the broad, compassionate perspective of the inner wisdom, in contrast with the limited perspectives of the various members of the personality system. The inner wisdom understands the relationship between past and present in a way that no personality does and can display possibilities for the future that no personality could have anticipated or believed attainable. The inner wisdom also understands the interconnectedness of the personality system and depicts it graphically and verbally in a variety of ways.

As in the case presented in the previous chapter, this case illustrates how the inner guidance clearly transcends anything suggested by the therapist. For example, I had never heard of, or thought of, the figure-8 breathing—although I confess that I now use it myself! Similarly, the image of the sieve or colander was wholly new to me. Although I knew that avoiding excess emotionality while communicating would increase the likelihood of one's valid point being acknowledged, I had never considered how valuable it would be to have a visual image to help one deconfound the elements of another's communication, thereby preserving one's emotional equilibrium. This feature of the messages received from the inner wisdom is entirely representative of experiences shared by DID clients.

Similarly, the inner guidance transcends the conscious intention of the personality seeking counsel. Charles and Thorin sometimes respond to the inner wisdom's recommendations by saying they don't know if they can do what the inner wisdom is promoting. For example, Thorin resists the inner guidance that he acknowledge his feelings of vulnerability in conference. He also responds with near-incredulity when the inner wisdom tells him that the system will be able to help Scott learn to take care of himself. His comment—"I'm not sure I believe it, but it *is* the inner wisdom"—clearly conveys that the guidance didn't emanate from his conscious mind.

Typical, as well, is the success of internal conferences in promoting systemic cooperation. Although Scott made an unusually early commitment to frequent at-home conferences, all of my DID clients have found conferences similarly productive once the host commits to holding them. The alters find them very gratifying, as conferences provide an opportunity for them to make their needs known and to play an appropriate role in decision making and planning for future happiness.

Unfortunately, Scott is also characteristic of most DID clients in the length of time he needed in order to implement some of the guidance he received. For example, it took Thorin many long, frustrating months to grasp and act upon the guidance that he not behave in an impulsive, intimidating, and destructive manner. It's important for the therapist to understand that the process can be slow, not because the therapy has been derailed but because some of the emotional paths may be seriously damaged and repair work takes time.

However, if Scott is typical in needing a great deal of time in order to make certain affective, cognitive, and behavioral changes, he is also quite typical in the speed with which his angry alters become allies in the therapeutic process. Therapists who are inexperienced with treating

DID clients may initially view these alters as threats to the host, the therapist, and the therapy. In their rage, they may appear sociopathic. It's important to bear in mind that, like Thorin, they have tender hearts that may be hidden even from their own awareness. They are grateful that the therapist believes they have something of value to say and is committed to helping them communicate with the host effectively. Ultimately, they want what the host wants—to be safe, respected, loved, and acknowledged for their contributions—and are willing to join the system in working towards these goals once they sense that together they can choose how they want to live.

Given the representativeness of many important features of this case, it isn't surprising that this narrative illustrates, in addition to the use of the conference room and the theater, a number of the other core intervention strategies of the Collective Heart model. One such strategy is the evenhanded articulation of a conflict within a personality or between personalities, as when Charles was ambivalent about preserving the image of his father and when Scott was encouraged to tell Charles why Charles' taking over creates a problem for him. By means of an unbiased rendering of the two perspectives, the therapist models for the client that healing work begins with acceptance rather than judgment. The approach is helpful for another reason. When the therapist articulates the conflict impartially and then suggests that the host or alter initiate a discussion of the dilemma in conference or consult the inner wisdom for guidance, it is clear to the client that the therapist trusts the group process and the inner wisdom and is not trying to control or influence the outcome of the intervention. Because this approach is respectful, nonleading, and nonjudgmental, it is especially useful in forming an empathic bond with an alter, as I did with Charles.

Also effective in engaging an alter in the therapeutic process is the reframing of an alter's disruptiveness. When "Dad" blocked Scott's and Charles' ability to enjoy the film about the good things they had done, I pointed out that perhaps Scott and Charles would only be able to achieve a limited appreciation of the good they had done without coming to terms with "Dad" and his objections to the process Scott and Charles were pursuing. This conveys to the disruptive alter that I understand that he has a valid point and that I will help him find ways to express himself constructively. By reframing the disruption as a valuable communication, you can invite the alter in, instead of shutting him out. This powerful intervention validates the angry alter and his essential role, engages him in therapy, emphasizes the potential value of facing painful affects, and highlights the interrelatedness of the alters.

Illustrated here, as well, is the technique of using shared videos of recent experience to increase empathy between members of the personality system. The very fact that they are able to show each other an internal video, the accuracy of which is verified by the personality whose experience is portrayed, provides additional evidence to the client that they really are one person and that the dissociative barriers in the mind are permeable.

The retrieved memory of the wedding day illustrates the applicability of the techniques to nontraumatic memories. This is an important point, as this treatment model places less emphasis on the retrieval of traumatic material and more emphasis on the retrieval of personal authority, relative to most other models. It addresses identity development that is informed not only by a painful life history but also by a history filled with meaningful, positive experiences that must be shared within the system so that they become part of the collective narrative. On numerous occasions, Scott received guidance regarding the retrievability of happy memories. For example, he reported having received the following guidance: "When I'm ready to experience some more of the times I've been loved, when I'm ready to experience them, I can have them."

Finally, this case illustrates the utility of suggesting a specific healing role for an alter whose protectiveness has historically been manifested paradoxically. Although all alters are essentially protective by nature, an alter who protects by preventing the host from getting his hopes up or by clinging to suicide as an option is experienced as a threatening presence rather than a protective one. For this reason, the recommendation of a specific healing role can be a potent intervention. Thorin was honored to take on the responsibility of promoting healing in the aftermath of surgery. Watch for opportunities to request assistance and they will present themselves. For example, an alter like Thorin, who habitually caused chaotic sleep by sharing memories through dreams, can be asked to be the one to promote restful sleep. Whether or not you have ideas for such a role, an alter can always be invited to ask the inner wisdom how he can help in a way that will be appreciated by the rest of the system. Alternatively, the host can ask an alter to help in a specific way or can request a volunteer from within the system when assistance is needed. The enthusiastic response to such requests is heart-warming. The Collective Heart model works because the alters want to help and because the inner wisdom shows them how, in the long run, they can do so in the most effective manner.

CHAPTER

Inner Lessons in Self-Advocacy

Nothing pleases an alter as much as collaborating with the host in self-advocacy. Typically, there is at least one alter who expresses needs in a hostile, heavy-handed, or explosive manner, and a host who, anxious about the possible consequences of confrontation, is not forceful enough in making needs known. Among the most satisfying moments in therapy for client and therapist alike are those moments in which the host and alter discuss their needs and collaborate in obtaining and implementing inner guidance about learning to speak up and take a stand.

Often the stage is set for this intervention when the host or an alter reports in session that she agreed to do something she didn't really want to do, or wasn't able to ask for what she really wanted, in her current life. The therapist then suggests that an internal conference, in which the participants discuss the pros and cons of speaking up, is often very helpful. After the conference, the client can describe the process to the therapist and all involved or interested personalities can visit the internal theater. There they can view a film, projected by the inner wisdom, about how the system will be able to work together to make their needs known and protect themselves from exploitation and manipulation. They can use the dials, as desired, to amplify emotions and sensations.

This is an elegant intervention because it not only addresses the client's difficulty with self-assertiveness, which has typically been quite an impediment to the client, but simultaneously promotes progress in terms of every goal of the first stage of therapy. For example, it engages the alters, who realize that the therapist values their input and wants to create opportunities for them to be heard by the host. Internal communication is increased when the host sees that the alters have something to offer and are eager to help. This is particularly important early in therapy, when the host may still believe that the alters are there to ruin her life with their anger, depression, fear, struggles for control, and other threatening behavior. The host is often quite moved by the alters' willingness to modify their behavior in response to inner guidance. The here-and-now focus of the intervention emphasizes that the alters are resourceful helpers who can promote more successful living, rather than mere receptacles of past pain. As a result, alters feel supported by the therapist and are more committed to therapy. Child alters, who are often fearful or overly responsible (or both), have reason to hope that older members of the system will work together to prevent people from hurting them. The host, too, experiences increased confidence in the therapeutic process, because she is reassured that the system can cooperate to solve problems and that change is possible. Acceptance of the diagnosis is fostered by the experience of the diverse personalities in conference and by the inner wisdom's vision of mutual support and safety. Furthermore, the lessons gleaned from the intervention can be applied to a variety of interpersonal situations on a daily basis.

☐ Case Illustrations

This chapter provides illustrations of inner lessons in self-advocacy drawn from three clinical cases. Each vignette portrays the application of the intervention strategy to a different stage of the first phase of therapy.

Marty

Marty, a 40-year-old married, employed male with a documented history of early trauma, was aware of the existence of alter personalities when he presented for therapy. A cautious, considerate man, Marty described a child personality who felt a great need to be comforted by Marty's wife and was very anxious when separated from her for more than a few hours. Marty experienced these needs as passive influence experiences. Marty was also aware of an adult male personality who tried to outdo Marty in various displays of mastery and appeared to derive pleasure from criticizing Marty's efforts. Marty called this alter "Harold" because this had been his father's name, and the alter's behavior was reminiscent of his father's behavior. Although I predicted that Marty would discover a protective purpose underlying Harold's apparently competitive and deprecating behavior, Marty insisted that I was wrong. He was sure Harold hated him and wanted to do away with him. Marty described several incidents in which Harold had put Marty's life in jeopardy. Like many DID clients during the early weeks and months of therapy, Marty had no reason to believe his angry alter held gifts for the system.

I told Marty I suspected that Harold might act the way he did because he couldn't yet see a range of options, and suggested that it might be helpful for me to talk with him. Marty consented. I told Marty that he could simply close his eyes, and Harold would come out if he wanted to talk to me. When Harold emerged, I thanked him for coming and expressed surprise that Marty felt Harold was trying to hurt him rather than help him. Harold explained why he was so critical of Marty: "He needs to stand up for himself. He's kind of a wimp. He needs to stand up to people." Harold reported that Marty was afraid to stand up to his wife because he was afraid she would leave him. Harold accepted my suggestion that he go inside and ask the inner wisdom for a film about how he could help Marty learn to stand up for himself. "I'll try," he responded, "but I don't think he has it in him."

After watching the film, Harold summarized the message and process:

> One thing Marty needs to know to stand up to everyone, not just his wife, is that he has the same rights they do. He needs to understand that just because he feels inadequate, that doesn't mean he has to let them take advantage of his inadequacy. When you see a person back down, you take advantage. He needs to stand up. The movie was about something that happened last weekend. I saw Marty talking with a neighbor, and the neighbor wanted Marty to do something for him. Even though Marty had things to do, he put it aside and did what the neighbor wanted. He always puts his rights aside.

Harold accepted my suggestion that he consult the inner wisdom about his role in helping Marty realize that he has rights and that his rights are just as important as anyone else's. He emerged from the inner consultation to report: "Whenever he gets in that situation, [I can] remind him that he can stick up for his rights." I then asked if Harold would be willing to invite Marty to join him in the theater to watch a two-part film. The first part, I explained, would be the film Harold had just seen, and the second part would be about how Marty could handle the situation differently with Harold's encouragement to stand up for himself. He consented, and closed his eyes. I waited.

Marty emerged and described the film he had seen about something that had happened the previous weekend. He had been painting his house when a neighbor stopped by and asked him to have a look at the neighbor's house and make a recommendation about preparing a room for painting. Marty had left his painting job to accompany the neighbor and had ended up spending several hours helping the neighbor with sanding and spackling. In the second part of the film, he saw Harold helping him handle the situation differently. "Harold," Marty explained, "tried to show me that when I have a problem like that, I can tell the person that my day is full. I have things I need to do. If they try to push me on it, I can offer to recommend a good painter."

Since many neighbors and coworkers had grown accustomed to taking advantage of Marty's difficulty in saying "no," it's not surprising that Marty had an opportunity to implement the guidance before his next therapy session. When a coworker asked Marty to take over a couple of projects so that the coworker could do some personal errands, Marty was able to tell him that his day was too full to take on anything extra. However, Marty was unaware of Harold's role in his self-assertive response. In session, I offered him an opportunity to go inside and see a film about the incident, so that he could determine whether Harold had performed a role. In the film, Marty heard Harold's voice telling him to stick up for his rights, reminding him that his day was full with his own projects and that he had the same right as everyone else to be ready to leave work on time.

This vignette illustrates Marty's early lessons in self-protection and self-advocacy. Perhaps even more importantly, these experiences provided evidence of Harold's willingness to perform a new, constructive role. They helped Marty see that he and Harold had something in common: They shared the discovery that he now had the power to do something about how he was treated, and mistreated, by others.

Olivia

This 24-year-old, employed, single female with a reported history of incestuous abuse had been diagnosed and treated for DID before she relocated to Virginia and sought therapy with me. In her previous therapy, she had become aware of a child alter who worked hard not to create any problems for her. Very early in our work together, Olivia realized that the "adult female presence" that seemed to periodically invade her life like a tornado was actually a second alter. Much of our early work focused on establishing a dialogue between Olivia and the adult alter, who had previously expressed herself by disrupting romantic attachments that Olivia had formed. It soon became clear to Olivia that the alter's violent reactions were borne of desperate efforts at emotional survival. When the alter felt that Olivia was being used sexually by her female partner, memories of the alleged incestuous abuse were triggered and the alter screamed and raged.

When Olivia had been in therapy with me for about 4 months, she reported an incident in which she had told Julia to back off, and Julia didn't respect the boundary that Olivia was trying to establish. Olivia began screaming and breaking furniture to demonstrate to Julia that she wasn't to be crossed. There was considerable damage to Olivia's property before Julia finally retreated.

Initially, Olivia felt pleased that she and her alter had participated in this situation co-consciously. In the past, Olivia had sensed the "tornado" approaching, felt like a distant, helpless observer during the ranting and raving, and was left totally depleted afterwards, aware only of the destructive rage that seemed to come out of nowhere. This time, Olivia noted progress in that she felt, for the first time, how the alter's anger was fueled by fear. Olivia felt that she was consenting to the destruction of her personal property, rather than watching helplessly from a distance. However, her initial satisfaction with what she perceived as progress soon gave way to depression about the course of her relationship with Julia.

I suggested that Olivia go inside with her adult alter and see a film about how, in the future, she and the alter would be able to make further progress in responding collaboratively to an attempted transgression of her boundaries. By this point in therapy, Olivia had had considerable experience in entering a meditative state independently and had been holding internal conferences at home between sessions. She agreed to my suggestion to go inside, but decided independently to restructure the intervention. She emerged from her meditative work to report:

> Okay. I'm done. I heard what you said, but I went back to the scene [revisited the recent conflictual experience instead of seeing a film about a future interpersonal interaction], with the inner wisdom and the alter present.... What I saw was that I would remain calm. I would just say to Julia, point out very clearly that she's overstepping my boundaries, that I feel very violated, express very clearly that this is very threatening. Then I'd give her an opportunity to withdraw. If she doesn't back off then, I would say "I have no choice now. I have to withdraw from the situation." All that can be done without screaming and breaking things. That *is* possible.

Olivia was understanding her alter's long history of destructive rages in a new way. She used to feel that the alter preferred to express herself in this way—in fact, insisted upon it. Having embarked on a collaboration with her, Olivia had a new perception of her alter's feelings about her habitual response to threat: "She feels guilty about it. That doesn't make her happy. It keeps her in a miserable rut, where she doesn't think there are any other choices."

The discovery that there are other options and that the client is free to choose among them is, of course, the key to the success of this intervention. A therapist can always tell a client that there are alternatives to maladaptive behavior, model the alternative behavior, discuss applications to a variety of life circumstances, and so forth. What distinguishes this treatment model is that there are also alternatives to the therapist imparting the broader vision. These vignettes illustrate that the client can discover within herself that there are safer and more satisfying ways to live, and that these insights emanate from the deepest aspect of her own collective being. Because they have access to the inner wisdom, alters don't need external pressure to change maladaptive patterns.

Scott

Scott (see chapter 8) had a plan in place to avoid continued emotional victimization by his abusive father. Scott's wife knew it and his alters knew it. The plan was never to be in his parents' home without his own vehicle, so that he could easily leave if the situation got out of hand. His wife knew that if he told her that they would be getting the children into the car right away, he was counting on her not to question his decision or delay the departure.

One day, when Scott had been in therapy for about 21 months, he and his wife hosted an extended family gathering in their home for the first time in many years. It hadn't occurred to him that advanced planning was necessary, that his old strategy of leaving the scene wasn't appropriate when he was the host. When his father began cruelly berating Scott's brother at the party and creating a scene, Scott felt emotionally paralyzed. With no workable plan in place, he simply didn't know what to do. He felt like he was 10 years old. During the interval between the party and his next therapy session, Scott felt that all of his alters were very angry at him and seemed to be criticizing everything he did.

In session, Scott decided to go inside and have a conference with his alters. He spoke to me, as was his habit, from his meditative state:

> One of the things I hadn't realized until just now is that Davy [a child alter] has been really scared. Thorin and Charles are just all over me because I haven't been realizing how it's affecting anyone. Davy has been cowering under the bed all day, because when that happened I didn't do anything to protect them. They were allowed to see and feel it all.... They don't realize that when this happens [when the alters all criticize him], I kind of start to shut down inside. Like when you say you're sorry, they completely discount it.... It really scares me when Thorin gets so mad. I'm afraid I'll just shut down and let him take over for a while. I'm trying to get him

to listen for a minute. We all make mistakes. I know I didn't plan well for what to do if Dad got angry at our house. I just didn't think about putting something into place in my house. Next time we'll do something different. My first thought was: We'll just leave. Thorin said "I'm not leaving my house 'cause of him." It's amazing how timid I feel lately, and how Davy is cowering under his bed. He's so afraid of getting hit. I'm trying to show him I'm not gonna let him [Dad] hit us. I say that, but if my Dad did hit me, I probably wouldn't have done anything. I think that's why Davy is so scared.

After discussing some concrete ways that Scott could be more self-protective in other areas of his life, he and his alters—still in the meditative state—returned to the question of how he could handle his father's escalation in Scott's home. Now that Scott understood that his alters were angry at him for leaving them vulnerable to the feelings of terror that arose within them when his father's abusive tirade began, he initiated consultation with the inner wisdom. He described what he was seeing:

What the inner wisdom is showing us is that I can't just leave my house, because that wouldn't be fair to my children, my wife, and my siblings. The inner wisdom is showing that I should have been able to pull Dad to the side, calmly but firmly. It's showing that if I do that, it will work. I see myself telling Dad: "You're acting in a way that's just not acceptable right now. I'd appreciate it . . . I need you to act in a more civil way." The inner wisdom is showing me that there's no repercussions. It's also showing that he might just leave, and that that's acceptable, not to feel guilt over that. The other parts [alters] are seeing how he [Dad] was in the past, but the inner wisdom keeps showing how it will be okay. Everyone is shaking their heads "no."

Because we were almost out of time, I encouraged Scott to bring his meditative work to a close. After he opened his eyes, he emphasized how hard it had been to accept the inner wisdom's message that he really could speak up to his father and that his father wouldn't escalate the verbal abuse or become physically assaultive. He reminded himself that his father was now an old man and that he himself was a strong adult. It was the inner wisdom's tenacity in showing the scene over and over that finally convinced Scott that it really was safe for him to set limits on his father's behavior. However, he was aware that his alters persisted in the belief that speaking up carried excessive risk.

I suggested that Scott replay the film for his alters in conference before our next session. He had a better idea. Since he was the only member of the system who believed that the inner wisdom's proposal was viable, he could show his alters a film about his own confidence in speaking up to his father. What Scott had done, in devising this particular plan, was to blend two of my intervention strategies into one. One is the vision of hope for the future: The inner wisdom projects onto the screen a scene of future possibility for the proximate or distal future (see chapters 7 and 8). The other is the shared videos of recent experience intervention, in which one personality shows another personality something that he has experienced and how he responded emotionally (see chapter 8). In both scenarios, the viewer can use the dial to amplify sensations and emotions in order to incorporate the film content experientially. Scott's plan was innovative: He decided to combine features of the film about future possibility with the film about past experience, because he had already experienced the confidence that the inner wisdom's suggestion of future possibility would work. He knew he could enhance the effectiveness of the inner wisdom's message for his alters if they could feel his confidence as they viewed it. I expressed my delight in Scott's creative solution to addressing his alters' skepticism.

☐ Discussion

These three vignettes illustrate how inner lessons in self-protection and self-advocacy can be learned in a variety of contexts. Marty's experience, which is typical of many DID clients early in therapy, involved overcoming his difficulty in speaking up for himself in relatively neutral everyday interactions with neighbors and coworkers. Scott's experience, on the other hand, involved the highly charged situation of witnessing the perpetrator of the childhood trauma behaving abusively. This latter application of the intervention strategy is appropriate when the collaboration between the alters is fairly well established. As we have seen, trust within the system was temporarily shaken even after 21 months of successful therapy, when core issues of vulnerability and capacity for self-protection were evoked.

Olivia's vignette illustrates a third application of the intervention. She needed to maintain safe boundaries in a highly significant relationship with an individual who, at times, triggered in her alter feelings of terror and rage associated with the incest she reported on initial evaluation. In Olivia's case, these issues surfaced early in therapy. In fact, her adult alter was induced to become involved in the therapy process when she was given an opportunity to express to Olivia her concerns about the relationship with Julia. It was in the ensuing internal dialogues that Olivia first observed that her alter was not out to ruin her life. Like Marty, Olivia had been terrified by the destructive potential of an alter who soon became an ally.

It should not be inferred from Scott's guidance that it's always advisable to challenge an abusive person. In some cases, the inner wisdom may counsel the client to avoid all contact with a dangerous person, who is likely to escalate. In other cases, the inner wisdom tells a client that the abuser is not the person he or she was during the client's childhood when the abuse occurred. In still other cases, such as Scott's, the inner wisdom focuses on the fact that the client is now an adult and will be able to prevent continued abuse. The point is, as always, that the inner wisdom has a perspective previously unavailable to the conscious minds of the host and the alters. By means of this intervention, the client learns to prevent victimization and exploitation in his or her current life, laying the groundwork for effectively processing experiences of past traumatization during the second stage of therapy.

Decreasing Anxiety to Remove Obstacles to Inner Guidance

The major focus of the second stage of therapy, the further dismantling of dissociative barriers between personalities, is addressed in chapter 11. Another important, but more subtle, process characteristic of the middle phase of therapy is discussed here. This process can be framed as the further dismantling of barriers between the inner wisdom and the conscious mind. While the dismantling of barriers between personalities is common to virtually all DID treatment models, the dismantling of barriers between unconscious guidance and conscious awareness is a distinctive feature of the Collective Heart model.

We saw in chapter 8 that as therapy progresses, the client becomes less reliant on formal questioning of his inner wisdom and more cognizant of the inner wisdom "chiming in" with unsolicited guidance. The client becomes increasingly receptive to guidance in normal waking consciousness throughout the course of therapy. We might conceptualize this process as the development of inner translucency, whereby the conscious mind receives enlightenment from the inherent radiance of the inner wisdom. In order for translucency to develop, certain obstacles must be identified and minimized. Foremost among these obstacles are anxiety and anger.

Scott, whose case was presented in chapter 8, had three meditative experiences during his second stage of therapy that are presented here to illustrate the guidance clients receive regarding the importance of decreasing anxiety and worry. The first experience occurred close to the end of his second year of therapy. He reported constant worry, for example, worry that he would "snap" and jeopardize his career, worry that he would lose control with his children and be perceived as a bad parent. He recalled that he had initiated fist-fights in his younger years, when he and his alters lacked the resources to explore their anger and had acted out instead. He was afraid he'd revert to this pattern. "If I don't worry about it," he explained, "then maybe it will happen." He felt his worrying might serve as a sort of insurance policy and that the discomfort of constant worry might not be an excessive price to pay for avoiding destructive behavior. I asked him what he thought his inner wisdom would say about maintaining this type of insurance policy. He had no idea and decided to enter a meditative state and inquire. Sitting quietly with his eyes closed, he reported what he was hearing:

> What the inner wisdom is saying is that when we all [all the members of the personality system] feel comfortable as a group, we can trust that the inner wisdom will let us know if we're veering off the right path, so to speak. What each one of us needs to trust is that if we get a warning that we're not acting right or we're acting the wrong way towards resolving something, we need to all trust each other that we'll listen to the inner wisdom, that warning sign, and kind of stop there and go inside, or do a conference. Basically it's just saying that we don't have to worry because there's enough checks and balances in place. But that we all have to feel comfortable with that.

After a brief pause, I asked: "When you're ready, may I make a suggestion?" He indicated his consent. "Is this a good time?" He nodded. "Do you think it would be helpful," I offered, "for all of you to see a film about the process of letting go of the worry?" "Okay," Scott responded.

I waited while Scott and his alters watched the internal film. Still in his meditative state with his eyes closed, Scott described what he had seen:

> It was kind of cute. It showed a really, really full attic, I mean, like you couldn't fit a toothpick in sideways in this attic. And then it showed everything disappearing bit by bit, to where it's nice and big and empty. And something—I don't know if it's the inner wisdom or what—these windows are being opened and the cool, the new breeze is being allowed to rush in, and a voice is saying "Look at how much room we have up here, without all this worrying clogging up the attic!" And it's just kind of like showing me all this room that's available for other things if you're not letting all this room be occupied by worrying.
>
> Then it kind of showed a dashboard on a car, saying that you don't drive around all the time worrying about whether or not there's oil in the car because you've got a little light that comes on when the oil is low. And if your gas is running low, there's a little light that says that the gas is running low. Kind of like saying that: It doesn't mean you don't ever check it, or

you don't ever have your oil changed, or fill your gas tank, but that you don't sit there and worry about that, you know. You don't have the car parked in the driveway and you're sitting in the house wondering if there's enough oil in it. You're just aware that if something were to happen to cause the oil to leak out, the light comes on. And every once in a while you change it. The same type of thing can happen here. Clear out all that room that's taken up worrying, and just replace all that stuff with a few warning lights.

Then it kind of takes it a bit further and says, If you don't heed the warning light in the car, you'll burn your motor up. [He laughs.] The whole idea is that you've got to heed the warning signs or the warning lights and take steps to rectify things, if in fact anything happens, but then day in and day out you don't have to worry about it. And really, the inner wisdom is pretty confident that we're not gonna revert. Kind of like saying, "Well, if you're worrying, then this is what you need to do, but you really don't need to be worrying."

Like Scott's image of the sieve or colander that allowed him to utilize the valid part of a critical remark while letting the mean-spirited aspect fall away (see chapter 8), these images of the attic and the dashboard helped Scott free himself from negative affect. It's unlikely that any rational challenge to Scott's strategy of using worry to protect himself against acting out would have had the impact of experiencing the tightly packed attic and then the spaciousness with the cool breeze rushing through. The inner wisdom essentially structured the experience as a two-part film. The first part showed Scott how much better he would feel if he cleared out his attic, or head, of burdensome and unnecessary clutter. The second part showed him why it was safe to do so. The key to releasing worry without fear of loss of control is the systemic agreement to heed the few warning signals that can replace all the anxious concern.

The need for systemic agreement explains why this therapeutic development is characteristic of the second stage of therapy. Commitment to heed the warning lights is not in place early in therapy, so the client is justifiably concerned about doing things that may put himself and others at risk. If there is a warning sign, such as anger, fear, discomfort, or internal conflict, the system needs to know that they will work in concert, consulting the inner wisdom as necessary, rather than have one personality respond impulsively on the basis of old associations and assumptions. Modifying the faulty circuitry of the mind (to use the imagery Scott received from his inner wisdom, described in chapter 8) requires refusal to use the familiar circuitry in an automatic manner. Alternative connections are formed and reinforced when the system acts multilaterally, consulting the inner wisdom as necessary to resolve impasses.

By the time the client reaches the second stage of therapy, he has the capacity to see the long-term consequences of behavior. He can interdict impulsive responding and gather the information needed for sound decision making. He can determine what is best for all concerned in the long run. Thinking in terms of long-range consequences becomes habitual. For example, Scott remarked during the second stage that "long term, it's worse if you just dissociate [when in distress] and let someone else [an alter] suck up the pain." After entering a meditative state to gain insight repeatedly during the first stage of therapy, the client is confident that he has the inner resources to create a healthier and happier way of living. As long as the full system is committed to using these resources consistently, there is no need to worry.

Within a month of his meditative vision of the attic and the dashboard, Scott had an opportunity to ask his inner wisdom for more help with creating new emotional pathways. He reported spiraling downward whenever he felt depressed or guilty because of associations between depression, guilt, inadequacy, and bad memories of his father abusing him emotionally or physically. He accepted my suggestion that he ask his inner wisdom how he could process his depression and guilt differently.

He closed his eyes and went inside. After several minutes, he described the idea that Charles was suggesting in conference:

> Charles thought about the Serenity Prayer. Grant me the—what is it?—the courage to change the things I can, accept the things I can't change, and the wisdom to know the difference. Then what the inner wisdom ... it's kind of difficult to understand, but I think what it's trying to show me is that I need to try to focus on the *actual point* where the feeling or the thought is initiated. What happens is that I'm not catching it quick enough, and it ends up going in the wrong way, kind of down the wrong path. So what it's saying is if I have a hint of guilt, I have that old pathway there where guilt goes back to feelings about my dad, and then it can end up getting stuck over there instead of getting processed. So what the inner wisdom is kinda trying to show me is I need to be more aware of when a negative emotion, or guilt, or a feeling of depression [starts] ... I need to get them right at the beginning. [Pause] That's interesting. And then use some of the same processes I have, where I put it through the sieve and realize what about it is material that I want to hold onto and what we can let wash over us. Kinda help determine if there's a path already existing that it can go down, because I just don't want to have to build a new path every time we have something else pop up. [Pause]
>
> The inner wisdom just gave me a really neat gift. It said if you don't plant the right seeds, all you end up with is a bunch of weeds ... and then you have to go back and pluck everything that grows that you don't want. If instead you took that seed before you planted it, and looked at it, and determined whether or not you wanted to keep it, and then only planted

the good ones, then you'll end up with the garden you want. It's kind of like saying, "Here, take this, break it down, [and see what's] the important part that stays up in the sieve. Determine what, as a system, we want to do about . . . those things up in the sieve. And the rest, acknowledge them for what they are, and let them go. And how to let them go is down some of those pathways that you already have in place."

Scott's first meditative experience presented in this chapter showed him how much better he would feel it he could let go of everything that he had crammed into his attic, his head. In a sense, this second meditative experience showed him how to avoid creating a crowded attic in the first place. This time, the inner wisdom offered a new image, that of a garden filled with weeds. Scott was shown how he could examine each seed before he planted it and choose whether or not he wanted to plant it. Again, the focus is on interdicting the pattern of responding on the basis of faulty assumptions and associations. The inner wisdom assured Scott that he could create the garden he wanted if he chose his seeds carefully. That is, he could create the life, the relationships, the experience of self he wanted if he became aware of the triggers to dysfunctional responding and used the resources that had become available to him.

The third meditative experience elaborating this theme of decreasing anxiety emerged from marital tension. Scott reported that he and his wife were in conflict over a major family decision. Between sessions, Scott had spent considerable time in conference discussing the matter, and he found that all of his alters agreed that they had reached the right decision, the one that would be best for all concerned in the long run. The inner wisdom confirmed that their decision was healthy. However, Scott was very troubled by the fact that his wife saw things differently, and he felt she was trying to coerce him into abandoning his convictions and supporting her preference. He also found that she had discussed their situation with others, although the two of them had agreed not to discuss it with others until after they had reached a decision. Scott realized that one of his alters was encouraging him to sleep on the sofa. He wasn't sure whether this proposal was intended as a punishment for his wife or as a way to achieve the necessary physical distance to protect himself from undue emotional influence. He decided to go inside and inquire.

Scott consulted his alters in conference and learned that Charles was indeed feeling the need to sleep on the sofa in order to punish Scott's wife for what he saw as her betrayal. While still in his meditative state, Scott continued to describe the guidance he was receiving:

But what the video the inner wisdom showed us was that if you withhold that intimacy of sleeping together in the same bed, all that's gonna do is cause more resentment, and kind of distance—put more distance between us. And what the inner wisdom is showing us is that long-term, the closer we get, the better—the better off we'll be. [Pause] If we wanted to kind of avoid some of the confusion . . . the inner wisdom is saying we should try to cut down on some of the external distractions. Like instead of having the TV on when you get home all the way through to the time you go to bed, leave it off when there's not a good show on. And what it's showing is that in those times when the TV's not on, they'll be more opportunity to discuss things like this. What you're seeing is like a discussion about [Scott's wife] talking to others, and getting a feel for who she talks to, and about what and why, being real careful not to pass judgment. But at the same time, to have firm rules in place. And that if anything, saying to her that I'm concerned about her trust and about her talking with others. Then . . . not discuss too many details with her, and to make her understand that the reason why you're not is because of the pattern in the past, and over time continuing to talk to her about the need for the privacy between us. [Long pause]

It's difficult for the different parts of me to hear the inner wisdom say this, but the inner wisdom is saying that I'm important to her and that it's kind of okay for me to be important to her, to . . . that it's okay for me to say no [about the important family decision they needed to make] and understand that she's going along with that because it's important to me. I don't know how that ties in, but it's okay for me to be important to her. That I'm kind of deserving of that. Then it shows that if I'm that important to her and she's talked to someone else [about something they agreed was confidential], it's either because she's confused or concerned or just, you know, not thinking at the moment she says something. But if I just make her understand how important it is [the agreement to keep certain matters in confidence], then we can trust her not to talk about it. But she needs reminding. She needs to be talked to a lot about things, more than I am now. It's important to put myself out there as a sounding board for her. [Long pause] It kind of makes sense.

Scott opened his eyes, reoriented to the room, and explained what preceded his acknowledgment that it makes sense. "It's a different point of view than I normally have," he explained. He described the final insight the inner wisdom had provided:

Growing up, you were either happy and close, or not happy and distant. There wasn't the ability to be upset with someone and remain close. . . . With both my parents it was that way. . . . The gap between you, you could almost see it [that is, Scott experienced it spatially while in his meditative state]. And that's what [we] were trying to do in saying "sleep on the sofa"—put that gap between us, physically. But what the inner wisdom was showing us is that you . . . don't want to have that gap right now. You want to try and stay close even though you're upset or even though you're having a conflict over it. That it's not that I need to be distant and upset. . . . Trying to show me how there shouldn't be a direct relation between the two. The whole idea is that if you do nothing but put distance between you, then it's not gonna accomplish anything. And that was what the video started out by showing us was, what if you do go to her and say "Hey, I'm upset, and because of that I'm gonna go sleep on the sofa." The distance between you not only stays the same but it gets even bigger. And then she has the opportunity to either escalate it or not. And that in any event, if I did do that, then it accomplishes nothing towards resolving the conflict. One of the things ... if she's talking to someone else about it, it's because I'm not talking to her enough, so regardless of how much I've talked to her about this, I haven't done it enough. . . . Basically, that's what the inner wisdom was showing.

Here we have three significant therapeutic developments that occurred within a 5-week period. Each contributed to Scott's ability to decrease anxiety. First he experienced, in a vivid sensory manner, the advantages of unburdening himself of extraneous worry. Then he saw how an effective warning system was in place, rendering anxious concern unnecessary. Next he saw how important it is to become aware of negative feelings when they begin, so that he gains control over the "pathways" they follow, processing what needs to be attended to and letting the rest go after acknowledging it for what it is. Finally, he saw how he could interdict a lifelong pattern of amplifying anxiety by compounding it with interpersonal rejection and isolation. He found that the inevitable disagreements and conflicts that arise needn't drive a wedge between people who love each other.

As anxiety is decreased, the client experiences a sense of inner spaciousness. Scott's image for this was the empty attic with the windows open and the cool breeze flowing through. This experience of inner openness greatly facilitates the flow of unconscious guidance into the conscious mind. There are fewer impediments, and a greater sense of inner attunement results.

Of course, the therapist could instruct the client in these principles or challenge the client to discover them through discussion and exploration of thoughts, feelings, and bodily sensations. But it is better to allow the client to discover them for himself with minimal direction by the therapist. Because the dissociative client can readily enter a meditative state and request internal assistance, doing so minimizes dependence on the therapist, reduces the power differential, and fosters feelings of self-efficacy in the client. Equally important, the guidance offered by the inner wisdom is more valuable than anything the therapist could present. The inner wisdom knows which images will be most meaningful to the client, so a therapeutic economy is achieved. The client receives exactly what he needs, what he is able to utilize at the moment, and nothing more. No external resource can rival the inner wisdom in achieving this exquisite balance.

CHAPTER

Working Through Trauma: Sharing Memories and Internally Challenging the Authority of the Abuser

> Do not be wedded forever
> To fear, yoked eternally
> To brutishness.
>
> —Maya Angelou

This chapter describes and illustrates the core work of the second stage of therapy. It focuses on the treatment needs of the prototypic DID client, the adult survivor of childhood abuse. Although Stage 2 culminates in the joining of the personalities into a harmonious whole, it is helpful to think of the goal of this phase as the restoration of personal power. This goal is achieved by sharing key memories and internally challenging the perceived authority of the abuser(s), thereby further dismantling the dissociative barriers between personalities so that the collective resources of the entire system are fully available to the host. Once the alters are liberated from their state of isolation and disempowerment, the actual joining process occurs spontaneously.

Successful completion of Stage 1 reflects the mobilization of essential resources that help prepare the client to effectively challenge the power of the abuser. As the client enters Stage 2, the personality system has learned to communicate productively and to cooperate in pursuing shared goals. The personalities have learned to trust and support one another. They have experienced co-consciousness. They've witnessed the fruits of their collaboration: less frequent episodes of amnesia and suicidal ideation, decreased internal conflict, better planning for managing the vicissitudes of life, and a greater sense of control. They've come a long way in dismantling the dissociative barriers between themselves.

However, until alters have shared their painful, often terrifying secrets, they are not ready to challenge, in a meditative state, the authority of the abuser. They need to operate from a collective knowledge base before they can prevail in this crucial therapeutic task. In some sense, all the healing work that is done prior to this stage can be understood as preparing the client for the challenge of sharing these secrets. The resources mobilized during Stage 1 prepare the host to tolerate the disclosures and prepare the alters to trust that they can now help more by telling than by continuing to conceal.

☐ The Act of Telling

The act of telling is a crucial step in the healing process, and one that should only be taken with great care. The very disclosure that would overwhelm and destabilize the host if made prematurely can significantly advance the therapeutic process if timed appropriately. The therapist must scrupulously avoid the suggestion that trauma has occurred and that the client is expected to recall trauma or disclose traumatic memories. Once the groundwork has been laid, that is, the goals of Stage 1 have been accomplished, any traumatic material requiring exploration and metabolism will emerge in due time.

Often, but by no means always, the youngest verbal alter spontaneously initiates this phase of treatment by presenting with distress associated with traumatic memories and resulting cognitive distortions. Typically the young alter experiences flashbacks, sometimes described as "bad pictures in my head," the belief that talking about it would be catastrophic, and the conviction that the scary things happened, and are happening, because she is bad and deserving of the abusive treatment. Alters are often unable to distinguish past and present and can derive limited comfort from the therapist's explanation that the event occurred a long time ago. After all, when the young alter is experiencing flashbacks, in some sense she is accurate in insisting, as one young alter did, that "it happens all the time." They typically require a great deal of help in learning to distinguish past from present so that they can stay grounded in the present moment (see chapter 3).

When an alter complains of flashbacks and intrusive memories at this stage of treatment, I suggest she ask the inner wisdom whether or not it's in the best interest of the system ("best for all of you") that she talk to me or the host about what she remembers. Generally, she is guided to talk to me first. Typically, she then expresses fear that something terrible will happen if she tells. Again, I suggest that she consult the inner wisdom. In response, she usually receives inner reassurance that it's safe to tell, as well as an explanation for why she has believed it would be catastrophic to do so. Sometimes the alter is told by the inner wisdom that the perpetrator was acting in self-interest in threatening the alter with the consequences of divulgence. However, there are sometimes other bases for the fear of disclosure. Not uncommonly, there are other alters whose primary or secondary roles are to prevent disclosure. They may do this by a variety of means, such as enforcing a "no crying" or "no telling" rule or by confusing the thought processes of the alters and host so that they doubt the veracity of their recollections. If the strategy of such an alter has not been detected and addressed in Stage 1, it should be addressed here to remove pressure from the alter ambivalent about divulgence. The therapist can address this strategy effectively by empathizing with the alter's desire to safeguard the system and then suggesting that the inner wisdom can show the alter how she has been protective in the past and can be even more protective now by adopting a new strategy. (See chapters 8 and 9 for illustration.)

Even after these obstacles to disclosure are removed, the alter may find it very difficult to put into words the terrible secret she's been concealing all her life. I empathize with how hard this is and may suggest she ask the inner wisdom why she should tell if it's so hard to do so. One young alter was told by the inner wisdom that someday all the bad pictures in her head would go into a big trash can inside her mind and burn up, and that the first step in getting them into the trash can was telling me. The concrete image provided her with hope. After disclosing the abuse to me, the inner wisdom counseled her to tell the host. The host, distressed by the disclosure, had trouble understanding why the alter appeared to be feeling so much better. I suggested she ask the inner wisdom. The reason the alter felt better, the inner wisdom explained, was that the minute she shared her secret, she was no longer alone.

There are many ways an alter can share her memories with the host. They may agree that the host will listen in as the alter reveals the memories to the therapist. Alternatively, the host and alter may meet in the conference room and the disclosure can be made verbally, visually, or tactilely: verbally by telling in words, visually by showing the memories on a screen (either in the conference room or in the theater), or tactilely by touching the palms of the hands. If the latter method (E. W. Flora, personal communication, 1992) is chosen, the host and the alter touch palms, causing the host to know and feel what the alter knows and feels. This is particularly useful when the alter is lacking or limited in language skills or speech production capacity. (Also see chapter 5 for a nontactile, nonverbal approach to the intrasystemic sharing of memories reported by Fine, 1994.) The host can choose among the various options or can consult the inner wisdom about their relative merits.

These methods of disclosure permit the host to control the dose. If the host is listening in while the alter speaks with the therapist, the host can choose to go to her inner room, thereby placing herself out of earshot, should the revelation threaten to overwhelm her. If the alter meets the host inside to share her memories verbally, the host can plan in advance to tell the alter when she's heard all she can handle at that time. If the traumatic scene is transmitted visually on the screen, the controls are used to titrate exposure. In particular, the dial for sensations and emotions can be turned down on initial viewing and gradually turned up, as tolerable, on repeat viewings. If the tactile transmission method is preferred, the host can simply remove her hands from the alter's, as necessary, to prevent emotional overload.

☐ The Pain of Hearing and Knowing

Despite the therapist's best efforts to help the host tolerate the alter's traumatic disclosures—by waiting until the inner wisdom encourages the disclosures and by suggesting techniques for titration—the experience is terribly painful for the host. As the inner wisdom explained to one client, there is no way it can feel okay to know that she has been hurt, especially if she was abused by someone who should have loved and protected her. Although the therapist strives to prevent the client from being overwhelmed, the client cannot be protected from feeling emotional pain and anger. These experiences are crucial to the healing process. Horevitz and Loewenstein (1994) emphasized that, in working with traumatic memories, "therapists should be less concerned with alleviating pain than with creating coping strategies that help the patient maintain personal integrity and purpose in life" (p. 307).

Host personalities vary in their responses to alters' disclosures. The nature of the disclosures, the number of alters and traumatic memories, and the host's coping style all influence the host's responses. It is not unusual for the client to contemplate termination of therapy in the days following transmission of painful memories. Suicidal impulses may be expressed. Suddenly, the host may feel that she simply cannot stand her own consciousness and is desperate to escape it. As always, ensuring the client's safety is the therapist's top priority. If the client is contemplating suicide or termination of therapy, encourage her to consult her inner wisdom about whether these steps are in the best interest of her system. Although hospitalization may be necessary to ensure safety, it can usually be avoided, particularly if more frequent sessions can be scheduled during the crisis.

Denial is common following transmission of traumatic memories. As always, it's important to maintain a stance of supportive neutrality regarding the veracity of memories (see chapter 2). If the client expresses doubt, suggest she consult her inner wisdom. Some clients report that they know intellectually that the traumatic event happened but have a hard time accepting it emotionally. One host announced, in the aftermath of a painful disclosure, that she decided that she was not DID and had no alters. She explained her reasoning: If she didn't have alters, then nothing bad ever happened that would have caused them to be created, and if nothing bad happened, then there was nothing to be angry about. I asked if this formulation solved all her problems. All but one, she explained. The remaining problem was that she must be crazy, she must be a bad person, to have been suicidal so many times when nothing bad had ever happened. Her problems must have been all her fault. Interestingly, it was not this flaw in her reasoning that induced her to abandon it. She was eventually persuaded by her alters, some of whom were furious at her for turning her back on them after all they had done for her.

When I first designed this treatment model, I made the mistake of rushing into the internal confrontation scene as a way of helping the host deal with the stress of absorbing painful memories. Of course, it's important to take as much time as the client needs to face the pain of her own history. It's helpful to ask the client what resources she has to help her cope with the challenges of this stage of therapy. This is far more effective than listing the resources for her. After she's completed her list, she can ask her alters to list additional resources. Finally, the host can ask the inner wisdom to complete the list. Items typically include increased safety in her current life, improved cooperation within the system, specific roles that the alters can play in promoting healing, confidence in the inner wisdom, visions of hope that she can recall and revisit, and external resources, such as family members, friends, and the therapist. Spiritually minded clients typically include in their lists God's ever-present love or the availability of transformative energy in the universe. It can be helpful to ask if any alters are willing to remind the host of these resources, should she forget them. Alters tend to respond enthusiastically to this challenge, thereby boosting the host's confidence that her alters are there to help.

Herman (1997) emphasized the importance of reframing mourning as an act of courage rather than an act of humiliation. As the host struggles with the task of absorbing traumatic memories into her life history and identity, she is empowered by viewing her struggle as courageous rather than humiliating. Similarly, it can be helpful to the alter to reframe the act of telling as an act of courage rather than an act of betrayal. Courage can be defined as following the guidance of the inner wisdom when it's hard to do so. This process of reframing strengthens the client's sense of attunement to the deepest aspect of her inner being, her truest nature.

After the alter does her part by disclosing her distressing secrets, the host must do her part by accepting the alter's experience in order to more fully release the alter from her isolation and despair. The host can ask the inner wisdom how she is to understand the disclosure, whether the memory was historically accurate, and to what extent it may have become blended with other memories or distorted over time. The host can also ask the inner wisdom to show or tell her what role her acceptance plays in the healing of the alter. The therapist can then point out to the host that she has the power to heal this wounded part of her through the act of opening her heart. She has the power to show her alter that she will never be abandoned again. Although it's very difficult to open one's heart to the experiences of terror, helplessness, and humiliation, the host sometimes feels a sense of calm afterwards. One client, at my suggestion, asked her inner wisdom why she felt so calm after listening to an alter's painful disclosure. She was told that she was no longer running away from herself and that the process of denial had been more stressful than she had realized.

After struggling to distance herself emotionally from the painful disclosures of two of her young alters, one host announced that she was slowly starting to accept what they had told her. "I don't know if I'm ready to talk about it yet," she explained, "but I realized that in order to fulfill my dreams, I need to get beyond the denial. . . . It's quite an impediment, to be stuck where I am forever."

☐ The Impact of Internal Confrontation

There are some DID clients whose pathological dissociation was triggered by accidents or natural disasters. For example, I treated one client whose first alter was created after the young host accidentally fell off a raft and was pulled under by a strong wave. In sheer terror, she utilized her innate capacity to dissociate before she was rescued. In metabolizing this type of trauma, the internal confrontation intervention is clearly inappropriate. However, the majority of DID clients were traumatized by abuse and benefit greatly from the opportunity to challenge, in a meditative state, the perceived power of the abuser.

This procedure involves an act of solidarity between the host and the alter who experienced the trauma (referred to here, for purposes of clarity, as "the working alter"). Also participating in this act of solidarity are any other alters who had a role in nurturing the working alter, were involved in some aspect of the trauma, or otherwise feel ready to participate. All alters wishing to participate must, of course, have access to the memory that will form the basis of the confrontation scene.

In introducing this intervention, the therapist reminds the client that she now has resources that were lacking at the time of the traumatic event—a strong alliance within the personality system and experience in utilizing inner guidance—and has thereby created a level playing field for the first time. On this level field she'll have an opportunity to challenge the abuser *inside*, where physical strength and social status do not confer power. I explain that the most profound kind of power is the power of moral authority which flows through the client's inner wisdom, or collective heart.

If the client is unsure whether or not to pursue the internal confrontation, she can request guidance from the inner wisdom. (If she chooses, or the inner wisdom advises, not to confront internally, she can seek guidance regarding an alternative therapeutic step.) If she consents, I explain that she and the participating alters can go to the theater together to watch the beginning of the abusive scene on the screen. At the appropriate time, they can enter the image on the screen together and confront the abuser about the abuse. I state clearly that this intervention does not rewrite history. (See chapter 3 for a discussion of wording the intervention when abuse is uncorroborated.) However, it can demonstrate that the abuser no longer has power over them. While I avoid coaching the client on what to say in confronting the abuser, I remind the client that she is acting on the authority of her inner wisdom. Had the abuser been following inner wisdom, the abuse would not have occurred. Therefore, the client can rise to the challenge of this inner confrontation with confidence that the deck is no longer stacked against her and moral authority is on her side.

Gretchen, a DID client in her 20s, chose to internally confront her great-uncle, who, she recalled, had sexually abused her on a single occasion in early childhood. By the time Gretchen retrieved memories of the abuse (several months before beginning therapy), the great-uncle was deceased. After retrieving the memory, Gretchen inquired and learned that other family members had continuous and recovered memories regarding the great-uncle's predatory sexual behavior toward them. On the basis of a continuous memory, her parents had agreed never to leave the children alone with the great-uncle, but did leave them with him on a single occasion when Gretchen was 5 years old, thinking that they would be safe because there was another adult in the home at the time.

Although, technically speaking, all uncorroborated abuse is alleged abuse, and although all clients reporting recovered memories need to be educated regarding the vagaries of the human memory process, there are certain circumstances under which it is clinically appropriate to evenutally join the client in her acceptance of the memories as historically accurate. Gretchen's case provides an illustration of such circumstances. She accepted my cautionary words about not jumping to conclusions, and made inquiries within the family. She learned of the continuous and recovered memories of others and the decision made by her parents during her early childhood. She arrived at her own conclusion that, although she could never prove that she had been abused, her memory was highly consistent with the pattern that had emerged. Because her great-uncle was deceased and litigation was not at issue, and because Gretchen was fully committed to the recovery process, it was clinically appropriate to support her conclusions and focus on therapeutic progress rather than on the uncorroborated status of her memories.

During the traumatic incident, 5-year-old Gretchen had dissociated, and 5-year-old Melissa had been created to cope with the victimization. When she, too, was overwhelmed, 13-year-old Allison came into being. During the first part of Stage 2, Melissa and Allison shared the terrifying details of the abuse with Gretchen. Gretchen (who had coined the term "collective heart" because she felt "inner wisdom" sounded too intellectual), turned to her collective heart for solace after Melissa's disclosure. Without any prompting from me or Gretchen, the collective heart informed her that the most painful of the memories had already been shared, and that although additional difficult work lay ahead, nothing could compare to the sheer terror of a helpless young child.

After both Melissa and Allison had shared their memories with Gretchen, Gretchen wondered how she could process all the anger that the abuse aroused within her. She asked whether she had to block it out of her consciousness or feel angry all the time, or whether there was a third alternative. I suggested she ask her collective heart for a vision of hope, a vision of how she could go on, given all the anger. She consented, entered a meditative state, and afterwards described her experience as follows: "We were driving a car, but I was filled with light—it was the light from the Tonglen exercises—that then was pouring out the headlights of the car and illuminating what was ahead of me."

Thus encouraged, Melissa and Allison shared their memories with the other alters (all adults), and the system agreed to challenge Uncle Ed internally. Several days after the intervention, 13-year-old Allison wrote the following description of the experience in her journal:

> I think I must have been able to keep my emotion control [dial for emotions and sensations] pretty much just right, because I didn't like seeing that picture or especially sharing it (just of him in there) but I didn't get sick. I'm proud of that. But I knew Gretchen was upset and confused and so I thought she and I needed to take care of him once and for all and so I talked to you and you said we could confront him with the here-and-now resources. And so ... we found some stairs ... that lead right up to the movie screen and we could all walk into the movie (but I had to go first and we had to all hold hands). Then when Uncle Ed saw us all there together *he* got scared. I told him he couldn't hurt me or Gretchen or Dad anymore by the things he had done a long time ago. And I said to him that *he* was the one who was bad and *he* was the one who was dirty. I didn't know if he would know who William and Heather and Emma [adult alters who had not been created at the time of the sexual abuse] were, but he did and he knew he was beat and then his side of the film started to *disintegrate* (Isn't that a neat word? While we're all working to integrate, Uncle Ed and his evil power are starting to disintegrate!!) Then all of the film around us sort of melted like the Wicked Witch of the West and we could all walk off of the screen together. I was very glad to have everyone's help on this and always and I feel even okay with sharing this with Gretchen because we've all been okay this week.

The sharing of memories and the act of confronting the abuser internally lead to a number of dramatic changes within, and between, personalities. The host and the working alter typically report observing major developmental strides following disclosures and internal confrontations. These changes are generally observed in the working alter, but distal effects are sometimes observed. For example, one DID client observed that an infant alter, who previously had only slept and cried, was crawling inside and smiling for the first time after the host listened empathically to the traumatic disclosures of two older child alters and demonstrated to them that she would no longer allow herself to be intimidated by family members. More commonly, the working alter announces that she is older, appears taller inside, learns to write or displays more mature penmanship, or displays some other evidence of increased maturity. For example, shortly after Allison's experience of confronting Uncle Ed internally, she confided in me that she had just had her first menstrual period. Previously, when the host menstruated, Allison was shielded from this aspect of the host's experience. Following the confrontation scene, the increased sharing of consciousness and enhanced self-esteem led to a developmental advance for Allison. Changes of this sort indicate that the alters' development, so long arrested, is starting to proceed. These developmental strides provide the system with evidence that the client has the power to heal, that the host can redeem the alters from a state of exile and stagnation.

While the primary developmental impact of significant healing work may be observed within one alter, the secondary impact on other personalities is not insignificant. For example, Gretchen's alter William, a spiritually minded alter who had always been a protector of Allison, shared his observations of the changes in Allison about ten days after the confrontation scene. "The impact of the solidarity on Allison," he announced joyfully, "was a wonderful thing to behold." The observing alter is not only gratified by the working alter's progress but also encouraged in terms of his own healing potential.

The impact of these developments on the host can be profound. After Allison shared the last of her traumatic memories, Gretchen observed feeling a new sense of intimacy with herself. "I feel," she reported, "more like a person and less like a body."

One very interesting change that often occurs during the second stage of therapy (without any prompting from the therapist) is that the host and working alter, while viewing a traumatic event on the internal screen, see the event happening to the host and not to the alter. The traumatic memory, so long held by the alter, involves the alter's experience of having endured the trauma. It is not until this stage of therapy that both parties observe that the abuse was perpetrated against the host, and that the host's body absorbed it even though the alter's consciousness registered it and retained it. For example, when Gretchen saw the internal film of the sexual abuse that led to Allison's creation, she observed that although these were Allison's memories, the body in the film was the body of a 5-year-old, not the body of a 13-year-old. This was particularly puzzling to Allison, who compared this viewing with a prior experience of viewing an internal film summarizing her therapeutic progress. In that previous experience, Allison had seen herself as a 13-year-old, involved in interactions with the other personalities inside. I helped her to understand the distinction. Earlier she had viewed internal events. Internally, the personalities appear to have separate bodies because the internal world is a sensory manifestation of their psychological reality, including the reality of their separateness as personalities. However, in viewing the traumatic event on the screen, Gretchen and Allison were witnessing an external event, a physical event that occurred during Gretchen's childhood. As an event that occurred in the physical world, Gretchen, and not Allison, was the victim. While it's quite challenging for the client to understand how the alter is the psychological victim and the host is the physical victim, the insight enhances the client's growing understanding of her fundamental unity. The alter is more clearly understood as a part of the client's consciousness who experienced certain events, responded to these events, and recalls these events.

The sharing of memories and the act of confronting the abuser internally lead to another dramatic change within the system. A blurring of boundaries between personalities becomes apparent. For example, Gretchen reported that, as Allison was writing the description of the confrontation scene in her journal, Gretchen was reading along, comparing her own experience with what Allison was recording. This co-consciousness, quite new for Gretchen, was made possible by Allison's disclosures and the act of solidarity. By this time, Allison had very few "mental contents," if you will, that were uniquely her own.

☐ Maintaining an Internal Boundary

Once an alter has shared whatever memories need to be shared and has acted in solidarity with the host, her separateness may cease to serve any useful function, and she may find it increasingly difficult to remain distinct from the host. In many cases, she spontaneously joins the host. However, sometimes an alter needs to remain distinct in order to perform a function for another alter. For example, because of the special relationship between Melissa and Allison, they decided to join Gretchen simultaneously. Melissa had shared all of her painful memories, had learned that she was not to blame for the abuse, and was ready to join. Allison, on the other hand, was retaining a single traumatic memory and could not join until the memory had been shared with Gretchen. As it turns out, Allison had had a key role in Heather's creation. Heather had been created to take over for Allison during a traumatic event that allegedly occurred in Gretchen's adolescence. The single traumatic memory retained by Allison was the portion of the abuse she experienced before Heather came into being. For this reason, Allison could not share her memory until Heather was ready to begin her memory work.

If Allison remained separate because she was holding onto one traumatic memory, what prevented Melissa from joining spontaneously once her painful memories had all been shared? It was not simply the intention to wait for Allison that permitted Melissa to maintain the boundary between her and Gretchen. Melissa discovered that by focusing on any unshared memories, however benign, she could preserve her own distinct identity and forestall the final step of the joining process. The memories she held onto were baking sugar cookies with her mother and rearranging magnetic alphabet letters on the refrigerator when she was learning to form words.

As the time for joining approached, Allison and Melissa spoke of the considerable effort involved in "maintaining a boundary." I emphasize this because it highlights the fact that fusion is not something the therapist initiates or controls. Although the joining process is dramatic, it is really nothing more than the natural consequence of the developments preceding it. When the dismantling of the dissociative barriers is complete, the joining simply occurs.

☐ The Process of Joining

Once Allison and Heather each shared their traumatic memories and Melissa shared her memories of baking cookies and reconfiguring the alphabet letters, it was inevitable that Allison and Melissa would permanently join Gretchen in a state of being "together as one." Allison came out to thank me for all I had done to help her and to say goodby. She remarked that she didn't really need to say goodby, because joining would be more like a "permanent hello," since she would never have to go away again. We planned a joining ritual to be conducted in a meditative state. In an internal sanctuary which they called "base," the seven personalities sat in a circle, holding hands. Gretchen held hands with Allison and Melissa, with Heather holding Allison's other hand and Emma holding Melissa's other hand, and William and Candice completing the circle. Gretchen closed her eyes and focused on breathing in all the gifts that Allison and Melissa held, and when she opened her eyes inside she found that she was holding hands with Heather and Emma. She had absorbed Melissa and Allison.

In due time, Gretchen's four other alters shared their traumatic memories, completed whatever work they needed to do as distinct entities, and joined Gretchen. Whereas Melissa and Allison had chosen to join in session and planned a joining ritual, each of the other four joined Gretchen between sessions. However, the news was never a surprise to me. In each case, Gretchen had experienced almost continual co-consciousness with the alter, and she and I both knew the joining was close at hand.

William was the last to join. He chose, as his day to join, the anniversary of the day when Gretchen had first begun experiencing flashbacks. Each year this particular day had been a time of emotional anguish. As William completed the process of sharing his memories with Gretchen, he decided to join on the anniversary date so that it would no longer be a day of degradation and suffering. It would become, instead, a day of release and transformation. He waited until the anniversary date to share a happy memory that he had been holding onto in order to remain separate. He explained to Gretchen that he planned to use this little trick that he learned from Melissa and Allison. The memory of the family singing around the campfire was his final gift to Gretchen as a separate entity. Finally, they were all together as one.

12
CHAPTER

Together as One:
The Postjoining Process

My mind is a safe place to be now.

—Gretchen

It's easy to assume that Stage 3 will be smooth sailing, now that the alters have joined the host. In fact, the final stage of therapy poses new challenges. Fortunately, the unification of the personality structure means that the collective resources of the system are now more consistently available, so the client is better equipped to face these challenges. Furthermore, these challenges are all anticipated, to varying degrees, during earlier phases of therapy. For example, the therapist encourages the client to articulate, during the first and second stages of therapy, whatever concerns she may have about being together as one. Clients voice many such concerns. What if I miss my alters? What if I need to go away and there's no one to take over for me? What if other people find me boring when it's just me? What if one of the alters was the one my boyfriend actually fell in love with? What if, after all my alters have done for me, I fail them because I'm still not happy or perfect once they've joined me? What if I'm lonely? What if I can't stand how quiet it is inside? These are all valid questions and can be explored in therapy. The inner wisdom can always be consulted for guidance and reassurance.

The complexity of third stage work depends, in large part, on the extent to which the client's progress through the developmental stages of childhood and adolescence has been disrupted by traumatization, dissociation, and multiplicity (see chapter 2). Bryant and Kessler (1991) provided a detailed account of postintegration work with a client whose severe, chronic abuse wreaked havoc on her development. Gretchen (see chapter 11), whose case is used here to illustrate the final phase of the Collective Heart model, is representative of those clients experiencing more limited childhood abuse. Fortunately, Gretchen had a nuclear family in which she was loved and protected. Three of her six alters were formed in the context of a single alleged incident of sexual abuse, and subsequent threats, by her great-uncle in early childhood. Her other three alters were formed during her high school and college years, when, in response to stimuli reminiscent of the earlier abuse, her existing alters became overwhelmed while struggling to shield the host from the memories evoked by these triggers, setting the stage for the creation of new alters. Some of her alters, hungry for love or excitement, became easy prey for abusive and opportunistic males.

☐ Present Orientation

Among the goals of Stage 3 are improved ability to differentiate past and present and increased capacity to stay in the present moment and build a satisfying future. As Gretchen approached the time when her last remaining alter would join her as one, she spoke to the other DID therapy group members, who were all in the first stage of therapy at that time. She described her capacity to differentiate past and present and the difference it made to the quality of her life. This vignette is presented as an illustration of how late second stage work lays the groundwork for the third stage.

> This stage in my life right now is just really spectacular, because I'm in the present more than I have ever, ever been in my entire life. And I can look at the past and I can remember ... but I'm not actually reliving [it]. ... I'm so glad to finally be able to recognize the difference. It's really exciting. ... It used to be like walking into a memory, like walking into that old nightmare, especially during this time of year, particularly painful, but this is the first year that I've ever really ... been so fully in the present that driving down these streets doesn't make me tear up, that just looking at the date doesn't make my stomach tie in knots and make me feel sick. So it's ... very exciting. I do feel sad about some of the stuff that happened in November and December around the holidays in previous years. I can feel very sad about that, and I can cry about it, but it's not going to ruin my holiday; it doesn't ruin where I'm at now, because the here and now is really exciting. I'm a newlywed and we have our first Christmas tree

together. And it's just spectacular, I have to say. It's just a great tree. And we have some really neat friends that we've had a couple of parties with so far to celebrate the holidays. And it's just everything I always wanted the holiday to be ... and it's really exciting to be able to do it for myself, create it for myself.... The biggest difference is not reliving [the traumatic memories]. Knowing it happened and being able to see it for what it was, and know it was *me* that all that stuff happened to, but not to be weighed down by that pain, like a rock in the heart.

A group member, who had not yet been in therapy for a full year, said he had been feeling angry and frustrated with himself because he let things that happened 25 and 30 years ago still affect him. Gretchen responded:

Well, the difference is, at least in my case, and I can't say this is true for you, the difference is that internally, not all of my alters realized that it wasn't 25 or 30 years ago. And that's why you can count on it to continue bothering you—consciously, subconsciously, whatever level you want to talk about it. The pain is real and intense and *there*, because it isn't in the past.... That's why just knowing what the day was on the calendar was enough to send me reeling, you know, right back into this black ball of depression.... It had nothing to do with where I was or what I was doing, but because somebody inside saw the date, and knew what happened on that day, and didn't know the difference between 1995 and 1989, 1990, 1975. They weren't able to distinguish.

The thing is, when you go back to a physical place where something bad has happened, if you're lucky you've got someone you love at your side, to hold your hand and remind you: "Okay, I'm right here with you. I may not have been with you last time when this bad thing happened, but I'm here now." When it's happening inside of you and you're reliving these feelings and these emotions, there's nobody to hold your hand except for your self. And it's your alter's hand you're holding, or another one of your alters may be holding another alter's hand. But, in the end, it's so empowering to realize that what can take place on the external, physical level can take place internally, too. That you've got the power and the resources to make these connections and hold your own hand.... You can ground yourself. And that, in the end, is so empowering. And every time you do it, you have to delight in that. Because that's what you're doing for yourself, and if you can't stand up for yourself in an outside relationship, if you can't stand up for yourself in the workplace or with your parents or spouse [group members had expressed difficulty doing these things], at least, when your insides are going through that crap, you can say "Whoa! Get it together. This is the here and now," and once you walk through that just one time successfully, and then twice, and then three times, even if it keeps on happening, even if you keep going back to that same spot, the ability to ground yourself each and every time is really something to delight in. I mean, that's a great gift you're giving yourself.

A group member expressed surprise that Gretchen could view this process so positively, because he considered it a personal flaw that he needed to ground himself. Gretchen explained:

> I'm lucky because I'm a little bit further along. And I can tell you this now: It's the pits when you're in the middle of it. We naturally train ourselves, others have trained us, to feel down about the things we just have to do to get by. But grounding yourself to get by, and get past a moment, is a lot better way than lashing out, or going for a pill or a knife, if that was ever your tendency. I mean, we have a lot of ways of coping, going for a drink, you know, just switching, just blocking the whole thing out, and every time you don't have to do that, it's a success. It's a success. And people may try to tell you otherwise, but they've never lived it. They just have no way of knowing.

☐ Increased Capacity to Handle Environmental and Internal Stress Adaptively

Due to stimulus generalization, traumatized individuals respond with hyperarousal not only to sensory stimuli associated with the trauma but also to intense, nonthreatening stimuli (van der Kolk, 1996). In the hyperaroused state, the individual is unable to make a realistic appraisal of current environmental threat and therefore cannot determine adaptive response options. The Collective Heart model addresses this difficulty early in therapy, helping the client recognize that deep within herself she has the wisdom to evaluate threats, compare a variety of response options, and select the approach most likely to ensure safety and promote growth. Although capacity to modulate affect and increased reliance on nondissociative defenses develop throughout the course of therapy, important strides are made during Stage 3, when the client's emotional and cognitive resources are integrated.

The case material presented below not only illustrates Gretchen's increased capacity to handle stress and respond to affective challenges but also reflects her progress toward attaining several other goals of the final stage of therapy: resolution of maladaptive cognitive and behavioral patterns, development of a sense of identity as a unified whole, and redirection of energy into personal, interpersonal, occupational, and spiritual growth. It also reflects her capacity to work independently and her associated preparation for termination.

By the time Gretchen's alters had all joined her as one, she was attending an individual and a DID group therapy session every other week. Nine months later, due to illness, she canceled her sessions. When she returned after a 4-week interval, she reported a major therapeutic passage that she had navigated independently: She had experienced her first depression since she was fully integrated. In her individual session, she described the process in detail. Initially, Gretchen had tried to talk herself out of the depression, telling herself that all her alters had joined her, there was no reason to be depressed, and that she didn't really have a right to be depressed. When the depression failed to lift, the appetite and sleep disturbance continued, and she found it harder and harder to get out of the bed in the morning, she knew she needed to consult her collective heart. At home, she entered a meditative state to ask inside why she was feeling so depressed. Her collective heart told her that there were several reasons for her depression: hormonal changes associated with her monthly cycle and anxiety about the physical health status of two loved ones. In addition, she learned that her recent completion of a long-term art project, which had engaged her and nourished her self-esteem, left a void in her life. She knew instinctively that she had obtained as much information as she needed during that meditative session and chose not to request assistance with resolving the depression. During the week that followed, she felt increased self-acceptance, knowing that there were, in fact, valid reasons to feel down. Her depression was no longer compounded by guilt and shame. She was able to reflect on her depression, comparing it with previous depressions, and observing that this time she had no suicidal thoughts. She described this depression as follows:

> I won't say it was debilitating, because I've been debilitated before. I know what that is, and this was by no means that bad. . . . To be able to go inside and get some answers sort of helped overcome that feeling of frustration and . . . lift me somewhat out of the depression by the feeling of competency: I know how to utilize my resources. I've got a start. I can take care of this. My husband . . . was right there with "Oh, my God. Why is she depressed? What is this about? What do I have to do? Do you need to go see Sarah?" And I was like "No, I mean, if I need to, I'll tell you. But I'm okay right now. I'm not feeling self-destructive or anything. I just need to work my way out of this. And it may take some time." And I did say that to him. I said it may not be overnight.

Gretchen reported that, by the following week, she felt ready to consult her collective heart about steps she could take to resolve her depression.

> I had to go down [inside] to figure out: Why am I not moving past this? What do I need to do to get beyond it? And one of the things I was told was that I need to stop filling my head with so much garbage, and by that it was meant . . . trash television, or trash novels, or trash music, but instead fill my life in those times with stuff that's more meaningful. And another thing that I was told was that I need to think about a comfortable way for me to start going back to church more regularly.

Gretchen continued her narrative about how she had handled her depression without my assistance. Later in the week, while in a normal state of consciousness, she had been struck by an additional precipitant of her depression. She realized that she needed to address some painful feelings she was experiencing at work. A coworker, with whom Gretchen had formed a close friendship, announced plans to resign and leave the company. Gretchen described how she had realized that her tendency to react impulsively reflected a maladaptive behavioral pattern she inherited when Heather joined her:

> When I feel I'm being abandoned, or what have you, then my inclination is to pick a fight before they can abandon me . . . so I've been trying very hard with Danielle to deal with her leaving the company in a more adult fashion. Which has been hard. I actually started to pick a fight with her . . . and then I . . . was so glad that I recognized . . . with the Heather-part of me, I knew exactly how I could hurt her the worst, and I didn't want to do that, but I could feel . . . that part of me that knew exactly how to go about it, so I was really struggling. So finally I called her at work and I said "Look, we need to talk this out." We talked, and *she* didn't realize how significant it was for me to talk with her like I was, but I knew as *I* was doing it. And in the beginning, like the first 5 minutes, I fiddled-faddled around . . . and then finally I was like "Okay, look, I've just got to be honest with you. This is how I'm feeling. This is what I'm going through." I told her: "Everyone else in the office just sees you once or twice a month, when we do these social things. You and I, we see each other every single day . . . this is going to be extremely hard on me. I've relied on you a lot here at the office, and I'm gonna miss you. And I have a great fear that when you leave, our relationship is going to be relegated to the once-or-twice-a-month kind of category." Now . . . I feel good, but at the time I felt awful, because, you know, it's that feeling of making yourself vulnerable. . . . Instead of getting angry, I'm allowing myself to feel the fear and the sadness, and that's hard. That's really hard. So that's where I'm at right now. And that's kind of what this depression is about. So that made sense.

I expressed enthusiastic support for the important healing work that Gretchen was conducting independently and asked whether she understood how her fear of abandonment was associated with the abuse. She had grasped the connection. Her great-uncle had enforced her silence by threatening her that, if she told her parents what had happened, they would get a divorce, she would lose her family, and there would be nobody to care for her. What she hadn't yet grasped on a deep, experiential level was that her great-uncle had invented her vulnerability to abandonment by her parents. I explained:

> It's important to remember that your great-uncle made all that up. . . . He invented all that, because you were in no danger of being abandoned by

your parents. He knew that. But he also knew he could prey on your fears, he could manipulate you by telling you the worst thing that a child could hear, as a way to keep you silent.

She listened intently as I spoke, and then responded:

I'm so glad you said that. . . . What you said just struck a chord in me, and that was when you said he made it up. . . . That really strikes a chord. That really gives me something to think about . . . because if he made that up, then all the other garbage that came out of his mouth, he was probably just making that up, too, right? . . . About me being a bad girl. . . . There's a part of me that still fears that that's true. I mean, it's that head-heart connection, you know. While my head knows, oh, that's just garbage, and that was a dirty old man saying something to keep me quiet, there's that little piece of me inside that is still healing, that still fears that he knew something that no one else does, when in reality, yeah, he did know something that everyone else didn't know, but it was that he was a filthy old man, and he was doing damage to some other people.

We spoke of the obvious healing work that remained to be done. She concluded:

It takes this reiteration. It's like trying to teach a child, you know, a new concept. And it is, it's a whole new concept. . . . It just has to be reiterated and reiterated and reiterated. And it just takes keeping going back to the collective heart, the piece of the cup that's not shattered, the part of the chalice that's never been broken. And you just have to keep going back down to that, to get that reassurance.

Gretchen found a number of ways to get that reassurance. She spoke with loved ones with increasing openness. She checked in with her collective heart. She also realized, during her third stage of therapy, that she had been "waking up in prayer" each morning. I asked how long this had been happening. "Now that you mention it," she responded, "ever since William joined me."

☐ Resolution of Anger and Grief

A major task of the final stage of therapy is the processing of anger and loss. The complexity of this task depends, in any given therapy, on the extent and nature of the abuse, the extent of the damage that has been done, and the extent to which the feelings have been acknowledged and worked through in previous stages of therapy. Regardless of the attention to these issues earlier in therapy, however, additional work must be done by the client during the third stage. This is because the trauma is an important part of her history and is therefore an integral part of the new identity she is forming as one whole person.

A crucial dimension of the resolution of anger and loss is the capacity to feel pain without feeling worthless and hopeless (see chapter 8). When mourning is reframed as an act of courage rather than an act of humiliation, self-esteem is enhanced (Herman, 1997). Although the descent into mourning has been described as a second stage task, additional work on both self-perceptions and processing of painful emotions is essential.

The final phase of therapy also provides an opportunity for the client to work her way through anger and grief unrelated to her traumatization. She may need to resolve other losses that have been experienced primarily by an alter, or experienced differently by the host and the alters, such as the death of a family member, friend, or pet. Part of the solidarity of the integrated personality system is the capacity to experience and metabolize, as one whole person, the life events that have affected various members of the system in diverse ways. Exploring responses to a variety of losses naturally helps the client prepare for the final challenge of therapy, the act of saying goodby to the therapy and the therapist.

☐ Termination of Therapy

Expressing and resolving feelings regarding termination is a complex task for both the client and the therapist. There are several features of the therapy that can make it somewhat easier. Obviously, when abandonment and loss have been explored adequately in other contexts, the client has an increased appreciation of her ability to tolerate leave-taking without loss of self-esteem. Similarly, when, throughout the therapy, feelings have been accepted with compassion, the client has learned that articulation of ambivalent or painful feelings is valuable. In addition, decreased frequency of sessions during the final months of therapy permits greater recognition of the client's capacity to proceed independently with her therapeutic work. Inherent in the Collective Heart model is the assumption that we all have ongoing healing and growth work to do throughout the life span, and we don't necessarily need to be in therapy in order to accomplish it. Therapy helps the client to remove the impediments and mobilize the resources so that the process of restoration, renewal, and self-actualization can proceed naturally.

The Collective Heart model encourages a strong collaborative alliance, rather than intense dependency, between therapist and client. The client benefits from consistent attention to minimizing the power differential inherent in the therapeutic relationship. The therapist can continue to

attend to this dimension of the therapy as the client approaches termination, by letting her know how much the therapist has learned from
the client and from the therapy process. As the case illustrations make
abundantly clear, working with these clients is a fascinating experience.
The client knows the therapist is sincere in conveying what an honor it
has been to join the client in such important, creative work. When I described the nature of the therapeutic relationship, I emphasized mutual
trust and respect. In the end, there is also mutual gratitude.

Current Status of the Collective Heart Treatment Model

The case material presented in the preceding chapters is intended not only to illustrate the Collective Heart treatment model, but also to provide a basis for preliminary evaluation of its efficacy. At this stage in model implementation, formal evaluation is not yet possible. There are several reasons for this. First, I am the only clinician who has utilized the model to date. Second, it has been used with a small number of clients who are not fully representative of the DID population. Finally, there are far too many uncontrolled variables to draw any reliable conclusions regarding the model's efficacy. Before empirical assessment is possible, however, the fairly consistent anecdotal evidence permits preliminary, qualitative evaluation to determine whether the model shows promise and whether it appears to carry excessive risk.

Continued implementation of new psychotherapy techniques typically proceeds on the basis of preliminary findings derived from anecdotal observations of this sort. Empirical assessment of new models comes much later. Clinical judgment of the risk-benefit ratio and similarity to established, accepted modalities guides decisions regarding continued implementation. Therefore, the limitations of anecdotal data notwithstanding, we can tentatively explore the following on the basis of the observations presented in this volume:

• To what extent is the model in compliance with the current standards of care?

- To what extent is the model innovative?
- What is the preliminary evidence supporting the fundamental assumptions of the model?
- What is the preliminary evidence supporting the efficacy of the model?

☐ Characteristics of the Clinical Series

Before addressing these four evaluative questions, we turn our attention to demographic and other characteristics of the clinical series on which the anecdotal observations are based. Although I have assessed and/or treated dozens of DID clients, these observations are drawn from the 12 dissociative clients I've treated since 1993, when I developed the Collective Heart treatment model. (In addition to these 12, there was one additional client who, with her regular therapist, sought my consultation for several sessions before deciding to seek psychotherapy from the psychiatrist who had been treating her psychopharmacologically. She is not included in this preliminary evaluation.)

Of the 12 clients constituting the clinical series, I diagnosed 10 DID and 2 DDNOS clients. Both DDNOS clients had alters as distinct as alters in DID, but in both cases the hosts experienced co-consciousness for the behaviors and emotional responses of their alters, did not experience amnestic episodes, and did not, therefore, satisfy the *DSM-IV* (American Psychiatric Association, 1994) criteria for DID.

Of the 12 clients, 9 (75%) were female and 3 (25%) were male; 10 (83%) were Caucasian, 1 (8%) was African American, and 1 (8%) was Asian American; 9 (75%) were heterosexual and 3 (25%) were gay/lesbian/bisexual. In terms of highest educational level achieved, 1 (8%) had earned a GED, 3 (25%) were high school graduates, 1 (8%) had a bachelor's degree, 2 (17%) had postbaccalaureate professional degrees, 1 (8%) had a doctoral degree, 1 (8%) was a college student, 1 (8%) was a graduate student, 1 (8%) completed a bachelor's degree while in therapy, and 1 (8%) completed a master's degree while in therapy. On the basis of these demographics, it is apparent that racial minorities are underrepresented in this clinical series and that males, more highly educated clients, and gays/lesbians/bisexuals are somewhat overrepresented.

In addition, the majority of these clients had relatively small personality systems: 2 (17%) had 1 alter, 1 (8%) had 2 alters, 4 (33%) had 3 alters, 2 (17%) had 5 to 7 alters, 2 (17%) had more than two dozen alters, and 1 (8%) terminated therapy after 12 sessions, before an accurate appraisal of the size of her personality system could be conducted. (She identified at least 10 alters on the basis of previous therapeutic exploration.) Because only 2 clients (17%) with more than 7 alters remained in treatment, complex DID cases are clearly underrepresented in this clinical series.

In terms of the marital status of the 12 clients, 3 (25%) were single, 2 (17%) were divorced, 5 (42%) were married, 1 (8%) was living with a long-term partner, and 1(8%) married while in therapy. None were remarried or widowed.

In terms of employment status, 5 (42%) were employed full-time, 2 (17%) were full-time students, 1 (8%) was a homemaker who began working part-time while in therapy, 1 (8%) had taken a disability leave from work due to her psychiatric symptoms and soon arranged full-time employment, and 3 (25%) were receiving social security disability insurance upon seeking therapy. (Of the 3 clients receiving disability income, 1 obtained full-time employment and relinquished her disability benefits while in therapy, 1 decided to return to school while in treatment, and 1 began part-time employment while in therapy and was making progress toward self-support at this writing.)

Most clients had struggled with suicidality. Of the 12 clients, 9 (75%) presented with suicidal ideation or had a prior history of at least moderate suicidal ideation. Seven (58%) had a prior history of attempting suicide or displaying suicidal behavior serious enough to alarm others. Six (50%) had a prior history of psychiatric hospitalization. In addition, 1 client (8%) avoided admission following treatment in the emergency room because he was able to convince the staff that his suicidal drug overdoses were accidental.

All 12 clients reported early childhood trauma. The nature of the reported initial trauma was as follows: sexual abuse in 7 cases (58%), physical and emotional abuse in 2 cases (17%), witnessing domestic violence in 1 case (8%), accidental trauma in 1 case (8%), and gross negligence and abandonment in 1 case (8%). One of the clients (8%) reporting early sexual abuse also reported childhood ritual abuse. Although only 58% of the clients reported that the initial trauma was sexual, an additional 3 clients (25%) reported a subsequent history of sexual abuse. Therefore, only 2 clients (17%) did not report having been sexually abused at some point in their lives.

In 10 of the 12 cases (83%), at least some corroboration was obtained. The nature of the corroboration ranged from the perpetrator's admission with apology in 3 cases (25%), report of witnesses in 4 cases (33%), and medical or legal documentation in 3 cases (25%). In the 2 cases (17%) where corroboration was not obtained, no efforts had been made to obtain it. In 4 cases (33%), the alleged perpetrator was deceased by the time our therapy began.

Overall, more stable clients, with smaller and less chaotic personality systems, were overrepresented in this clinical series. These clients tended to be fairly stable relative to the general DID population in terms of capacity to maintain employment and marriage or partnership, and to avoid psychiatric hospitalization. Although there are many DID clients who function fairly well and are able to mask their multiplicity quite effectively, ideally even anecdotal observations such as these should be drawn from treatment of a more balanced pool of higher and lower functioning clients.

☐ Preliminary Evaluation of the Model

Compliance with the Standards of Care

This model conforms to the three-phase approach to treating clients with posttraumatic and dissociative symptoms which has received wide support in recent years. The early attention to symptom reduction, improved daily functioning, and increased capacity for self-protection and sound decision making are all consonant with the phase-oriented approach. Consistent with the professional consensus, the Collective Heart model avoids the suggestion that the client is likely to have been a victim of childhood abuse and should attempt to recall abuse in order to progress therapeutically. It avoids premature and excessive attention to trauma, focusing instead on mobilizing coping resources and developing ego strength. It avoids confronting the client and attacking existing defenses, instead accepting dissociation and denial as responses to overwhelming experiences and framing resistance or hesitation as self-protective. It does not encourage the client to confront the alleged perpetrator or initiate litigation. It avoids body work. Consistent with the consensual standards of care, this approach is characterized by caution, restraint, and respect.

The Collective Heart model is consistent with Kluft's (1993c) 12 ground rules, and is in compliance with the ISSD *Guidelines for Treating Dissociative Identity Disorder (Multiple Personality Disorder) in Adults (1994)*. Although the ISSD guidelines include a statement that the "minimum recommended frequency of sessions for the average DID patient with a therapist of average skill and experience is twice a week" (p. 4), they do allow for less frequent sessions for "patients of high motivation and strength" (p. 4). Typically, I see clients presenting complex cases twice a week, with once a week as the mode for less complex cases. As described in chapters 8 and 12, some clients are seen only once every other week, with frequency decreasing further during the third stage, as these clients are able to maintain stability and make significant progress independently between sessions.

In an effort to further evaluate whether this treatment model is in full compliance with the standards of care, I raise three concerns that a cautious reader might consider.

1. *Does this approach actually avoid the hazards associated with hypnosis where recovered memories are at issue?* Although I report the use of the self-induced meditative state rather than the formal hypnotic trance state, one could argue that I'm merely calling hypnosis by another name to avoid the reservations that have been expressed regarding hypnosis (clinically and legally). Similarities between the self-induced meditative state and the heterohypnotic state with regard to memory distortion and erroneous inflation of confidence in the veracity of memories have not, to date, been explored empirically. However, there are several distinctions between this type of meditative work and formal hypnosis that are crucial to our preliminary evaluation of risk.

One important distinction is that I don't use the meditative state for purposes of memory retrieval. It may be during a meditative state that the inner wisdom guides an alter to share memories with the host or guides the host to start to listen more attentively to a given alter, but the memories are continuous on the part of the alter who holds them. Although the alter may choose to share the memory with the host or other alters by means of meditative techniques described in chapter 11, the alter chooses the means of conveyance while in a normal state of consciousness.

Similarly, I don't generally use the meditative state for purposes of age-regression. The only age-regressive intervention I use is the inner challenging of the apparent authority of the abuser (see chapter 11), which I describe to the client as nonhistorical. That is, I tell the client she is not rewriting history but has an opportunity to bring her current collective resources to bear on her memory of an overwhelming experience that had produced a distorted self-image, thereby dismantling the distortion. Because the client has continual awareness of her current resources throughout this intervention, it is only age-regressive in a limited sense.

Another important distinction is that this approach avoids the amplification of the power differential between the therapist and the client that can occur with hypnosis. Spanos (1996), in describing the components of the hypnotic situation, wrote:

> Standard hypnotic induction procedures include interrelated suggestions that the subject is becoming relaxed, going to sleep, and entering a hypnotic state. Furthermore, these suggestions are usually phrased in such a way that it is implied that the suggested events are happening to the subject rather than initiated by the subject (e.g., "you are drifting deeper and deeper asleep"). (p. 20)

My approach contrasts sharply with this traditional hypnotic induction approach. I describe all imagery to the client before she decides whether or not to enter the meditative state. For example, the inner structures, such as the conference room and the theater, are described as mechanisms that can foster specific kinds of therapeutic progress. The client provides or declines informed consent while in a normal state of consciousness. By avoiding telling the client what she sees, hears, or feels while she is "inside," the therapist avoids a stance of authority, thereby minimizing contamination of the client's experience. Furthermore, I use therapist-guided imagery (after describing it to the client and obtaining consent) only for purposes of relaxation early in the treatment process, before the client has learned to enter the meditative state independently.

My general approach to meditative work is to interfere as little as possible. As has been seen, some clients prefer to provide a running description of their meditative experiences, while most tell me what they learned after emerging from the meditative state. If I'm inclined to offer a suggestion while they are inside, I typically ask, "May I make a suggestion?" This approach emphasizes that the client is always in control and I am only there to assist her.

These dissimilarities between hypnosis and meditation notwithstanding, it is essential to reiterate that no DID treatment is free of hypnotic elements. This is such a trance-prone population that clients should be assumed to enter trance states frequently even when formal hypnotic induction is avoided (ISSD, 1994). The question is whether some of the risks of hypnosis can be avoided by eliminating formal hypnosis from treatment. This is an empirical question that has yet to be addressed. On the basis of these anecdotal observations, I feel that, by using the auto-hypnotic or meditative techniques described here in the context of the therapeutic relationship described in chapter 6, we may be able to avoid some of the risks associated with the use of hypnosis with this particular treatment population.

However, because complex cases are underrepresented in this clinical series, the possibility remains that this model may be inadequate for treating difficult cases and that formal hypnotic interventions may be necessary for bringing about acceptable clinical outcomes with these individuals. It is hoped that even in these cases, the model offered here would complement the more traditional procedures.

We turn now to the second concern that might be raised regarding the extent to which this model is in compliance with the standards of care.

2. *Is this model suggestive?* It certainly is. As discussed in the preface, all therapy is suggestive. The therapist commonly suggests that the client's needs are worthy of attention, that there is a basis for hope, that the client has untapped resources with which to promote healing, and so

forth. The important thing is that the therapist take responsibility for what is suggested. In presenting this model, every effort has been made to take responsibility for what I suggest and to avoid countertherapeutic suggestions that encourage pathological responses, such as pseudomemory production, regression, and excessive dependency.

My belief is that this method, by training the client to trust herself, actually decreases her susceptibility to external suggestion. Again, there is no empirical support for this belief. There is, however, an interesting anecdotal observation supporting this speculation. Once, in one of my DID group therapy sessions, a client was describing her experience as the time approached for an alter to join her as one. The host reported that, when she saw her alter inside, the alter appeared to be growing translucent. Although I said nothing, I wondered what impact, if any, her disclosure would have on other group members. Because I had never heard a client describe the imminent fusion in this way, I felt that if a group member later reported similar experiences, it could be attributed to the influence of suggestion. Interestingly, it did not affect the subsequent joining experiences of other clients in the group. Many alters have joined since that time, and none of them signaled their evolution through translucency.

3. *Is this approach overly endorsing?* While it is not overly endorsing of the veracity of memories, one might argue that it is overly endorsing of the guidance of the inner wisdom. There are two important points here. One is that, although the inner wisdom is introduced as a source of reliable guidance (an endorsing statement), the client is always encouraged to evaluate the guidance received, considering whether it is helpful, whether it seems accurate given the client's past experience, and so forth. If the client doesn't understand the guidance or doesn't accept it, I suggest that she challenge the inner wisdom with her reservations. The other important point is that the therapist is cautioned never to make clinical decisions on the basis of the inner guidance alone. For example, in handling a suicidal crisis, the therapist is cautioned to make a decision regarding hospitalization based on sound clinical judgment (see chapter 6). By the same token, the therapist is advised to discourage a client from taking any action advocated by the inner wisdom if it appears to be countertherapeutic. Although this type of dilemma is rarely encountered, the therapist must be prepared to explore further any guidance that challenges clinical judgment, such as quitting a job precipitously, confronting an alleged abuser, entering into a hasty marriage, and so forth. Should the client report receiving inner guidance that appears risky or unsound, she should be encouraged to ask the inner wisdom to help her understand the counsel in light of her own, or the therapist's, skepticism.

To What Extent Is the Model Innovative?

If this treatment model is a three-phase model in compliance with the emerging professional consensus, to what extent does it involve novel and distinctive elements? I explore this issue from both a theoretical and a procedural standpoint. The theoretical consideration is whether or not the notion of the inner wisdom of the unconscious mind is novel, and the procedural considerations are whether specific interventions are original.

The Concept of the Inner Wisdom

Consider the following descriptions of the benefits of mindfulness meditation:

> We learn to be aware of our fears and our pain, yet at the same time stabilized and empowered by a connection to something deeper within ourselves, a discerning wisdom that helps to penetrate and transcend the fear and the pain, and to discover some peace and hope within our situation *as it is*. (Kabat-Zinn, 1990, p. 29)

Kabat-Zinn (1990) elaborated:

> When you touch base in any moment with that part of your mind that is calm and stable, your perspective immediately changes. You can see things more clearly and act from inner balance rather than being tossed about by the agitations of your mind. (p. 53)

The concept of a powerful inner wisdom is by no means an original contribution. Diverse psychological, spiritual, and philosophical traditions acknowledge, by many different names, the inner resource, representing the individual's true nature, that can guide him or her to right action and psychological and/or spiritual health. In the mystical Jewish tradition of Kabbalah, the subconscious mind is considered closer to the Divine Infinite than are the intellect, emotions, and body (Wolf, 1999). Certainly Puységur (see chapter 1) found, over 200 years ago, that some mesmerized subjects tapped into valuable inner guidance not ordinarily available to consciousness.

In psychology and psychiatry, this inner authority or guide is apparent in the Jungian archetypes of The Wise Old Man and the Magna Mater (Jung, 1959), Hilgard's (1994) "hidden observer" (one can only wonder what Hilgard would have found if he had asked the hidden observer to do more than observe), Allison's (1974) Inner Self-Helper (ISH) (see chapter 2), and the Self of the Internal Family Systems model (Goulding

& Schwartz, 1995). Putnam (1989) pointed out the relationship between the ISH and a construct more widely recognized by therapists treating nondissociative clients, that of the observing ego function:

> The principle embodied in the ISH is that at some level the patient has an observing ego function that can comment accurately on the ongoing processes and provide advice and suggestions as to how to aid the rest of the patient in achieving some insight and control over his or her pathology. One can often find this type of function in non-MPD patients as well as in one's own self. (p. 204)

Although my notion of the inner wisdom of the unconscious mind is similar to these various psychological constructs, there are certain distinguishing characteristics. In particular, I contrast it with the ISH (Allison, 1974) and its apparent derivative, the Self of the Inner Family Systems model (Goulding & Schwartz, 1995). While the inner wisdom, the ISH, and the Self are presumably all manifestations of the same inner resource, conceptually and procedurally they are somewhat different.

Although Allison and Schwartz (1998) stated explicitly that the ISH is an entity—the "Essence" of the person, rather than an alter—most clinicians and researchers have conceptualized the ISH as an alter personality. The ISH is generally understood as a higher order alter with spiritual qualities and extensive knowledge regarding the rest of the alters, while the inner wisdom is understood as transcending and subsuming the personality system. The inner wisdom is not one of the alters, but the foundation upon which the entire personality system rests. I feel that this theoretical distinction is clinically relevant, because it provides a seamless mechanism by which the client's identity fragmentation and underlying unity are simultaneously acknowledged. It also avoids the appearance of favoring the contributions of one alter over the contributions of the others.

It is obvious that the inner wisdom is closer to Allison's (1974) original conceptualization of the ISH than it is to the modifications of the ISH concept offered by other contributors to the professional literature. However, the inner wisdom and Allison's ISH are rather distinct with regard to affect. Allison stated: "The ISH lacks emotion; it answers questions and communicates in the manner of a computer repeating information" (p. 122). My clients have reported that the inner wisdom is experienced as a warm, compassionate presence. One client reported that while she experienced suicidal impulses, her inner wisdom was "pleading with [her] to hang on." This description is certainly at odds with Allison's experience of a dispassionate ISH.

The inner wisdom and the ISH can also be contrasted procedurally. While Allison (1974) consulted the ISH himself, I never speak directly with the inner wisdom. With the Collective Heart model, the client's capacity to access inner guidance is emphasized from the outset. The host and alters all learn to seek inner guidance as desired. Although this assumption hasn't been tested empirically, it appears likely that my approach fosters greater independence, self-confidence, and therapeutic progress between sessions. Another possible advantage of my approach is that, because the inner wisdom provides visual guidance as well as verbal counsel, reliance on the therapist's consultation with the inner wisdom would result in the loss of the valuable visual data. It will be recalled that it is the visual guidance that allows the client to easily amplify the emotional component of the experience via the dial, thereby assisting the client in selecting the most rewarding course of action and modifying unhealthy behavior.

Finally, the nature of the guidance of the ISH and the inner wisdom can be, at times, quite discrepant. For example, Allison (1974) reported that his patient's ISH counsels the host to rid herself of a troublesome alter, as follows: "Betsy . . . is just one piece of you . . . a completely bad piece, and we're going to get rid of it" (p. 22). The ISH elaborates:

> I'm going to be with you and if you can just try to think strong thoughts and hate the kind of person that Betsy is and the things that Betsy has made us do, hate all that she stands for, which is the Devil itself. Hate it all and then you and I become one and be one solid person, solid in every way. (p. 23)

The inner wisdom, in contrast, recognizes the potential contributions of each member of the system as valuable to the eventual harmonious functioning of the client. Of course, one could argue that the distinction derives from individual or therapist variables, rather than theoretical distinctions between Allison's model and my own. It certainly is possible that my clients report the inner wisdom's valuation of each alter because I have suggested that the inner wisdom will provide guidance regarding what's best for all concerned in the long run and because I have shared my belief that even apparently threatening behavior on the part of alters is fundamentally protective. This is not intended to imply that the guidance of the inner wisdom is determined by the therapist's suggestions, or that the therapist manipulates the inner wisdom. Rather, the inner wisdom is wise about many things, including the resources the therapist can offer the client, and the inner wisdom wants to form a partnership with the therapist, if possible. My belief is that the more the therapist acts in accordance with what is best for the client in the long run, the more powerful will be the collaboration between the therapist and the client's inner wisdom, and the more useful will be the inner wisdom's visual and verbal guidance.

One of Allison's (1974) names for the ISH is the Self. The Internal Family Systems model (Goulding & Schwartz, 1995), which construes the various personalities as members of an internal family, involves a notion of the Self that is similar to the Collective Heart model's inner wisdom. Goulding and Schwartz (1995) described the Self as follows: "In addition to the parts, people contain a 'self', an innate core of the psyche that differs significantly from parts due to its meta-perspective and its many leadership qualities, like compassion, curiosity, and courage" (pp. 11–12). This Self is similar to the construct of inner wisdom not only in that both reflect a transcendence of the personality system, but also in that both provide an ever-available and ever-nurturing inner source, freeing the client from dependence on others to inform her self-esteem. Goulding and Schwartz (1995) explained:

> The good parent/bad child sequence ... changes when the survivor's parts believe that she does not *need* the abuser to love her or take care of her, because she now has access to her Self, and her Self will ensure her safety and ensure that she will receive the love and support that all people need. (pp. 287–288)

The Internal Family Systems and Collective Heart models differ theoretically in two important ways. The first distinction is that, while in the Collective Heart model the inner wisdom guides the personality system to reunify the personality system fragmented by trauma, in the Internal Family Systems model multiplicity is viewed as normative. All people are seen as having parts, but the parts become more extreme and polarized and the Self becomes obscured, in response to trauma. When the Self resumes its rightful authoritative role, the system's functioning is more balanced and harmonious, although, in contrast with the Collective Heart approach, the system is considered healthiest when the parts remain distinct. The second distinction is that the Self guides the other parts by assuming a leadership role. One client's Self addressed the parts as follows: "It's true that some parts are very wise, but I am the one who ultimately makes final decisions, although those decisions will be made with as much input from you as possible" (Goulding & Schwartz, 1995, p. 90). In the Collective Heart model, the roles are reversed: The inner wisdom provides input, but decision making is the responsibility of the personality system.

Procedural Considerations

We now explore the extent to which the Collective Heart model involves original therapeutic techniques. The use of meditation in psychotherapy is by no means an original contribution. Meditative techniques have been incorporated into the practice of psychotherapy for some time, with an increasing number of publications appearing in this area in recent years. Neither is the use of the future perspective original. As discussed in chapter 5, Fine (1994) mentioned utilizing a future orientation in her work with dissociative patients. The Solution-Focused Therapy model (de Shazer et al., 1986) draws on Milton Erickson's practice of having the client consult, while in a trance state, a vision of future success to establish a map for therapeutic work. Specific techniques derived from Ericksonian hypnosis include Dolan's (1991) healing letters, either addressed to the internal "Older, Wiser Self," who then responds with nurturing guidance to the client in her current state, or written from the perspective of a successful future, as in the "Letter From the Future" (Capacchione, 1979, cited in Dolan, 1991). Both techniques take advantage of the client's capacity to tap unconscious resources by visualizing a desired state, articulating it, and then using it to determine a series of steps the client can take toward actualizing it.

Similarly, the use of screen techniques is not an original contribution. A brief history of screen techniques is found in chapter 5. What is new here is the combination of these three techniques that appear individually in the professional literature: the incorporation of meditation into psychotherapy, the articulation of a positive future state as a guide to therapeutic progress, and visualization techniques for dissociative clients utilizing an internal screen. In addition, this model enhances the dial on the internal remote control (see chapter 5), previously used to reduce or eliminate physical and emotional responses to internal visual stimuli, by introducing the capability for amplification of bodily sensations and emotions to help clients identify rewarding behavioral alternatives. This new combination of techniques makes possible an array of novel interventions, which can be used to instill hope, enhance empathy between personalities, and guide the healing process.

I am not aware of any of the following appearing in the professional literature: the visions of hope for healing; the shared videos of recent experience (although, as stated in chapter 5, they bear a resemblance to the earlier contribution of Fine, 1994); and the two-part videos, in which a habitual response can be compared with an alternative offered by the inner wisdom. The use of the dial to amplify the experiential component significantly enhances the potency of these interventions. The technique in which the client challenges, while in a meditative state, the perceived authority of the abuser is only partially innovative. Watkins and Watkins (1993), for example, presented a case in which the therapist offers to go inside with the client's young alter to confront the parents in the recalled traumatic context. The therapist makes an offer of support to the frightened alter:

> I could go in there and you could just stand behind me, or beside me, and I could hold your hand, and tell them what I think of this. . . . I'm a lot bigger than they are, and I'm going to make sure they don't hurt you. And any time you want to interrupt and say what you want to say, that's O.K. (p. 295)

The Collective Heart model proposes that instead of having the therapist assist the alter, the intervention is deferred until the collaboration within the personality system is sufficiently evolved to permit the host and other alters to perform the protective function served by the therapist in the Watkins and Watkins approach. Although there has been, to date, no empirical comparison of the two approaches, there is a theoretical advantage to using the approach that fosters greater trust in the system's capacity to support and protect its vulnerable members.

What Is the Preliminary Evidence Supporting the Fundamental Assumptions of the Model?

As discussed in chapter 3, there are three fundamental assumptions of the Collective Heart model. The first is the universality of the intact inner core capable of guiding the individual to a state of harmonious functioning. The second is that severely traumatized, fragmented clients typically need respectful, therapeutic assistance with mobilizing this inner core. The third assumption is that highly dissociative clients have easy access to the guidance of the intact inner core, which they can experience in a vivid, sensory manner.

The case illustrations presented in chapters 7 through 12 provide anecdotal support for the existence of the intact inner core in a number of dissociative survivors of childhood trauma. However, these illustrations cannot be expected to support the assumption that all human beings, including nondissociative individuals and those more severely traumatized than the members of this clinical series, possess this inner resource. The universality of the inner wisdom remains an assumption, but one that has not been assessed, even anecdotally, by the work presented in this volume.

There is no support whatsoever for the second assumption of the Collective Heart model. Because there was no comparison between individuals receiving and not receiving psychotherapy, the need for psychotherapy in the process of mobilizing the inner wisdom was not explored, even anecdotally. It is theoretically possible that even a severely traumatized, dissociative individual could learn to utilize her inner wisdom without the benefit of a therapeutic relationship.

The third assumption, which addresses the ease with which dissociative clients can obtain inner guidance in a vivid, sensory manner, is well supported by the anecdotal observations presented. All 12 clients were able to obtain inner guidance using the relatively simple, straightforward techniques described in chapter 5. Of course, one cannot conclude that all highly dissociative clients are able to do so. However, the natural dissociative tendencies of this population, combined with these anecdotal observations of this relatively small clinical series, strongly suggests that highly dissociative clients are likely to be good candidates for this approach.

What Is the Preliminary Evidence Supporting the Efficacy of the Model?

While empirical evaluation of the Collective Heart model has not yet been undertaken, there is significant anecdotal support for its effectiveness. Clinical outcomes are summarized here without comparing them to outcomes for clients receiving other treatment modalities and for individuals receiving no therapy. Therefore, the strongest claim that can be made is that this approach appears promising at this time.

Of the 12 clients in the clinical series, 10 (83%) made a commitment to the therapy process and made significant progress. Of the other 2 clients (17%), one terminated prematurely in order to take advantage of an out-of-town employment opportunity after only 18 therapy sessions. She expressed a high level of satisfaction with the therapy process. The other client expressed some dissatisfaction with the therapy model. In particular, she resented the inner wisdom as an authority figure, albeit an internal one, because she felt it compromised her autonomy. Her ambivalence manifested itself in a continuing pattern of missed sessions and canceled appointments, culminating in termination after only 12 sessions over an 8-month period.

Of the 10 clients who made a commitment to the therapy process, none expressed dissatisfaction with the treatment model, care received, or any aspect of the therapeutic relationship. Two of them, however, did terminate prematurely due to pressure from family members. One reported that her husband was very disturbed by her diagnosis. When efforts to address his concerns failed, she chose to terminate therapy before attaining her therapeutic goals in the hopes of minimizing marital discord. It is impossible to know whether she would have continued therapy longer if another treatment had been offered for her dissociative disorder. The other client who terminated prematurely due to family influence was a young adult whose parents insisted she leave the area and return to their home in another state. She was financially dependent on them and was not able to manage without their support. She expressed gratitude in a letter following termination, thanking me for introducing her to her inner wisdom, which she described as an enduring gift.

All 10 clients whose therapy lasted beyond 18 sessions demonstrated a marked improvement in functional level. They all made significant progress in terms of communication and cooperation within the personality system. Spontaneous switching in session was rare, perhaps suggesting that the alters' needs were adequately addressed in internal conferences. However, it should be noted that spontaneous switching in session was significantly more common in the two complex cases.

While I was treating them, 1 of the 12 clients (8%) attempted suicide, a total of 2 clients (17%) required hospitalization for suicidality or homicidality, and there were no completed suicides, homicides, or assaults. These observations should be viewed in light of the fact that 6 clients (50%) had a prior history of psychiatric hospitalization and that 1 additional client (8%) had been previously treated in the emergency room following suicidal drug overdoses.

All 17 fusions achieved by clients to date have been enduring fusions. To my knowledge, none have been unstable or reversed, even upon 3-year follow-up. All client fears regarding fusion were effectively addressed by the future-oriented visual presentations provided by the inner wisdom. The notion that the entire system would someday be "together as one" reassured each alter that he or she would always perform a valuable function and that joining would maximize the alter's contribution.

None of the 12 clients has brought legal charges against either me or an alleged abuser. At this writing, 3 clients (25%) reported discussing the abuse with the perpetrator during the course of therapy (between sessions) and receiving confessions and apologies. As mentioned earlier, in 4 cases (33%), the alleged perpetrator was deceased by the time our therapy began.

In general, therapeutic relationships with the clients remaining in therapy beyond the 18th session have been strong and healthy. The reader will recall how a client, who wondered why a professional psychologist would value the client's inner guidance so highly, was informed by her inner wisdom that she is like a house, with the personalities as rooms and the inner wisdom as the foundation (see chapter 6). This approach is consistent with decreased dependency on the therapist, who was described as a person standing outside the house.

There have been few phone calls, relatively few crises (that is, relative to the degree of psychopathology), and very little evidence of idealization or devaluation of the therapist. Criticism of, or antipathy toward, the therapist by the alters has been extremely rare and has never persisted after alters have been encouraged to verbalize their concerns and criticisms. Overall, clients have conveyed a high level of satisfaction with the therapeutic relationship and with the therapy process.

In addition to the possible risks that have been discussed in the context of conformity with the standards of care, two potential risks, specific to this model, should be considered. One is the possibility that the approach could produce feelings of inadequacy in a client who couldn't enter a meditative state, couldn't see the screen in the theater, or couldn't see alters in the conference room. Although this situation has not arisen, it is worth anticipating. This can be done by describing the meditative work as something that many dissociative clients find useful, to be embarked upon by the consenting client with an open mind. As stated previously (see chapter 8), sometimes it takes a bit of experimentation and a lot of acceptance of whatever comes, before the client receives clear verbal and visual guidance.

The other potential risk is that the client could become too dependent on the inner wisdom, preferring to enter a meditative state rather than relying primarily on conscious resources. No client displayed this tendency. Should this problem occur, it appears highly likely that the inner wisdom would guide the client to trust her conscious mind more. This surmise is consistent with the guidance Lynn received from her inner wisdom (see chapter 7). She was told to stop asking so many questions and to stop playing the "what if?" game. Lynn reported receiving the following guidance: "If you just do what you're supposed to do every day it will work out. Just try to be flexible. It told me to go and enjoy my time and not worry."

☐ Conclusions

As has been emphasized, no firm conclusions can be drawn from anecdotal observations, and this clinical series was neither large nor fully representative of the DID population. However, the model appears to be promising on the basis of reasonably consistent client responses and outcomes. Clients have found this to be a welcome, ego-syntonic approach. Each of the 12 clients obtained valuable verbal and visual guidance, and no client has obtained guidance from the inner wisdom that I judged to be countertherapeutic. There have been no adverse developments associated with inner conferences conducted by a client independently between sessions. Overall, clients demonstrated significant progress in terms of increased affective stability, improved internal communication and cooperation, healthier interpersonal relationships, and improved energy level with associated productivity. Spontaneous dissociation in session was rare. Some of the problems commonly encountered by DID clients, such as resistance to fusion, unstable fusion, and excessive dependency on the therapist, have, to date, been avoided with this model.

Although the model can be said to be *suggestive*, it does not appear to be *misleading*. The distinction is crucial. The model suggests that the client possesses inner resources that can be mobilized to restore mental health. The anecdotal evidence supports the assumption that these resources exist, and illustrations have been provided (see chapters 7 and 8) to demonstrate that inner guidance transcends both therapeutic suggestions and the client's conscious knowledge and wishes.

My clinical experiences in working with these 12 clients has convinced me that this approach holds promise. I hope that my colleagues will be persuaded of the promise of this model and that eventual broader implementation will lead to research efforts permitting formal assessment. Outcome studies could provide answers to two important questions. The first is whether the memories reported by clients receiving this form of treatment are corroborated at least as frequently as is the case for clients receiving other forms of appropriately cautious psychotherapy. The second is whether this model is effective relative to other models, as evidenced by functioning at termination and maintenance of treatment gains at long-term follow-up. Both are empirical questions.

I have made every effort to anticipate and address the reservations of potential critics of this treatment model. On the basis of these concerns and clinical observations, I feel that the model is free of significant risks and that continued implementation is ethically defensible. However, critical response to this volume, as well as continued observations regarding treatment outcomes, will inform my ongoing appraisal of the efficacy and appropriateness of this approach.

Herman (1997), in discussing countertransference dynamics in working with trauma survivors, noted that "repeated exposure to stories of human rapacity and cruelty inevitably challenges the therapist's basic faith" (p. 141). No therapist can make an empathic connection with a DID client without experiencing this profound personal challenge. I feel an immeasurable gratitude that my work with these 12 clients has also strengthened my basic faith. This has been engendered by the discovery that no trauma, however horrific and psychologically damaging, has the power to eradicate what is deepest within us, our own truest nature and inherent authority.

Preservation of Life Contract (Avoiding Self-Harm)

As part of our therapy plan, we understand and accept the following:

- We, as personalities within the larger system, all share the desire to experience more happiness and less emotional pain than we now have.
- Because we all share one body, we all share the responsibility for keeping it safe.
- Because we all share the same inner wisdom, and because the inner wisdom has provided visions of hope to all who have sought this guidance, it is unfair to the system for a personality who declines a vision of hope to declare that there is no hope for a good and satisfying life.
- Any personality who feels so discouraged that he or she considers suicide in any form or damaging the body in any way agrees to communicate his or her distress in therapy so that this distress can be addressed in a constructive manner.
- We understand that our therapist, _____, is committed to helping us with each phase of the healing process.
- We understand that the healing process takes time, but we feel noticeably better once we know that our needs are acknowledged and validated and that a commitment has been made to respond to our needs as the system is able to do so. We have observed how the inner wisdom can provide guidance by identifying which step we are ready to take each day in the complex process of healing.

- Because we know how painful it is to be coerced or controlled, we agree not to be controlling or coercive within the personality system. We agree to learn to influence each other in respectful, supportive, and cooperative ways. This means, among other things, that no personality will try to overwhelm the rest of the system, do away with any part of the system, or make any decisions potentially involving health or safety risks without first consulting the rest of the system to make sure that the entire system supports the decision.
- Any personality who disagrees with any part of this contract will take the initiative to discuss concerns in therapy rather than sabotage the contract.
- For all of these reasons, we, the undersigned, and all those within the system who cannot or choose not to sign personally, do hereby promise to call our therapist, _____, at _____, if we feel unable to resist suicidal or self-destructive impulses, or impulses to physically harm other members of the personality system. We understand that she can be reached at this number 24 hours a day, 7 days a week, in an emergency, unless she is on vacation. In the event that she is on vacation, we understand that the answering service will contact the therapist who is providing coverage in her absence. If we feel unable to resist these impulses and cannot reach her or the covering therapist for any reason, we agree to call _____ Hospital at _____.

[At the bottom of the contract, add lines for the date and signatures of each member of the client's personality system and for the therapist.]

Preservation of Life Contract (Avoiding Physical Harm to Others)

As part of our therapy plan, we understand and accept the following:

- We, as personalities within the larger system, all share the desire to experience more happiness and less emotional pain than we now have.
- Our angry feelings make sense in light of our experiences. Whether or not we're ready to talk about these experiences, and whether or not others within the personality system are ready to hear about these experiences, we can remind ourselves that someday the full system will understand and accept our angry responses to what we've experienced. We can also remind ourselves that the inner wisdom can show us how we can find ways to express our feelings that do justice to our anger, our need for safety and respect, and our ability to create a more satisfying life.
- We're not to blame for how we feel, but we are responsible for our behavior. Because we all share one body, we all share the responsibility for any damage done by the body.
- Because we all share the same inner wisdom and because the inner wisdom has provided guidance for expressing anger constructively to all who have sought this guidance, it is unfair to the system for a personality who declines such guidance to declare that there is no hope for expressing anger except through violence.

233

- Any personality who is preoccupied with violent expressions of angry feelings agrees to communicate his or her distress in therapy so that this distress can be addressed in a constructive manner.
- We understand that our therapist, _____, is committed to helping us with each phase of the healing process.
- We understand that the healing process takes time, but we feel noticeably better once we know that our needs are acknowledged and validated and that a commitment has been made to respond to our needs as the system is able to do so. We have observed how the inner wisdom can provide guidance by identifying which step we are ready to take each day in the complex process of healing.
- Because we know how painful it is to be coerced or controlled, we agree not to be controlling or coercive within the personality system. We agree to learn to influence each other in respectful, supportive, and cooperative ways. This means, among other things, that no personality will try to overwhelm the rest of the system, behave in a physically destructive manner, or make any decisions potentially involving health or safety risks without first consulting the rest of the system to make sure that the entire system supports the decision.
- Any personality who disagrees with any part of this contract will take the initiative to discuss concerns in therapy rather than sabotage the contract.
- For all of these reasons, we, the undersigned, and all those within the system who cannot or choose not to sign personally, do hereby promise to call our therapist, _____, at _____, if we feel unable to resist assaultive or homicidal impulses. We understand that she can be reached at this number 24 hours a day, 7 days a week, in an emergency, unless she is on vacation. In the event that she is on vacation, we understand that the answering service will contact the therapist who is providing coverage in her absence. If we feel unable to resist these impulses and cannot reach her or the covering therapist for any reason, we agree to call _____ Hospital at _____.

[At the bottom of the contract, add lines for the date and signatures of each member of the client's personality system and for the therapist.]

REFERENCES

Allison, R. B. (1974). A new treatment approach for multiple personalities. *American Journal of Clinical Hypnosis, 17*(1), 15–32.

Allison, R. B., & Schwartz, T. (1998). *Minds in many pieces: Revealing the spiritual side of multiple personality disorder.* Los Osos, CA: CIE.

Alpert, J. L. (Ed.). (1995). *Sexual abuse recalled: Treating trauma in the era of the recovered memory debate.* Northvale, NJ: Jason Aronson.

American Psychiatric Association. (1980). *Diagnostic and statistical manual of mental disorders* (3rd ed.). Washington, DC: Author.

American Psychiatric Association. (1987). *Diagnostic and statistical manual of mental disorders* (3rd ed. revised). Washington, DC: Author.

American Psychiatric Association. (1994). *Diagnostic and statistical manual of mental disorders* (4th ed.). Washington, DC: Author.

Angelou, M. (1999). On the pulse of morning. In *Kol Haneshamah: Prayerbook for the Days of Awe.* Elkins Park, PA: Author.

Armstrong, L. (1978). *Kiss daddy goodnight: A speakout on incest.* New York: Hawthorne Books.

Armstrong, L. (1994). *Rocking the cradle of sexual politics: What happened when women said incest.* New York: Addison-Wesley.

Auerbach, C. F. (2000). Trauma shatters the self and the world. *New York State Psychologist, 12,* 7–12.

Barrett, D. (1994). Dreams in dissociative disorders. *Dreaming: Journal of the Association for the Study of Dreams, 4*(3), 165–175.

Bass, E., & Davis, L. (1988). *The courage to heal: A guide for women survivors of child sexual abuse.* New York: Harper & Row.

Belli, R. F., & Loftus, E. F. (1994). Recovered memories of childhood abuse: A source monitoring perspective. In S. J. Lynn & J. W. Rhue (Eds.), *Dissociation: Clinical and theoretical perspectives* (pp. 415–433). New York: Guilford Press.

Bernstein, E., & Putnam, F. W. (1986). Development, reliability, and validity of a dissociation scale. *Journal of Nervous and Mental Disease, 174,* 727–735.

Borysenko, J. (1995, April). *Meditation, imagination, and healing.* Workshop presented at the University of Maryland, College Park.

Bowers, M. K., Brecher-Marer, S., Newton, B. W., Piotrowski, Z., Spyer, T. C., Taylor, W. S., & Watkins, J. G. (1971). Therapy of multiple personality. *The International Journal of Clinical and Experimental Hypnosis, 19,* 57–65.

Braun, B. G. (1984a). Towards a theory of multiple personality and other dissociative phenomena. In B. G. Braun (Ed.), *Symposium on Multiple Personality Disorder, 7*(1), 171–193.

Braun, B. G. (1984b). Uses of hypnosis with multiple personality. *Psychiatric Annals, 14,* 34–40.

Braun, B. G. (1988). The BASK model of dissociation. *Dissociation, 1*(4), 4–23.

Breuer, J., & Freud, S. (1959). On the psychical mechanism of hysterical phenomena. In J. Riviere (Trans.) *Sigmund Freud: Collected papers* (Vol. 1, pp. 24–41). London: Hogarth Press. (Original work published 1893)

Briere, J. N. (1992). *Child abuse trauma: Theory and treatment of the lasting effects.* Newbury Park, CA: Sage.

Brown, D., Scheflin, A. W., & Hammond, D. C. (1998). *Memory, trauma treatment, and the law: An essential reference on memory for clinicians, researchers, attorneys, and judges.* New York: Norton.

Brown, L. S. (1994). *Subversive dialogues: Theory in feminist therapy.* New York: Basic Books.

Brown, L. S. (1997). The private practice of subversion: Psychology as Tikkun Olam. *American Psychologist, 52,* 449–462.

Bryant, D., & Kessler, J. (1991). *Beyond integration: One multiple's journey.* New York: Norton.

Butler, K. (1996). The latest on recovered memory. *Family Therapy Networker, 6,* 36–37.

Cardeña, E. (1994). The domain of dissociation. In S. J. Lynn & J. W. Rhue (Eds.), *Dissociation: Clinical and theoretical perspectives* (pp. 15–31). New York: Guilford Press.

Carlson, E. B., & Armstrong, J. (1994). The diagnosis and assessment of dissociative disorders. In S. J. Lynn & J. W. Rhue (Eds.), *Dissociation: Clinical and theoretical perspectives* (pp. 159–174). New York: Guilford Press.

Carstensen, L., Gabrieli, J., Shepard, R., Levenson, R., Mason, M., Goodman, G., Bootzin, R., Ceci, S., Bronfenbrenner, U., Edelstein, B., Schober, M., Bruck, M., Keane, T., Zimering, R., Oltmanns, T., Gotlib, I., & Ekman, P. (1993, March). Repressed objectivity. *APS Observer,* p. 23.

Chu, J. A. (1998). *Rebuilding shattered lives: The responsible treatment of complex post-traumatic and dissociative disorders.* New York: Wiley.

Chu, J. A., Matthews, J. A., Frey, L. M., & Ganzel, B. (1996). The nature of traumatic memories of childhood abuse. *Dissociation, 9*(1), 2–17.

Coons, P. M. (1980). Multiple personality: Diagnostic considerations. *Journal of Clinical Psychiatry, 41,* 330–337.

Coons, P. M., Bowman, E. S., & Milstein, V. (1988). Multiple personality disorder: A clinical investigation of 50 cases. *Journal of Nervous and Mental Disease, 176,* 519–527.

Courtois, C. A. (1995). Scientist-practitioners and the delayed memory controversy: Scientific standards and the need for collaboration. *The Counseling Psychologist, 23,* 294–299.

Courtois, C. A. (1996). Informed clinical practice and the delayed memory controversy. In K. Pezdek & W. Banks (Eds.), *The recovered memory/false memory debate* (pp. 355–370). San Diego: Academic Press.

Courtois, C. A. (1999). *Recollections of sexual abuse: Treatment principles and guidelines.* New York: Norton.

Crabtree, A. (1993). Multiple personality before "Eve." *Dissociation: Progress in the Dissociative Disorders, 6*(1), 66–73.

de Shazer, S., Berg, I., Lipchik, E., Nunnally, E., Molnar, A., Gingerich, W., & Weiner-Davis, M. (1986). Brief therapy: Focused solution development. *Family Process, 25,* 207–221.

Dolan, Y. M. (1991). *Resolving sexual abuse: Solution-focused therapy and Ericksonian hypnosis for adult survivors.* New York: Norton.

Eitinger, L. (1962). Pathology of the concentration camp syndrome: Preliminary report. *Archives of General Psychiatry, 5,* 371–379.

Ellenberger, H. F. (1970). *The discovery of the unconscious: The history and evolution of Dynamic Psychiatry.* New York: Basic Books.

Enns, C. Z., Campbell, J., Courtois, C. A., Gottlieb, M. C., Lese, K. P., Gilbert, M. S., & Forrest, L. (1998). Clients who experienced childhood abuse: Recommendations for assessment and practice. *Professional Psychology: Research and Practice, 29*(3), 245–256.

Enns, C. Z., McNeilly, C. L., Corkery, J. M., & Gilbert, M. S. (1995). The debate about delayed memories of child sexual abuse: A feminist perspective. *The Counseling Psychologist, 23*, 294–299.

Fine, C. G. (1988). Thoughts on the cognitive perceptual substrates of multiple personality disorder. *Dissociation, 1*(4), 5–10.

Fine, C. G. (1994). Cognitive hypnotherapeutic interventions in the treatment of multiple personality disorder. *Journal of Cognitive Psychotherapy, 8*(4), 289–298.

Fremouw, W. J., dePerczel, M., & Ellis, T. E. (1990). *Suicide risk: Assessment and response guidelines*. New York: Pergamon Press.

Freud, S. (1953a). The aetiology of hysteria (1896). In J. Riviere (Trans.) *Sigmund Freud: Collected papers* (Vol. 1, pp. 9–23). London: Hogarth Press. (Original work published 1924)

Freud, S. (1953b). Charcot (1893). In J. Riviere (Trans.) *Sigmund Freud: Collected papers* (Vol. 1, pp. 9–23). London: Hogarth Press. (Original work published 1924)

Gold, S. N. (2000). *Not trauma alone: Therapy for child abuse survivors in family and social context*. Philadelphia: Brunner-Routledge.

Goulding, R. A., & Schwartz, R. C. (1995). *The mosaic mind: Empowering the tormented selves of child abuse survivors*. New York: Norton.

Gravitz, M. A. (1993). Etienne Félix d'Hénin de Cuvillers: A founder of hypnosis. *American Journal of Clinical Hypnosis, 36*, 7–11.

Harvey, M. R., & Herman, J. L. (1997). Continuous memory, amnesia, and delayed recall of childhood trauma: A clinical typology. In P. S. Appelbaum, L. A. Uyehara, & M. R. Elin (Eds.), *Trauma and memory: Clinical and legal controversies* (pp. 261–271). New York: Oxford University Press.

Herman, J. L. (1981). *Father-daughter incest*. Cambridge, MA: Harvard University Press.

Herman, J. L. (1997). *Trauma and recovery: The aftermath of violence from domestic to political terror*. New York: Basic Books.

Hilgard, E. R. (1994). Neodissociation theory. In S. J. Lynn & J. W. Rhue (Eds.), *Dissociation: Clinical and theoretical perspectives* (pp. 32–51). New York: Guilford Press.

Horevitz, R. P. (1983). Hypnosis for multiple personality disorder: A framework for beginning. *American Journal of Clinical Hypnosis, 26*, 138–145.

Horevitz, R. (1994). Dissociation and multiple personality: Conflicts and controversies. In S. J. Lynn & J. W. Rhue (Eds.), *Dissociation: Clinical and theoretical perspectives* (pp. 434–461). New York: Guilford Press.

Horevitz, R., & Loewenstein, R. J. (1994). The rational treatment of multiple personality disorder. In S. J. Lynn & J. W. Rhue (Eds.), *Dissociation: Clinical and theoretical perspectives* (pp. 289–316). New York: Guilford Press.

International Society for the Study of Dissociation. (1994). *Guidelines for treating dissociative identity disorder (multiple personality disorder) in adults (1994)*. Skokie, IL: Author.

Janet, P. (1973). *L'automatisme psychologique: Essai de psychologie expérimentale sur les formes inférieres de l'activité humaine*. Paris: Felix Alcan. (Original work published 1889)

Jung, C. G. (1959). *The basic writings of C. G. Jung*. New York: Random House.

Kabat-Zinn, J. (1990). *Full catastrophe living: Using the wisdom of your body and mind to face stress, pain, and illness*. New York: Bantam Doubleday Dell Publishing Group.

Kluft, R. P. (1982). Varieties of hypnotic interventions in the treatment of multiple personality. *American Journal of Clinical Hypnosis, 24*, 230–240.

Kluft, R. P. (1984a). Aspects of the treatment of multiple personality disorder. *Psychiatric Annals, 14*, 51–55.

Kluft, R. P. (1984b). An introduction to multiple personality disorder. *Psychiatric Annals, 14*, 19–24.

Kluft, R. P. (1987). First-rank symptoms as a diagnostic clue to multiple personality disorder. *American Journal of Psychiatry, 144,* 293–298.

Kluft, R. P. (1991). Multiple personality disorder. In A. Tasman & A. Goldfinger (Eds.), *American Psychiatric Press review of psychiatry* (Vol. 10, pp. 161–188). Washington, DC: American Psychiatric Press.

Kluft, R. P. (1993a). Basic principles in conducting the treatment of multiple personality disorder. In R. P. Kluft & C. G. Fine (Eds.), *Clinical perspectives on multiple personality disorder* (pp. 19–50). Washington, DC: American Psychiatric Press.

Kluft, R. P. (1993b). Clinical approaches to the integration of personalities. In R. P. Kluft & C. G. Fine (Eds.), *Clinical perspectives on multiple personality disorder* (pp. 101–133). Washington, DC: American Psychiatric Press.

Kluft, R. P. (1993c). The treatment of dissociative disorder patients: An overview of discoveries, successes, and failures. *Dissociation, 6*(2/3), 87–101.

Kluft, R. P. (1997). The argument for the reality of delayed recall of trauma. In P. S. Appelbaum, L. A. Uyehara, & M. R. Elin (Eds.), *Trauma and memory: Clinical and legal controversies* (pp. 25–57). New York: Oxford University Press.

Krakauer, S. Y. (1991). *Assessing reading-deficit patterns among adolescents' MMPI-A profiles.* Unpublished doctoral dissertation, Virginia Consortium for Professional Psychology, Norfolk & Williamsburg, VA.

Lindsay, D. S. (1997). Increasing sensitivity. In J. D. Read & D. S. Lindsay (Eds.), *Recollections of trauma: Scientific evidence and clinical practice* (pp. 1–24). New York: Plenum Press.

Loewenstein, R. J. (1993). Posttraumatic and dissociative aspects of transference and countertransference in the treatment of multiple personality disorder. In R. P. Kluft & C. G. Fine (Eds.), *Clinical perspectives on multiple personality disorder* (pp. 51–85). Washington, DC: American Psychiatric Press.

Loewenstein, R. J. (1994). Diagnosis, epidemiology, clinical course, treatment, and cost effectiveness of treatment for dissociative disorders and MPD: Report submitted to the Clinton Administration Task Force on Health Care Financing Reform. *Dissociation, 7*(1), 3–11.

Loftus, E. F. (1993). The reality of repressed memories. *American Psychologist, 48,* 518–537.

Loftus, E. F., & Ketcham, K. (1994). *The myth of repressed memory.* New York: St. Martin's Press.

Maslow, A. H. (1954). *Motivation and personality.* New York: Harper and Row.

Mulhern, S. (1991). Letter to the editor. *Child Abuse and Neglect, 15,* 609–611.

Peale, N. V. (1954). *The power of positive thinking.* New York: Prentice-Hall.

Phillips, J. (1995). *The magic daughter: A memoir of living with multiple personality disorder.* New York: Viking.

Pope, K. S., & Brown, L. S. (1996). *Recovered memories of abuse: Assessment, therapy, forensics.* Washington, DC: American Psychological Association.

Prince, M. (1930). *The dissociation of a personality.* London: Longmans, Green, and Co. (Original work published 1905)

Putnam, F. W. (1989). *Diagnosis and treatment of multiple personality disorder.* New York: Guilford Press.

Putnam, F. W. (1992) Discussion: Are alter personalities fragments or figments? *Psychoanalytic Inquiry, 12*(1), 95–111.

Putnam, F. W. (1994). Dissociative disorders in children and adolescents. In S. J. Lynn & J. W. Rhue (Eds.), *Dissociation: Clinical and theoretical perspectives* (pp. 175–189). New York: Guilford Press.

Putnam, F. W. (1997). *Dissociation in children and adolescents: A developmental perspective.* New York: Guilford Press.

Putnam, F. W., Guroff, J. J., Silberman, E. K., Barban L., & Post, R. M. (1986). The clinical phenomenology of multiple personality disorder: Review of 100 recent cases. *Journal of Clinical Psychiatry, 47,* 285–293.

Ross, C. A. (1989). *Multiple personality disorder: Diagnosis, clinical features, and treatment.* New York: Wiley.

Ross, C. A., Norton, G. R., & Wozney, K. (1989). Multiple personality disorder: An analysis of 236 cases. *Canadian Journal of Psychiatry, 34,* 413–418.

Rubin, L. J. (1996). Childhood sexual abuse: False accusations of "false memory"? *Professional Psychology: Research and Practice, 27*(5), 447–451.

Sandberg, D., Lynn, S. J., & Green, J. P. (1994). Sexual abuse and revictimization: Mastery, dysfunctional learning, and dissociation. In S. J. Lynn & J. W. Rhue (Eds.), *Dissociation: Clinical and theoretical perspectives* (pp. 242–267). New York: Guilford Press.

Saxe, G. N., van der Kolk, B. A., Berkowitz, R., Chinman, G., Hall, K., Lieberg, G., & Schwartz, J. (1993). Dissociative disorders in psychiatric inpatients. *American Journal of Psychiatry, 150,* 1037–1042.

Schreiber, F. R. (1974). *Sybil.* Chicago: Henry Regnery.

Schultz, R., Braun, B. G., & Kluft, R. P. (1989). Multiple personality disorder: Phenomenology of selected variables in comparison to major depression. *Dissociation 2,* 45–51.

Shay, J. (1995). *Achilles in Vietnam: Combat trauma and the undoing of character.* New York: Simon & Schuster.

Spanos, N. P. (1996). *Multiple identities and false memories: A sociocognitive perspective.* Washington, DC: American Psychological Association.

Spiegel, D. (1984). Multiple personality as a post traumatic stress disorder. *Psychiatric Clinics of North America, 7,* 101–110.

Steinberg, M. (1994). *Interviewer's guide to the Structured Clinical Interview for DSM-IV Dissociative Disorders-Revised* (SCID-D-R). Washington, DC: American Psychiatric Press.

van der Hart, O., Brown, P., & van der Kolk, B. A. (1989). Pierre Janet's treatment of post-traumatic stress. *Journal of Traumatic Stress, 2,* 379–395.

van der Hart, O., Lierens, R., & Goodwin, J. (1996). Jeanne Fery: A sixteenth-century case of dissociative identity disorder. *Journal of Psychohistory, 24*(1), 18–35.

van der Kolk, B. A. (1996). The complexity of adaptation to trauma self-regulation, stimulus discrimination, and characterological development. In B. A. van der Kolk, A. C. McFarlane, & L. Weisaeth (Eds.), *Traumatic stress: The effects of overwhelming experience on mind, body, and society* (pp. 182–213). New York: Guilford Press.

van der Kolk, B. A., Brown, P., & van der Hart, O. (1989). Pierre Janet on post-traumatic stress. *Journal of Traumatic Stress, 2,* 365–378.

van der Kolk, B. A., van der Hart, O., & Marmar, C. R., (1996). Dissociation and information processing in posttraumatic stress disorder. In B. A. van der Kolk, A. C. McFarlane, & L. Weisaeth (Eds.), *Traumatic stress: The effects of overwhelming experience on mind, body, and society* (pp. 303–327). New York: Guilford Press.

van der Kolk, B. A., Weisaeth, L., & van der Hart, O. (1996). History of trauma in psychiatry. In B. A. van der Kolk, A. C. McFarlane, & L. Weisaeth (Eds.), *Traumatic stress: The effects of overwhelming experience on mind, body, and society* (pp. 47–74). New York: Guilford Press.

Watkins, H. H. (1980). The silent abreaction. *International Journal of Clinical and Experimental Hypnosis, 28*(2), 101–113.

Watkins, H. H., & Watkins, J. G. (1993). Ego-state therapy in the treatment of dissociative disorders. In R. P. Kluft & C. G. Fine (Eds.), *Clinical perspectives on multiple personality disorder* (pp. 277–299). Washington, DC: American Psychiatric Press.

West, C. (1999). *First person plural: My life as a multiple.* New York: Hyperion.

Wilbur, C. B. (1984). Treatment of multiple personality. *Psychiatric Annals, 14,* 27–31.

Wolf, L. (1999). *Practical Kabbalah: A guide to Jewish wisdom for everyday life.* New York: Three Rivers Press.

Yates J. L., & Nasby, W. (1993). Dissociation, affect, and network models of memory: An integrative proposal. *Journal of Traumatic Stress, 6,* 305–326.

Zelikovsky, N., & Lynn, S. J. (1994). The aftereffects and assessment of physical and psychological abuse. In S. J. Lynn & J. W. Rhue (Eds.), *Dissociation: Clinical and theoretical perspectives* (pp. 190–214). New York: Guilford Press.

INDEX

241